THE BOOK OF

REVELATION

UNLOCKING THE FUTURE

AMG *Publishers*

CHATTANOOGA, TENNESSEE

TWENTY-FIRST CENTURY
BIBLICAL COMMENTARY SERIES

THE BOOK OF

REVELATION

UNLOCKING THE FUTURE

EDWARD
HINDSON

GENERAL EDITORS

MAL COUCH & ED HINDSON

Unless otherwise noted, Scripture quotes are taken from the NEW AMERICAN STANDARD BIBLE, © 1960, 1962, 1963, 1968, 1971, 1972, 1973, 1975, 1977, by the Lockman Foundation. Used by permission

The previous edition of this book was published as *Approaching Armageddon*.

ISBN 0–89957–810–1

Cover Design by Phillip Rodgers
Editing and Text Design by Warren Baker

Printed in the United States of America
07 06 05 04 03 02 –S– 7 6 5 4 3 2 1

*To John F. Walvoord
and J. Dwight Pentecost
for a lifetime of teaching others
to prepare for His coming*

Acknowledgments

Special appreciation should be expressed to several of my colleagues with the Pre-Trib Research Center in Arlington, Texas for their helpful advice and suggestions: Tim LaHaye, Thomas Ice, James Combs, Paul Benware, Robert Gromacki, Mal Couch, Robert Thomas, Paige Patterson, and Randall Price. Thanks also to Mrs. Emily Boothe who typed the original manuscript.

Twenty-First Century Biblical Commentary Series

Mal Couch, Th.D. and Ed Hindson, D.Phil.

The New Testament has guided the Christian Church for over two thousand years. This one testament is made up of twenty-seven books, penned by godly men through the inspiration of the Holy Spirit. It tells us of the life of Jesus Christ, His atoning death for our sins, His miraculous resurrection, His ascension back to heaven, and the promise of His second coming. It also tells the story of the birth and growth of the Church and the people and principles that shaped it in its earliest days. The New Testament concludes with the book of Revelation pointing ahead to the glorious return of Jesus Christ.

Without the New Testament, the message of the Bible would be incomplete. The Old Testament emphasizes the promise of a coming Messiah. It constantly points us ahead to the One who is coming to be the King of Israel and the Savior of the world. But the Old Testament ends with this event still unfulfilled. All of its ceremonies, pictures, types, and prophecies are left awaiting the arrival of the "Lamb of God who takes away the sin of the world!" (John 1:29).

The message of the New Testament represents the timeless truth of God. As each generation seeks to apply that truth to its specific context it becomes necessary for an up-to-date commentary to be created just for them. The editors and authors of the Twenty-First Century Biblical Commentary Series have endeavored to do just that. This team of scholars represents conservative, evangelical, and dispensational scholarship at its best. The individual authors may differ on minor points of interpretation, but all are convinced that the Old and New Testaments teach a dispensational framework for biblical history. They also hold to a pretribulational and premillennial understanding of biblical prophecy.

The French scholar René Pache reminded each succeeding generation, "If the power of the Holy Spirit is to be made manifest anew among us, it is of primary importance that His message should regain its due place. Then we shall be able to put the enemy to flight by the sword of the Spirit which is the Word of God."

This volume on the book of Revelation deals with the most significant book of prophecy in the New Testament. The Revelation is the grand and noble conclusion to the Bible. It is the crown jewel of biblical literature and concludes the books of the New Testament and the entire Word of God. Doctrinally, Revelation shows the living relationship between the risen Christ and His Bride, the Church. The book also records the final days of this world and reveals the glorious new world yet to come. Historically, the Revelation was already being quoted by Christians early in the second century, only a few years after it was written. Though many have debated how it should be interpreted, all believers cherish the book of Revelation because it gives us hope for the future when God will make "all things new" (Rev. 21:5).

Contents

FOREWORD

Looking Ahead

The book of Revelation is the most fascinating book ever written. It claims to be a vision of the end of the world. We are swept up into another time and another place as the panorama of the future unfolds before us. This final book of the biblical record is the capstone of divine revelation. In it, God reveals the great end-times drama that leads to Armageddon and beyond.

All of us are curious about the future. There is something in human nature that wants to know what is going to happen next. God speaks to that need in our lives by revealing the future before it happens. We call that process a *prophecy* of future events. This book is a study of the prophecies in the book of Revelation.

As we examine these prophecies of the future, it is my goal to help simplify the message of the Revelation so that you can easily understand it for yourself. We will survey the general content of this great book of prophecy with a view to keeping the big picture in mind, rather than being lost in all the details. I have observed over the years that too many people get sidetracked on the details and lose sight of the main focus of the book.

I have had the privilege of teaching the Bible to over fifty-thousand students in the past twenty-five years. Others have often described my teaching style as taking the complicated and making it simple. It is my prayer that this style will come through in this book. My greatest joy is in making the Bible come alive for the average reader.

I have divided the book of Revelation into an outline of seven major points. These include the letters to the seven churches, the seven seals, the seven trumpets, and the seven bowls. My approach is to keep the study focused on the key issues in each chapter.

The book itself is divided into seven sections following the seven points of the outline. The chapters of the book follow the chapters of the Revelation to make it easier to find one's way through each section. I have endeavored to cover the main issues without getting bogged down in the details. I have also included the best and most profound quotes from other commentators, regardless of their eschatological viewpoints. My own position is pretribulational; however, I have attempted to show respect and appreciation for other viewpoints.

The general outline that I have developed for the book of Revelation is as follows:

1. Preface (chap. 1)
2. Proclamation (chaps. 2—3)
3. Problem (chaps. 4—5)
4. Process (chaps. 6—11)
5. Players (chaps. 12—18)
6. Plagues (chaps. 19—20)
7. Postscript (chaps. 21—22)

The most important person in the Revelation is Jesus Christ. The penman is John the apostle. The *problem* around which the entire book revolves is the seven-sealed scroll. The *process* of judgments includes the seven seals and the seven trumpets. The *plagues* are the seven bowls of judgment that lead to Armageddon. Right in the middle of the Revelation is a "scorecard" that lists the seven symbolic *players* in the great end-times drama.

I have included a series of study questions at the end of each chapter to enable the reader to study the details of the Revelation for himself or herself. Filling these in will be an education in itself. May God bless your reading and may your reading challenge your heart.

Keep looking up!

Ed Hindson
Liberty University
Lynchburg, VA

Keys to Unlocking the Future

The book of Revelation is the greatest book of apocalyptic literature ever written. It captivates our attention, stirs our imagination, and points us to our glorious future destiny. In this singular book of New Testament prophecy, the curtain is removed and the future is revealed for all to see. In a series of seven visions and numerous symbolic word pictures, the whole climax of human history is foretold in lucid detail.

The term *revelation* means to "unveil" or "uncover" that which was previously hidden. It translates the Greek term *apokalupsis*. Thus, the book is often known as the Apocalypse. It is the last book of the Bible and describes the final consummation of all things. In so doing, it serves as the capstone of the entire biblical library of sixty-six books.

The general nature of the Revelation has been described as both *apocalyptic* and *prophetic*. Jewish apocalyptic literature can be seen in Isaiah 24—27, Ezekiel 38—39, Daniel 7—12, and Zechariah 9—14. Similar elements appear in the apocryphal books of Enoch, Baruch, Fourth Ezra, the Ascension of Isaiah, and the Apocalypse of Zephaniah. But none of these are quoted in the Revelation, which draws most of its symbolic imagery from the canonical Old Testament books. Apocalyptic writings may be distinguished by dreams or visions of end-times conflicts between the supernatural forces of good and evil. Persons or kingdoms are represented as animals; historical events take the form of natural phenomena. Colors and numbers have secret meanings. And everything points to the end of the world.

The Apocalypse calls itself a "prophecy" of future events (cf. Rev. 1:3; 22:7,10,18,19). While it combines apocalyptic visions with epistolary instructions, the Revelation is essentially a book of New Testament prophecy. It is an inspired book of prophetic visions of the future. These focus on scenes both in heaven and on earth, both of Israel and the Church, and cover a span of time including the Tribulation period, the Millennial Kingdom, and the eternal state.

New Testament scholar Bruce Metzger reminds us: "In order to become oriented to the book of Revelation one must take seriously what the author says happened. John tells us that he had a series of visions. He says that he 'heard' certain words and 'saw' certain visions." Metzger then adds, "Such accounts combine cognitive insight with emotional response. They invite the reader or listener to enter into the experience being recounted and to participate in it, triggering mental images of that which is described."[1]

Themes of the Revelation	
The Christ	Chapter 1
The Church	Chapters 2 — 3
The Consummation	Chapters 4 — 22

It is this exciting sense of personal participation that raises one of the problems encountered in studying the Apocalypse: There is always a great temptation to read about the future through the eyes of the present! From our current standpoint in history, we presume to speculate on how the events predicted in the Revelation will eventually be fulfilled. The problem is that each generation tends to assume that it is the terminal generation and that the end will come in their lifetime.

Ages of the Revelation	
Church Age	Chapters 1 — 3
Tribulation Period	Chapters 4 — 19
Kingdom Age	Chapter 20
Eternal State	Chapters 21 — 22

Nature of Symbolic Language

The events predicted in the Revelation are stated in *symbolic language.* Many of these symbols are taken from Old Testament passages.[2] These include: tree of life, Lion of Judah, song of Moses, book of life, Lamb of God, throne of God, Wormwood, Sodom, Babylon, Jezebel, Gog and Magog, and Armageddon. Some symbols are drawn from other New Testament passages. These include: Word of God, "first-born of the dead," eternal gospel, Son of man, marriage supper, the Bride, "first resurrection," and "second death." In fact, of the 404 verses that are contained in the Revelation 278 are drawn from Old Testament passages.

Some of the symbols in the Apocalypse have no biblical parallel and are left unexplained. These include: mark of the beast, image of the beast, beast of the sea, scarlet beast, seven thunders, synagogue of Satan, "hail and fire, mixed with blood," great army of the Euphrates, little book, and great white throne. Other symbols are specifically explained and identified: Alpha and Omega = Jesus Christ; seven lampstands = seven churches; "new song" = song of the Lamb; "great day of their wrath" = Great Tribulation; 144,000 = Jews from the tribes of Israel; Dragon = Satan; scarlet beast = Rome (city on seven hills); New Jerusalem = Church (Lamb's Bride). Other symbols are self-explanatory: numbers, angels, open door, golden bowls (vials), seals, trumpets, songs, horses, fire, death and hell, holy city, and glory of God.

We must also remember that these are prophecies of real events. Reading the Apocalypse is like watching a movie of end-time events. It is literally going "back to the future." Therefore, many of the things referred to in the book of Revelation can be understood only by a *literal interpretation*. John was really on the island of Patmos. The risen Christ literally appeared to him. The seven churches actually existed in Asia Minor in the first century A.D. The predicted future judgments are real, involving armies, weapons, and mass destruction. Earthquakes are earthquakes. Tears are tears. Nations are nations. Jews are Jews. Gentiles are Gentiles. Heaven is real. So is the lake of fire!

The key to interpreting the Apocalypse is discerning what is literal and what is symbolic. Even then we must remember that the symbols themselves depict real people, things, situations, and events. For example, the "seven lampstands" (1:20) symbolize real churches that actually existed when the book was written. The "male child" (12:5) is Jesus Christ. The sounding of the "seven trumpets" (8:2—11:15) results in the actual devastation of the earth.

Unfortunately, much of what has been written about the Revelation has been unfounded speculation or what Graham Scroggie calls "an ill-digested rehash of someone else's views." In commenting on the controversy surrounding the interpretation of the Revelation, he says, "Much of this could have been avoided if more regard had been shown for sound principles of interpretation, and if controversialists had been more anxious to reach the truth than to establish a theory."[3]

Keeping this in mind, we must proceed with both guarded caution and keen insight. This is the "book of the unveiling," as the title indicates. It is meant to be understood! Thus, the *promise:* "Blessed is he who reads, and those who hear the words of the prophecy, and heed the things which are written in it" (Rev. 1:3). As you read and study this great "vision of the End Times," you will be blessed time and time again.

Who Really Wrote the Apocalypse?

Much has been written about the author and the date of his writing. The vast majority of biblical scholars favors identifying John the apostle as the human author and assigns a date of A.D. 95 for the composition. Some argue for the separate identity of John of Patmos (not the apostle). Others argue for an earlier date of authorship.

The arguments in favor of the apostle's authorship rest upon a similarity in style and vocabulary. John's Gospel, epistles, and the Revelation contain several commonalities: the words *true, lamb, I signify, tribulation, out of, witness, thunder, life, tabernacle* (verb), and *Word* of God. John's writings show the highest usage of articular participles in the New Testament, as does the Revelation. He also shows a fondness for the present tense of "I am coming" (Greek, *erchomai*) and the verb "I worship."[4]

There are certain irregularities of grammar throughout the Revelation that are unique to it: use of participles, broken sentences, additional pronouns, mixed genders, and several unusual constructions.[5] However, most of these are due to the visionary nature of the text. John was writing as fast as he could to record the visions he was seeing. In some cases, there just weren't first-century words to describe what he saw (e.g., flying objects). It is clear, however, that the author was a Palestinian Jew with a vast knowledge of the Old Testament. It is also evident that he was currently living in Asia Minor late in the first century A.D. and had a personal knowledge of the local churches in that region.

John's arrival in Asia came in circa A.D. 66, just after Paul's last visit in A.D. 65. It coincided with the migration of Palestinian Christians from Judea to the province of Asia just before the outbreak of the Jewish Revolt of A.D. 66–70. The condition of the churches of Asia Minor described in the Revelation reflects the widespread persecution under Domitian, the Roman emperor (A.D. 81–96) at the end of the first century.

Attempts to date the Apocalypse in the decade of the sixties fail all external criteria. Metzger notes that Nero's mad acts at the time were restricted to the city of Rome and had nothing to do with emperor worship. In contrast, Metzger states: "The first emperor who tried to compel Christians to participate in Caesar worship was Domitian."[6]

In the meantime, the general condition of the churches of Asia Minor is described as wealthy, prosperous, lukewarm, tolerant of heresy, and having lost their first love. These hardly fit the newly founded churches of the sixties to which the apostle Paul wrote his epistles. The bottom line on the evidence for the date of A.D. 95 is the general acceptance of the early church fathers: Irenaeus (A.D. 180), Clement of Alexandria (200), Origen (254), Victorinus (270), and Eusebius (325).

Why Is Revelation So Unique?

There are several elements that make the Revelation the most unique book in the Bible. The basic structure of the book is woven around a series of threes and sevens. The overarching triplet reveals past, present, and future:

1. *Past:* "the things which you have seen" (chap. 1).

2. *Present:* "the things which are" (chaps. 2—3).

3. *Future:* "the things which shall take place after these things" (chaps. 4—22).

The *seven visions* are as follows:

1. Seven churches (1:9—3:22)

2. Seven seals (4:1—8:1)

3. Seven trumpets (8:2—11:19)

4. Seven symbolic figures (12:1—14:20)

5. Seven bowls (15:1—16:21)

6. Seven judgments (17:1—19:10).

7. Seven triumphs (19:11—22:5)[7]

The use of symbolic numbers is found everywhere in the Apocalypse. These include: 1/2, 1, 2, 3, 4, 5, 6, 7, 10, 12, 24, 42, 144, 666, 1,000, 1,260, 1,600, 7,000, 12,000, 144,000, 100 million, and 200 million. The term *hour* is used ten times in Revelation (3:3,10; 9:15; 11:13; 14:7,15; 17:12; 18:10,17,19), always referring to a brief period of time (e.g., "in one hour your judgment has come").

The most significant numbers in the Apocalypse are as follows:

Three is the symbolic number of the Trinity. It is one of John's favorite numbers, and his use of it dominates his writing style. He constantly expresses himself in triplets: "Blessed is he who reads . . . those who hear . . . heed" (1:3); "Jesus Christ: faithful witness . . . first-born of the dead . . . ruler of the kings of the earth" (1:5); "[He] loved us . . . released us . . . made us to be a kingdom, priests to His God" (1:5-6); "says the Lord God, who is and who was and who is to come" (1:8); "the living one . . . was dead . . . am alive forevermore" (1:18); "I know your tribulation . . . the poverty . . . the blasphemy" (2:9); "remember . . . keep it. . . repent" (3:3), "Buy . . . gold . . . white garments . . . eye salve" (3:18). There are scores of these triplets throughout the book of Revelation.

The number three also figures prominently in several passages referring to judgment. There are three series of judgments: seals, trumpets, and bowls. Judgment consists of three elements: fire, smoke, and brimstone. These elements kill a third part of mankind (9:17–18). A third of the trees are burned up (8:7), and the sun is blacked out a third part of the day (8:12). There are three evil agencies (the satanic trinity): Dragon, beast, and False Prophet (16:13) behind all opposition to the reign of Christ on earth. Finally, there is the threefold defeat of Satan: on earth (12:9), into the abyss (20:1–3), and into the lake of fire (20:10).

Four is a number generally related to the earth, which has four regions (north, south, east, west) and four seasons (spring, summer, fall, winter). In the Revelation there are four living creatures (4:6); four angels at the four corners of the earth, holding the four winds (7:1); four angels are bound in the Euphrates River (9:14–15); the inhabitants of the earth have a fourfold description: tribes, tongues, peoples, and nations (5:9; 10:11); the New Jerusalem lies foursquare (21:16).

Six is the number of man, who was created on the sixth day. In Revelation 13:18 it represents the number of the ultimate man, the Antichrist: 666.

Seven is the most significant number in the Apocalypse. There are seven spirits, seven churches, seven lampstands, seven stars, seven lamps of fire, seven horns, seven eyes, seven seals, seven trumpets, seven bowls, seven songs, seven angels, seven thunders, seven "worthy's," seven heads, seven crowns, seven mountains, seven Kings, and seven last plagues. In addition, there is the sevenfold description of Christ (1:14–16), sevenfold message to each of the churches (chaps. 2—3), sevenfold praise of the Lamb (5:12), sevenfold result of judgment (6:12–14), seven divisions of mankind (6:15), sevenfold blessing (7:12), sevenfold description of the "locusts" (9:7–10), 7,000 were killed (11:13), sevenfold triumph (11:19), and the seven "new things" (chaps. 21—22). Then there is the number three and a half, which is half of seven.

Twelve is the number of completeness. There are twelve tribes of Israel, twelve apostles of Christ, twenty-four elders (a double twelve), tree of life has twelve types of fruit (22:2), New Jerusalem has twelve gates guarded by twelve angels (21:twelve), the city has twelve foundations (21:14). There are twelve precious stones adorning the foundation stones and twelve pearls (21:19–21). There are also multiples of twelve: Each of the twelve tribes contains 12,000 people, making a total of 144,000 (12,000 times 12); the wall measures 144 cubits (12 times 12).

What Is the Apocalypse All About?

The central theme of the Apocalypse is given in the title to the book. It is "the revelation of Jesus Christ which God gave Him to show to His bond-servants, the things which must shortly take place" (1:1). Jesus Christ is the central theme of the Revelation. He is the most important key to understanding the book. He is both the author of the Revelation and the subject of it.

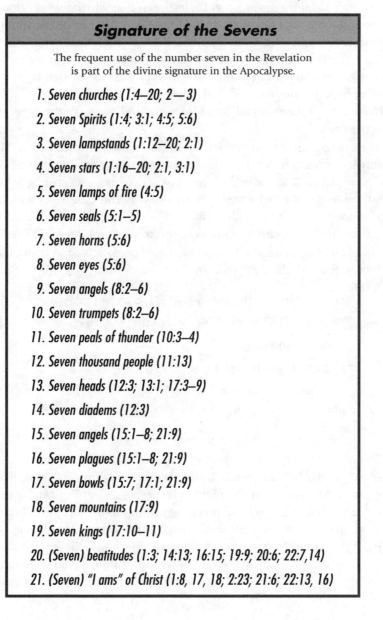

Signature of the Sevens

The frequent use of the number seven in the Revelation
is part of the divine signature in the Apocalypse.

1. Seven churches (1:4–20; 2 — 3)

2. Seven Spirits (1:4; 3:1; 4:5; 5:6)

3. Seven lampstands (1:12–20; 2:1)

4. Seven stars (1:16–20; 2:1, 3:1)

5. Seven lamps of fire (4:5)

6. Seven seals (5:1–5)

7. Seven horns (5:6)

8. Seven eyes (5:6)

9. Seven angels (8:2–6)

10. Seven trumpets (8:2–6)

11. Seven peals of thunder (10:3–4)

12. Seven thousand people (11:13)

13. Seven heads (12:3; 13:1; 17:3–9)

14. Seven diadems (12:3)

15. Seven angels (15:1–8; 21:9)

16. Seven plagues (15:1–8; 21:9)

17. Seven bowls (15:7; 17:1; 21:9)

18. Seven mountains (17:9)

19. Seven kings (17:10–11)

20. (Seven) beatitudes (1:3; 14:13; 16:15; 19:9; 20:6; 22:7,14)

21. (Seven) "I ams" of Christ (1:8, 17, 18; 2:23; 21:6; 22:13, 16)

Jesus appears in chapter 1 as the glorified, risen Savior. In chapters 2—3, He is Lord of the Church. In chapters 4—5, He is the Lamb of God. In chapters 6—11, He is the Judge of all mankind. In chapters 12—13, He is the miracle-born male child. In chapters 14—19, He is the coming King. In chapters 20—22, He is Lord of heaven and earth.

The purpose of the book is to reveal the future. David Jeremiah observes: "The word 'revelation' means the disclosure of that which was previously hidden or unknown. The book of Revelation tells us that Jesus is coming again, how He is coming, and what the condition of the world will be when He comes."[8] The concept of *revelation* is that of unveiling a "mystery" which was previously unknown. Merrill Tenney states, "It was not written to mystify, but rather to explain the truth of God more clearly. For this reason one should approach it with the expectation of learning, and not with the expectation of being confused."[9]

The expectation of the Revelation points to the return of Christ. The risen Savior who appears to John on Patmos is the same One who returns with His triumphant Church at the end of the book. He who walks among the churches (lampstands) as our heavenly High Priest is the One who will take His Bride to reign and rule with Him in His Millennial Kingdom on earth. Everything in the Apocalypse points to the second coming of Christ.

David Hocking observes that the concept of our Lord's soon return is emphasized seven times in the Revelation by the words "shortly" or "quickly":[10]

> "Things which must *shortly* [Greek, *en tachei*] take place" (1:1).
>
> "Repent therefore; or else I am coming to you *quickly*" (2:16).
>
> "I am coming *quickly*" (3:11).
>
> "The third woe is coming *quickly*" (11:14).
>
> "And behold, I am coming *quickly*" (22:7).
>
> "Behold, I am coming *quickly*:"(22:12).
>
> "Yes, I am coming *quickly*" (22:20).

The phrase "I am coming quickly" (Greek, *erchomai* and *tachus*) must refer either to "suddenly" or "shortly." The first meaning implies "speedily," as in an instant ("like a thief in the night" [1 Thess. 5:2]). It indicates a rapid-fire sequence of events. The second meaning implies in a short period of time, as in "soon." This focuses on the imminence of the events. Scholars are divided on how this should be interpreted. Robert L. Thomas believes that the events predicted by Daniel and foreseen by Christ now (after the resurrection) stood in readiness to be fulfilled. Thus, John could speak of them as imminent, though they still were yet to be fulfilled—the final aspect of which will occur *suddenly.*[11]

Where Are We Headed?

Critics of Bible prophecy have often characterized it as a message of "doom and gloom." In reality the prophetic message is one of doom and boom! It is both negative and positive. For the unbeliever, the bottom line is, "Bad news—you lose!" But for the believer, the bottom line is, "Good news—we win!"

Biblical history is always written from the divine perspective. The viewpoint of heaven supersedes that of earth. God sees the past, present, and future all at once. For Him, all things are in the present tense. He sees future events as though they were already happening. A perfect example of this is in the prediction of the virgin birth of Christ in Isaiah 7:14. The Hebrew text refers to the virgin (*almah*) as having already conceived (*harah*). The translation should actually read: "Behold the pregnant virgin bearing a son."[12] The prophet sees this future event as though it were a present reality.

John the revelator sees the future as though it were happening before him. He records these events as he sees them unfold. Several key chronological terms indicate the *progression* of this revelation of future events. These include "then," "when," "after this," "immediately," "another," "and there followed," and "after these things."

The predominant term which keeps the book of Revelation constantly moving is the word *and* (Greek, *kai*). The term *kai* is used over 1,200 times in the Revelation and is generally translated "and," although it also appears translated as "but," "even," "both," "also," "yet," and "indeed." The average reader does not realize that nearly every verse of the Apocalypse begins with *kai* (*and*). This phenomenon is known as *polysyndeton,* meaning "many ands." These are used to bind together the numeric units of the Revelation in a pattern known as *kaimeter.*[13]

Some examples of the kaimeter pattern are as follows:[14]

Write in a book what you see, and send it to the seven churches:

—to Ephesus

—and to Smyrna

—and to Pergamum

—and to Thyatira

—and to Sardis

—and to Philadelphia

—and to Laodicea. (1:11)

The Lamb who was slain is worthy to receive

power

and riches

and wisdom

and might

and honor

and glory

and blessing (5:12)

In these examples, six "ands" (*kais*) tie together a list of seven items. Sometimes the text uses seven "ands" to tie together a list of seven. For example:

And I looked when He broke the sixth seal,
and there was a great earthquake;
and the sun became black as sackcloth made of hair,
and the whole moon became like blood;
and the stars of the sky fell to the earth,
as a fig tree casts its unripe figs when shaken by a great wind,
and the sky was split apart like a scroll when it is rolled up;
and every mountain and island were moved out of their places. (6:12–14)

"Come up here."
And they went up into heaven in the cloud
and their enemies beheld them;
and in that hour there was a great earthquake,
and a tenth of the city fell;
and seven thousand people were killed in the earthquake,
and the rest were terrified
and gave glory to the God of heaven. (11:12–13)

The *kaimeters* can also tie together units of two, three, four, five, six, ten or twelve. The use of *and* (*kai*) is the literary cement that holds the Revelation together and keeps it moving. One cannot read this book without being swept up in a sense of movement. The pattern reads like this:

This happened,
and that happened,
and then this,
and then that, etc.

It is this constant sense of progression that clearly indicates the Revelation is moving the reader toward a final climax. One cannot read this book and mentally stand still. The reader will sense, consciously or unconsciously, that he or she is moving through a series of events that appear like instantaneous flashes on a video screen. These glimpses of the future are intended to keep us moving toward the final consummation of human history. The closing chapters actually fast-forward us into eternity itself!

What Lies Ahead?

The book of Revelation presents a series of panoramic pictures, followed by a series of snapshots. You get the big picture first, then the specifics. The pattern of the book is generally, Bad news—details to follow, or good news—details to follow. Therefore, things are *not* necessarily in precise sequential order.

Consider these examples. The seven churches are introduced in 1:20, but the letters sent to them follow in chapters 2 and 3. The Lamb appears to take the seven-sealed book in 5:5-7, but the seals are not opened until 6:1—8:1. The seven trumpets are introduced in 8:2, but the final trumpet does not sound until 11:15. Armageddon is mentioned in 16:16, but the details about the fall of "Babylon" and the triumphal return of Christ don't come until chapters 17—19. The Bride of Christ appears at the Marriage Supper in 19:7-9, but she is not described in full detail until 21:9-27.

The contents of the Revelation move in a *series of progressions:*

1. Christ appears to John—on Patmos (chap. 1).

2. He dictates the letters to the seven churches—on earth (chaps. 2—3).

3. John is transported into God's throne room—in heaven (chaps. 4—5).

4. He sees the future judgments—from heaven (chaps. 6—11).

5. John sees the seven symbolic players—from heaven and earth (chaps. 12—13).

6. He sees the seven last plagues—from heaven (chaps. 14—18).

7. John witnesses the marriage of the Lamb in heaven and His triumphal return to earth (chap. 19).

8. He views the Millennial Kingdom—on earth (chap. 20).

9. John sees the new heaven and the new earth in eternity (chaps. 21—22).

10. He hears the final invitation appeal and adds his own: "Amen. Even so, come, Lord Jesus" (22:16–21).

The Big Picture

When we compare the contents of the Revelation with other biblical prophecies, certain *basic patterns* emerge:[15]

1. *The Church will continue to grow.* But it will have varying degrees of success and difficulty. Jesus promised to continue to build His Church and empower it to attack the gates of hell (Matt. 16:18). But He also warned of persecution and rejection (Matt. 24:9–12).

2. *Satanic opposition will intensify.* Things will get worse as we get closer to the time of the end. "Difficult times" will come (2 Tim. 3:1–5). Scoffers will mock the idea of Christ's second coming (2 Pet. 3:3–4; Jude 17–18). False prophets will increase and apostate religion will rival the true Church (1 Tim. 4:1; 2 Pet. 2:1–3; 2 Cor. 11:13–14).

3. *Israel will return to the Promised Land.* The great end-times regathering has already begun (since 1948). Israel is once again a nation in her own land (Ezek. 20:34; 37:12–21; Is. 43:5–6). But her return will touch off a storm of protest and conflict in the Middle East (Joel 3:2–14; Ezek. 38:1–6).

4. *The Church will be raptured to heaven.* When our Lord departed to heaven, He promised His disciples He would return to take them home with Him (John 14:3). The apostle Paul predicted that the dead in Christ shall rise first, and we that are alive and remain shall be caught up into heaven (1 Thess. 4:16–17; 1 Cor. 15:51–52).

5. *Judgments of the tribulation period will follow.* The great judgments of the End Times vividly described in the book of Revelation are called "the hour of testing" (3:10), "the great day of their wrath" (6:17) or "great tribulation" (7:14). These judgments relate to the seals, trumpets, and bowls of the Apocalypse.

6. *Marriage of Christ and the Church.* The Church's absence from chapter 4 through chapter 18 is best explained by the fact that she has already been raptured to heaven to participate in the marriage supper of the Lamb (19:7–9). Here she receives her rewards, crowns, and robes of righteousness prior to her procession back to earth with the Savior.

7. *Triumphal return of Christ.* The climax of the Apocalypse comes in 19:11–21, when the glorified Christ returns as King of kings and Lord of lords with His Bride, the Church, at His side. He returns to conquer all opposition to His reign and to establish His Millennial Kingdom on earth (19:19—20:4).

8. *Millennial Kingdom.* Jesus Christ will reign upon the earth for one thousand years (a millennium) while Satan is bound in the "abyss." During this time, God's promises to Israel will be fulfilled. The Messiah shall reign from Jerusalem over all the earth in peace, blessing, and prosperity (Rev. 20:1–6; Is. 2:2–4; 9:6–7).

9. *Final triumph.* Even after one thousand years of earthly blessing, Satan will once again attempt to destroy the kingdom of God by one final act of rebellion. This time his defeat is final, and he is cast into the lake of fire (20:7–10). The Great White Throne Judgment follows, when even death and hell are cast into the lake of fire (20:11–15).

10. *Eternal state.* The Revelation describes eternity as "a new heaven and a new earth" (21:1). It also emphasizes the significance of the New Jerusalem in the celestial state (21:2). God is pictured dwelling with His people in an eternity of peace and blessing. Suffering and death are no more and every tear is wiped away. Paradise is truly restored, and the saved have access to the tree of life (21:3—22:5).

How Do We Get There?

The final question to ask ourselves as we begin our study of the Apocalypse is, How do we interpret this great book with its highly symbolic language? Students of biblical prophecy have wrestled with this question for almost twenty centuries now. But several things are clear from the text of the Revelation itself:

1. John is looking into the *future* ("things which shall take place after these things," 1:19).

2. He sees a *succession of events* taking place in heaven and on the earth ("what must take place after these things," 4:1).

3. These events involve a series of *catastrophic judgments* on the earth (trees, grass, nations, rivers, mountains, islands, etc., are destroyed, chaps. 6—19).

4. These judgments result in the final *triumph and return* of Christ and the establishment of His kingdom on earth for one thousand years (19:11—20:6).

5. Beyond this is the *eternal state* of the new heaven and new earth, which remains for all eternity (21:1—22:5).

How are we to read this book? The early church was unanimous in its belief that it was speaking about *future events*. Only later did Christian authors begin to propose other ways of interpreting the Apocalypse. But each of these has failed to do justice to the obvious intention of the book itself. Variations have included:

1. *Preterist view:* sees the entire book, with few exceptions, as being fulfilled in the past—in the first century A.D. with the fall of Jerusalem and the persecution of the church by the Roman Empire. It allows no real future fulfillment of any of the judgments (seals, trumpets, bowls).

2. *Historicist view:* looks for the fulfillment of these prophecies throughout church history. This has led to endless speculation that is totally without biblical support. Identifications have included monks and friars as "locusts," Muhammad as the "fallen star," Alaric the Goth as the first trumpet, Elizabeth I as the first bowl, Martin Luther as the angel of Sardis, Adolf Hitler as the red horse, *ad infinitum.*

3. *Idealist view:* interprets Revelation as a series of ideal principles related to the struggle between good and evil. Allegorizes the entire book as a spiritual conflict unrelated to actual historic events. The "tribulation" becomes one's internal conflicts. The "return of Christ" takes place in one's own heart and mind. It views the prophecy as having nothing to say about real future events.

Robert L. Thomas summarizes his defense of the *futurist view* with this cryptic observation:

> The futurist approach to the book is the only one that grants sufficient recognition to the prophetic style of the book and a normal hermeneutical pattern of interpretation based on that style. It views the book as focusing on the last period(s) of world history and outlining the various events and their relationships to one another. This is the view that best accords with the principle of literal interpretation.[16]

The Apocalypse reveals the future. It is God's road map to help us understand where human history is going. The fact that it points to the time of the end is clear throughout the entire book. It serves as the final consummation of biblical revelation. It takes us from the first century to the last century, from persecution to triumph, from the struggling Church to the Bride of Christ, from Patmos to paradise.

The Apocalypse has been called the epilogue of the unfolding drama of redemption.[17] In the biblical record, human history begins in a garden and ends in the eternal city. It begins with tragedy and ends in triumph. It begins with man's failure and ends with his exaltation. In between, there stands a cross! And on that cross, Jesus Christ changed the course of human history forever. Hallelujah! What a Savior!

SECTION I: PREFACE

Vision of the Coming King

Revelation 1

CHAPTER 1

What in the World Is Happening?

Preview:
The Revelation opens with a clear statement of purpose: to reveal the future. Then it moves immediately to John's vision of the risen Savior. The glorified Christ assures John that He has the future under control and the stage is set for the great "unveiling."

Everyone is curious about the future. We all want to know what lies ahead. The same was true for the early Christians. They were undergoing tremendous persecution by the end of the first century A.D. Many felt abandoned and betrayed. Others began to feel hopeless. Some even began to ridicule the hope of Christ's return. They were not unlike our own generation.

We cannot imagine things getting worse than they already are. Every new public expression of sinful behavior or blatant unbelief shocks us. We all wonder how much time is really left on God's timetable. As the clock of history winds down, we sense that the end may be near.

Back in the apostle John's time, believers had many of the same concerns. But their concerns were intensified by political persecution from the Roman government. The Roman beast seemed to control the whole world. Its tentacles reached everywhere—threatening even the churches of Asia Minor. Many Jewish Christians had fled there to escape persecution from their own countrymen in Judea. But now the Gentiles posed an even greater threat to the future of the young churches.

It was in this context that John found himself. By the end of the first century, he was Jesus' last personal disciple still alive. All the others had perished long before. Each one had been martyred for his faith in Christ. But rather than make a martyred hero of John, the local Roman authorities decided to exile him to the island of Patmos off the coast of Asia Minor.

Tradition claims that John had come to Ephesus in A.D. 66. That meant he had been there for nearly thirty years. Scholars have often thought he was the youngest of Jesus' disciples. By A.D. 95, he was an old man—probably in his eighties.[1] Sixty-five years had passed since the crucifixion and resurrection of the Savior. John had been faithful all those years. But now he faced the greatest trial of his life. He was being abandoned on an unpopulated and deserted island. A political prisoner, he was left to die alone in exile.

Here we find the disciple whom Jesus so dearly loved. John had been with the Savior from the beginning. He had left the family fishing business to follow the carpenter from Nazareth. He was in the "inner circle" with Peter and James. At the Last Supper, he was seated next to Jesus and leaned over on his shoulder to talk to Him. He was the *only* disciple to show up at the cross. It was there that Jesus entrusted the care of His mother, Mary, to His beloved disciple (John 19:25–27).

But now, John was alone, abandoned on an isolated island. He was facing death and wondering about the future. What would happen to those fragile churches on the mainland? How long would the persecution last? What about the Savior's promise to return? All these questions probably filled his mind.

The Heavenly Intruder

Sunday morning came. It was the Lord's Day—resurrection day. John knew the churches would be assembled. He also knew they would be praying for him. That's when it happened! A booming voice broke the silence, announcing: "I am the Alpha and the Omega . . . who is and who was and who is to come" (Rev. 1:8).

When John turned to see who was speaking to him, he saw the risen Christ in all of His divine glory and heavenly splendor. The Savior had not abandoned him. Indeed, He had come for His faithful disciple who had cared for His earthly mother. Now it was the Savior's turn to care for John. And it was time to take him home to glory.

There are many unanswered questions about the book of Revelation. Did they find it beside John's body? Did he live to be recalled from exile? How did the book pass from the seven churches of Asia to the other Christian communities? We may never know the answers to some of these questions. But several things are clear from this first chapter:

1. John was exiled on Patmos.
2. Christ appeared to him there.
3. The Revelation was given to John.
4. Then it was sent to the seven churches for each to read.

The Divine Intruder had come for His disciple. He had come with a vision of the future and a message of hope for His Church. It was a glorious morning for every true believer. Unlike the Old Testament prophecies that often remained sealed up (Dan. 12:9), the Savior had come to reveal the future (Rev. 22:10). And what an incredible future it would be!

The Great Unveiling

Revelation opens with the preface to the book. This gives the reader an introduction to all that follows in the succeeding chapters. It is virtually impossible to understand the Apocalypse without a grasp of this first chapter. Its key elements include the following.

Title: The Revelation of Jesus Christ (1:1). Most Bible versions title the book: "The Revelation of St. John the Divine." However, such titles were not in the original New Testament Greek manuscripts. The actual title of the book is given in the opening verse: "The Revelation of Jesus Christ." He is the divine author of the book. It is His revelation ("unveiling") of the future. John is the human author who recorded what he saw and heard (1:2, 19). In many ways, John acts as a recording stenographer. He jots down, as fast as he can, future events that transpire before his eyes.

Testimony: All that he saw (1:2). Immediately, in verse 2, John begins with one of the many "triplets" which appear throughout the book. These are typical of the Johannine writing style. Notice John 1:1: "In the beginning was the Word, and the Word was with God, and the Word was God." In Revelation 1:2 the triplet reads: "Who bore witness to:

1. the word of God,
2. and the testimony of Jesus Christ,
3. even to all that he saw.

This passage tells us that the Apocalypse is an *eyewitness account*. This is not secondhand information that John has heard from someone else. He stakes his apostolic reputation on the fact that he actually saw and experienced these things.

Terms: "Blessed is he" (1:3). John then adds another triplet as he announces the first of seven *beatitudes* that appear throughout the book. This one reads: "Blessed is:

1. he who reads

2. and those who hear the words of the prophecy,

3. and heed the things which are written in it; for the time is near."

The scope of this promise covers the entire book, which is described as a "prophecy" (Greek, *prophēteias*). The Revelation thus describes itself as a prophetic book (cf. 22:7,10). It promises a threefold blessing to those who read it, hear it, and keep it. This emphasis reminds us that the purpose of reading or hearing the Word of God is that we might obey it.

There are *seven beatitudes* ("blessings") scattered throughout this amazing book. They are part of the unique "arithmalogue" structure of the book. The beatitudes are:

1. "*Blessed* is he who reads and those who hear the words of the prophecy, and heed the things which are written in it; for the time is near" (1:3).

2. "Write, '*Blessed* are the dead who die in the Lord from now on!' " (14:13).

3. "Behold, I am coming like a thief. *Blessed* is the one who stays awake and keeps his garments" (16:15).

4. "Write, '*Blessed* are those who are invited to the marriage supper of the Lamb' " (19:9).

5. "*Blessed* and holy is the one who has a part in the first resurrection" (20:6).

6. "And behold, I am coming quickly: *blessed* is he who heeds the words of the prophecy of this book" (22:7).

7. "*Blessed* are those who wash their robes" (22:14).

Time: "The time is near" (1:3). There are no dates set in the Revelation! No matter what anyone tries to read into the text of this prophecy, there are no specific time indicators of when it will be fulfilled. The only indication of time is the phrase "the time is near" (Greek, *kairos engus*). This may be translated "near" or "soon." Taken with the phrase "must shortly take place" (Greek, *en tachei*, "soon") in verse 1, the reader is left expecting the imminent return of Christ.[2]

John the Revelator

The preface (vv. 1–3) is followed by the introduction to the book. This takes the form of an epistolary greeting, which is typical of apostolic letters.

Following the pattern of triplets, John is identified three times (1:1, 4, 9).[3] This fits the pattern of the book and is understandable in light of his exile to Patmos. He had no way of knowing whether he would ever see them again, so he made certain they knew the book was from him.

The fact that the introduction is written to the seven churches of Asia Minor indicates that the entire book, not just the seven letters, was intended for all the churches to read. While there were other churches in the area (e.g., Colosse, Magnesium), these seven seem to be representative of the Church as a whole. John's greeting is "grace . . . and peace." These words are always stated in this order. There can be no real peace apart from God's grace.

The reference to the seven Spirits (1:4) is found only here in the Revelation. Commentators are divided as to whether it refers to seven angels (cf. Rev. 8:2) or the sevenfold aspects of the Holy Spirit (cf. Is. 11:2). The most persuasive position views the "seven Spirits" as originating in Zechariah 4:1–10, which speaks of the "seven lampstands" (cf. Rev. 4:5) that are the "eyes of the Lord" (cf. Rev. 5:6). New Testament scholar Bruce Metzger believes, "John uses the expression in order to symbolize the plentitude and power of the Holy Spirit."[4]

Jesus Christ is introduced with a double triplet (1:5). He is the:

1. Faithful witness (Greek, *marturia*)

2. First-born of the dead

3. Ruler of the kings of the earth

In light of the persecution they were facing, John reminds them who Jesus really is: the faithful martyr, risen Savior, King of kings. They need not fear death because He has gone before them and triumphed over it.

Next, John emphasizes what the Savior has done for us:

1. Loved us

2. Released us

3. Made us to be a kingdom, priests to His God and Father

These designations of the Savior remind us that we have both a heavenly and earthly destiny in Him. He is King of the *earth* and we shall reign as kings with Him on the earth (cf. Rev. 5:10). From the very beginning, the Apocalypse has an earthly focus. Premillennialists have always understood this, but other eschatological viewpoints have missed this altogether. We are promised that we will rule with Him on earth, not just in a "spiritual" sense, but literally.

Names and Titles of Christ in Revelation

1. Jesus Christ (1:1, 2, 5)
2. Faithful witness (1:5)
3. First-born of the dead (1:5)
4. Ruler of the kings of the earth (1:5)
5. Alpha and Omega (1:8; 21:6; 22:13)
6. He who is and who was and who is to come (1:4, 8; 4:8)
7. The Almighty (1:8; 15:3)
8. Son of man (1:13; 14:14)
9. The first and the last (1:17; 2:8; 22:13)
10. The living One (1:18)
11. The One who holds the seven stars (2:1)
12. The One who walks among the seven golden lampstands (2:1)
13. The One who has the sharp two-edged sword (2:12)
14. Son of God (2:18)
15. He who has eyes like flame of fire (2:18)
16. He whose feet are like burnished bronze (2:18)
17. He who searches the minds and hearts (2:23)
18. He who has the seven Spirits of God (3:1)
19. He who is holy, [and] who is true (3:7)
20. He who has the key of David (3:7)
21. The Amen (3:14)
22. Faithful and true witness (3:14)
23. Beginning of the creation of God (3:14)
24. Lion from the tribe of Judah (5:5)
25. Root of David (5:5; 22:16)
26. The Lamb (28 times)
27. Lord, holy and true (6:10)
28. Their Lord [who] was crucified (11:8)
29. Male child (12:5, 13)
30. King of the nations (15:3)
31. Lord of lords and King of kings (17:14; 19:16)
32. Word of God (19:13)
33. Bright morning star (22:16)

The King Is Coming

Theme: "Behold, He is coming" (1:7–8). John states the theme of the Revelation in another triplet. He points to the imminent return of Christ as the basic theme of the entire book: "Behold, He is coming with the clouds." Then he adds the triplet using the triple *kai:*

1. *And* every eye will see Him

2. *Even* those who pierced Him

3. *And* all the tribes of the earth will mourn over Him

The promise is one of future triumph. The Savior is ultimately coming to take over the earth. He will not return as the lowly servant, humble shepherd, or rejected prophet. This time He will return as King of kings, and the whole world will know it. The focus here is on the final aspect of His return in judgment on an unbelieving world. Then, and only then, will the apostle Paul's words be fulfilled: "That at the name of Jesus every knee should bow . . . and that every tongue should confess that Jesus Christ is Lord, to the glory of God the Father" (Phil. 2:10–11).

John the revelator states the theme of the book in 1:7, and Christ, the Source of the Revelation, repeats it in 1:8. "I am the Alpha and the Omega" refers to the first and last letters of the Greek alphabet (like *A* and *Z* in English). Thus, Christ is both the beginning and the ending. In Him, all things were created (John 1:3), and in Him all things will be consummated (Rev. 21:6). The Savior is then described as the Lord who:

1. "is" (present tense),

2. "was" (past tense), and

3. "is to come" (future tense).

He is the eternal Son of God. Like the Father, He always was, He is, and He will always be. The emphasis, however, is on the present tense and focuses on the eternal presence of God. He is the ever-present One: "I am who I am" (Ex. 3:14). Since all things are present to the mind of God, He sees the end from the beginning as though it were already happening. Thus, He can disclose the future to John in the visions of the Apocalypse.

The Final Victory

Triumph: "behold, I am alive for evermore" (1:9–20). John explains that he had been exiled to the island of Patmos "because of the word of God and the testimony of Jesus Christ" (1:9). Patmos was the Alcatraz of the ancient world. It was an isolated place from which there was no escape. There, on the rocky promontory (ten miles long and six miles wide), the aged apostle met the risen Savior face-to-face. John explains that he was "in the Spirit" on the Lord's Day (Sunday) when the Savior appeared to him. The phrase "in the Spirit" is an explanation of an out-of-the-body "trance" (called "ecstasy" [Greek, *ekstasis*] in Acts 10:10; 11:5; 22:17). John never slept during this experience; thus, it was a vision, not a dream. Robert L. Thomas explains it as "the ecstatic condition into which God placed John for the sake of granting him the revelations of this book."[5]

John heard the Master's voice and turned to see who it was. As he turned, he saw *seven golden lampstands*—probably in the shape of a Jewish menorah (1:12). These were representative of the seven churches to which the book is addressed (1:20). In the middle of the *lampstands*, he saw the Son of man dressed in the high priestly garments—the floor-length white robe with the golden sash (cf. Ex. 39). The rest of the description of the risen Savior is symbolic of His Shekinah glory and deity and follows a *sevenfold pattern:*

1. Hair: white like white wool
2. Eyes: flame of fire
3. Feet: burnished bronze
4. Voice: sound of many waters
5. Right hand: held seven stars
6. Mouth: sharp two-edged sword
7. Face: shining like the sun

David Hocking writes, "This is no ordinary look at the man we know from the gospel as Jesus Christ. To say that His appearance is unique is also an understatement: it is supernatural, a glorious description that could be given to God alone."[6] The grandeur of this description points to the majesty, purity, and authority of the One described. This is the risen Savior. This is the glorified Christ. This is the coming King!

The Savior's description also introduces one of the most powerful symbols in the Apocalypse: the sword of His mouth. He is the One who spoke the world into existence. He is also the One who spoke and calmed the storms, stilled the waves, and spoke peace to men's hearts. No wonder John loved to call Him "the Word of God" (cf. John 1:1; 1 John 1:1; Rev. 19:13). The *sword* of His mouth symbolizes the power of His spoken word, which cuts both ways: it creates and it destroys. Ultimately, it is His word that will defeat the forces of the Antichrist and slay his armies (cf. Rev. 19:15, 21).

John, the beloved disciple, collapses at the Savior's feet (1:17). He cannot stand in his own strength before his divine King. Remember, this is one of

Jesus' dearest and closest disciples. If he cannot stand before Him, how dare we think we can! Throughout the Revelation it is clear that approaching God is no trivial matter. We can come into His presence only by the permission of the blood of Christ (cf. Heb. 10:19–21).

John lay prostrate on the ground before the King of kings, the High Priest of heaven. But then came that familiar tender touch: "He laid His right hand upon me" (1:17). The nail-scarred hand of the Savior touched His beloved servant. It had been more than 60 years since he had watched in the upper room when Jesus said to doubting Thomas, "Reach here your finger, and see My hands . . . and be not unbelieving, but believing." And Thomas answered, "My Lord and my God" (John 20:27–28)!

That same nail print will be there for all eternity, reminding us of the Savior's love. And it was that loving voice that said, "Do not be afraid." John had heard those words before—the night He calmed the storm. "Take courage," He said that night, "it is I; do not be afraid" (cf. Matt. 14:24–27; John 6:20).

When John looked up, he saw the Savior looking down. "And I was dead, and behold, I am alive forevermore," He announced. Then He added the most important statement of all: "And I have the keys of death and of Hades" (1:18). Jesus had already triumphed over the forces of Satan in His crucifixion and resurrection. He had already descended into hell, announced Satan's doom, "stolen the keys," and risen victorious.

Now the Lord had come for His beleaguered servant, His beloved disciple, and His dear friend. He was going to unlock the mystery of the future and unveil the sequence of events that would lead to Armageddon and the End Times.

He commanded John to "write" those things which:

1. "You have seen" (past)

2. "Things which are" (present)

3. "Things which shall take place after these things" (future)

Many have used that simple threefold designation to outline the entire book: past (chap. 1), present (chaps. 2—3); future (chaps. 4—22). The chapter closes by uniting each of these elements. The Savior who died and rose again in the past is still alive and moving in His Church in the present and will come again in the future. He has already triumphed, and so shall we!

Study Questions

1. Read John 14:3. What key to the prophetic significance of Revelation 2 do you find in this verse?

2. What is the biblical title of the book (cf. 1:1)?

3. According to Revelation 1:2, what is the unique nature of the Apocalypse?

4. What is promised to everyone who reads, hears, and keeps the words of this prophecy (1:3)?

5. Where was the book of Revelation sent (1:4)?

6. Describe Jesus' appearance in Revelation 1.

7. Why had John been exiled to Patmos (1:9)?

8. What was John doing when he received his visions (1:10)?

9. What is the significance of the Greek letters Alpha and Omega (1:11)?

10. Though Jesus is depicted in all of His deity in Revelation 1, by what name is he referred to in Revelation 1:13?

11. What does the sword in Jesus' mouth symbolize (1:16)?

SECTION II: PROCLAMATION

Letters to the Seven Churches

Revelation 2–3

CHAPTER 2

Judgment Begins at The House of God!

Preview:

The second section of the book of Revelation contains the Letters to the Seven Churches. These are personal epistles from the risen Christ to seven literal churches in Asia Minor. Imagine that Jesus wrote a personal letter to your church. What would He say in that letter? These letters give us an idea of what Christ thinks of the Church.

John the Revelator has already introduced us to the seven churches in chapter 1. The risen Christ has appeared to him and instructed him to write a book and "send it to the seven churches" (1:11). These churches are symbolized by the seven golden lampstands (1:12, 20). Thus, the connection is made between the preface (chap. 1) and the proclamation (chaps. 2–3). Jesus Christ, the Lord of the Church, is moving actively in the churches as our heavenly High Priest. His love and concern for these churches has already been demonstrated on the cross. Now, as the risen, living Lord of the Church, He sends a personal message to those churches which were under John's care and influence.

Before the Apocalypse presents any message of judgment on the unbelieving world, it first calls the churches to repentance. Judgment must begin at the house of God. If the local churches are not a proper expression of God's truth and righteousness, how can they influence the world for Christ? In these letters, we find the Lord of the Church lovingly but firmly speaking to His Church. Some have called these "love letters from the Lord of heaven."[1]

The seven churches were seven literal churches that existed in Asia Minor (see map) in the first century A.D. Ephesus was the largest city in the area and presumably the largest church. Thus, it served as a "mother" church to the others. All seven were connected by the local Roman highway. They were arranged in a circular pattern going from Ephesus to Smyrna, on to Laodicea, and back to Ephesus.[2]

Attempts to find prophetic parallels between these churches and a supposed "seven ages of church history" are forced and fanciful at best. Such parallels have been suggested since medieval times, but have always proven unsatisfactory as time moved on. Even the seven suggested in the old *Scofield Reference Bible* hardly do justice to the facts of church history.[3] A careful reading of these chapters, and indeed the entire Apocalypse, will reveal that there is *nothing in the text itself* to indicate that these seven churches are symbolic of church history!

What Do the Seven Churches Represent?

A basic reading of these letters reveals that they are simply seven local churches that all existed at the same time and in the same general area. Each had its own unique characteristics, strengths, and weaknesses. At best, we can suggest only that they represent seven different types of churches.

The message to each church follows the same sevenfold pattern:

1. *Commission:* "To the angel of the church in . . ."
2. *Character:* "The One who . . . says this"
3. *Commendation:* "I know your deeds . . ."
4. *Condemnation:* "But I have this against you . . ."
5. *Correction:* "Repent, turn, change . . ."
6. *Call:* "He who has an ear, let him hear . . ."
7. *Challenge:* "To him who overcomes . . ."

The only exceptions to this pattern may be seen on the following chart of the seven churches of revelation. Notice there are no words of commendation for Sardis or Laodicea, and no words of condemnation for Smyrna or Philadelphia. Certainly the latter two are upheld as ideals for the others. Notice also that all seven churches still had a lampstand, including Laodicea (1:20). Of the Laodicean church, the Lord also said, "Those whom I love, I reprove and discipline" (3:19). Here we see the Lord of the Church appealing to His churches in love and concern. The appeal of these letters is personal to each *local* church. At the same time, the principles dealt with are *universal* in nature.

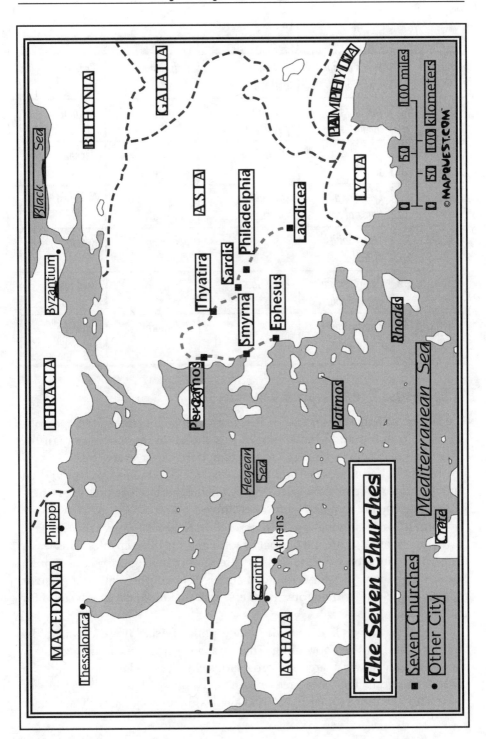

The Seven Churches

Seven Churches
Other City

	Christ	**Commends**	**Condemns**	**Corrects**
Ephesus	Walks among lampstands	Toil and perseverance	Left first love	Repent
Smyrna	The first and the last	Tribulation and poverty		Be faithful
Pergamum	Sharp two-edged sword	Did not deny My faith	False doctrine	Repent
Thyatira	Eyes like a flame of fire	Love and ministry	False doctrine	Hold fast
Sardis	Seven Spirits of God		Spiritually dead	Repent
Philadelphia	Opens and no one will shut	Open door		Hold fast
Laodicea	Faithful and true witness		Lukewarm	Open the door

1. Ephesus: Preoccupied Church

The church at Ephesus was one of the outstanding churches of the apostolic era. Paul, Timothy, and John all served this church in the first century of the Christian era (cf. Acts 18–19). Aquila and Priscilla were also very actively involved at Ephesus, as was Apollos (cf. Acts 18:24–26). This was a privileged church, indeed! Yet, as time wore on, they had begun to lose their first priority and became preoccupied with other things.

John himself is thought to have resided in Ephesus for over thirty years.[4] It was here that he wrote the Gospel of John and his three epistles. This was a time when emperor worship was the predominant religion of the Roman Empire. Christians like John found themselves in conflict with the popular religion of their time. Therefore, it was essential that they take a clear stand for their beliefs.

City. Ephesus was known as the "metropolis of Asia." It was considered a "free city" and was self-governing. There was no permanent Roman military stationed there. It was a large and prosperous city. Even today, its ruins are the most extensive in the whole region. Ancient Ephesus had a population of more than 250,000 people! It also had a large Jewish population. The theater seated 25,000 spectators and was the scene of the riot in Acts 19:28–29. The marble-paved main street was lined with shops and public buildings.

The greatest structure of all at Ephesus was the Temple of Diana—one of the seven wonders of the ancient world. This temple stood on a platform measuring over 100,000 square feet (twice the size of a football field). The temple itself was supported by one hundred marble columns. Each was a monolith (single stone) fifty-five feet in height. Inside the temple stood the statue of the goddess Diana (Greek, *Artemis*).

Church. The apostle Paul visited Ephesus at the end of his second missionary journey (Acts 18:19) in about A.D. 51. Aquila and Priscilla assisted Paul there and influenced Apollos (Acts 18:25–26). On his third missionary journey, Paul returned to Ephesus and ministered there for three years (circa A.D. 52–55). Paul later left Timothy in charge of the church at Ephesus (1 Tim. 1:3). In circa. A.D. 60, Paul wrote his epistle to the Ephesians from prison in Rome. In A.D. 66, the apostle John arrived and stayed some thirty years.[5]

The Ephesian church was one of the great apostolic churches. The Lord commends them for their labor, patience, fidelity, and endurance (Rev. 2:2–3). They had stood true to the faith despite their pagan surroundings. The constant lure of temptation was all around them, but they remained true to Christ. "But I have this against you," He said, "that you have left your first love" (2:4).

The church's "first love" could refer to several things: its love for Christ, the fervency of new believers, or the basic priorities of the church. As time had passed, their love had diminished. Their church life was filled with other priorities. The basics of Christian living were being neglected. So the Lord of the Church calls them back to their original commitment to those basic priorities.

Challenge. The glorified Savior challenged the Ephesians to *remember* their original position in Christ—seated in heavenly places (cf. Eph. 1:3). Then He calls upon them to *repent* and reinstate their original commitments ("first works"). Otherwise, He threatens to come and remove their lampstand. This indicates that any church can cease being a true church. Once the light of the gospel goes out, it ceases to be the "light of the world."

2. Smyrna: Persecuted Church

Smyrna was located about thirty-five miles from Ephesus. It was the next major city on the Roman road. Known today as Izmir, ancient Smyrna was a beautiful and prosperous city. As early as 195 B.C., a temple had been built there to *Dea Roma* (the personification of Rome as a goddess). In A.D. 25, a temple was built there to Emperor Tiberius. Thus, emperor worship became a matter of great pride and loyalty to the people of Smyrna.

In contrast to the deification of Rome and its emperors stood the Christian church at Smyrna. There is not one hint of compromise in our Lord's letter to them. Their devotion to Christ was such that they refused to burn incense at Caesar's bust. But in time, they paid dearly for their fidelity to the Savior. In the middle of the second century (ca. 156), the aged and godly Polycarp, bishop of the church for forty years and John's personal disciple, was burned at the stake for his faith in Jesus Christ.

"Swear by the genius of Caesar and I will release you. Revile Christ!" the proconsul demanded.

"For eighty-six years I have served him and he has done me no wrong," Polycarp replied. "How then can I blaspheme my King who saved me? I am a Christian!"

Condemned as "the teacher of Asia, the father of the Christians, the destroyer of the gods," Polycarp died with calm dignity and unflinching courage. A century later, in A.D. 251, during the Decian persecution, Pionius the Presbyter was arrested on the anniversary of Polycarp's death and executed for his faith in Christ. His last words were, "I have chosen to die in obedience to my Master, rather than transgress His commands."[6]

City. Ancient Smyrna was named for a perfume whose aroma was released by crushing the resin of a small thornbush. The perfume was known to the Greeks as *Smyrna.* The city itself was ruled in turn by Anatolians, Lydians, and Persians. It was eventually totally destroyed and left in ruins. In 334 B.C., Alexander the Great rebuilt it as a Greek city, but it later gave its allegiance to Rome. Cicero called the city "our most faithful and most ancient ally."[7] By New Testament times, Smyrna was a large Roman city with a prosperous Jewish community.

In A.D. 178 and again in 180, Smyrna was badly damaged by earthquakes and was rebuilt by Emperor Marcus Aurelius. In A.D. 325, during the Council of Nicea, Bishop Eytychius represented Smyrna. In the fifth century, Attila the Hun conquered the city. In A.D. 673 it fell to the Arabs, but was liberated until A.D. 1402 when it fell to Tamerlane, who massacred the Christian population in the name of Islam.[8]

Church. Persecution was the watchword of this church. They had suffered often at the hands of the Romans and would suffer even more in the years to come. The Jewish population in Smyrna was particularly anti-Christian. They led the chant demanding the martyrdom of Polycarp and other believers. But as was so often the case, the blood of the martyrs was the "seed of the church." The church at Smyrna grew into one of the most revered and influential churches of its time because its leaders were willing to lay down their lives for Christ and the gospel.

Four things characterizing the suffering of the believers at Smyrna were mentioned in our Lord's letter to them:

1. *Poverty:* They had been excluded from the financial prosperity of the city and were rich only in Christ (2:9).

2. *Slander:* The unbelieving Jews slandered them as heretics and troublemakers. But Jesus said such were of the "synagogue of Satan."

3. *Prison:* Many of them would be imprisoned for their faith in Christ as were so many of the apostles.

4. *Death:* Like Polycarp and others, many of these believers died for their faith rather than worship the Roman emperor. They were indeed "faithful until death" (2:10).

Challenge. There are no words of condemnation for this church. There is no call to repentance. They are told they are rich in Christ and exhorted to be "faithful until death" (2:10). The heavenly epistolary expresses no regret. Their deaths are but temporary in light of eternity. They will be rewarded with a "crown of life" and shall overcome the "second death" (2:10–11).

It is difficult, if not impossible, for most modern Christians to comprehend what it must be like to risk all you have for Christ. Most of us struggle with concerns about public embarrassment or social rejection. We know little or nothing about laying down our lives for the gospel.

Joseph Tson, a Romanian Baptist pastor, survived great personal persecution during the Communist regime in Romania. He and members of his church became part of the revival God used to break the Soviet grip on his nation. When faced with the possibility of imprisonment and death, he met a fellow believer who challenged him with what he calls the "theology of martyrdom." Tson calls it the "greatest privilege of the Christian life—to give your life for Christ." "But," he adds, "you must be counted worthy to die for Christ!" Despite all his personal suffering and that of his family, Tson laments, "We were not worthy!"

3. Pergamum: Political Church

Forty miles north of Sardis sits ancient Pergamum in the Caicus Valley. Pliny, the Roman writer, called it "the most famous city in Asia." It was the center of Roman power and authority in the province. In fact, the Pergamanians worshiped power. As early as 29 B.C., it became the site of the first temple of the Caesar-cult, erected in honor of Augustus Caesar. The city also housed an ancient temple to the god Zeus—the god of power. The altar from that temple is in the Berlin Museum and was often visited by Adolf Hitler. Pergamum (also, Pergamos) was the epitome of the hunger for power in pagan society.[9]

There was no distinction between religion and politics in Pergamum. The city's coins depicted intertwined serpents to represent the interconnection between the sacred and the secular. For the pagans in this city, politics was religion and religion was politics. And for the Christians, there was a constant temptation to compromise their beliefs and practices for political gain.

Religion has always had a precarious relationship to political power. When power is on the side of religion, it tends to corrupt it. But when power is against religion, it tends to persecute it. Unfortunately, the pressure of persecution often drives religion to seek power as a means of protection and self-preservation. In time, religion itself often falls victim to the very thing it opposes. It has been observed more than once that the ultimate subversion of Christianity occurs whenever we confuse spiritual authority with political power.[10]

City. Pergamum was an incredible city. Pillared temples, public buildings, and massive fortifications sat atop the acropolis. And above all was the great Temple of Zeus, king of the gods. When Attalus III of Pergamum died in 133 B.C., he bequeathed the city to the Romans, and they made it their political capital in Asia. The local library was one of the greatest in the ancient world, boasting a collection of 200,000 volumes.

Pergamum was also known for its famous *asklepium* (healing and medical center). Here, religious meditation, dream interpretation, snake-handling, and medical arts were combined for healing purposes. The Sacred Way led from the Asclepion, built in honor of the god of healing, toward the acropolis, which rose a thousand feet above the plain. Near the summit stood the immense altar to Zeus. A short distance away was the elegant Temple of Athena (Greek goddess of war). But more than anything else, the imperial cult of Caesar worship dominated all else at Pergamum.[11]

Church. Christ began His letter to the church at Pergamum by reminding them, "I know where you dwell" (Rev. 2:13). He was fully aware that these believers were surrounded by a non-Christian society and exposed to its values, standards, and pressures. Confrontation between the power of the state and the young Christian church was inevitable.

Christian tradition claims that Gaius (3 John 1) was the first bishop of Pergamum and that he was succeeded by Antipas, whom the Lord refers to in His letter as "My witness, My faithful one" (2:13). His name (Greek, *anti pas*) means "against all" and may refer to his willingness to stand against all compromise and temptation.

Despite this wonderful heritage, the Lord had great concerns for this church. Christ is depicted as holding a two-edged sword. The *jus gladii* ("right of the sword") was viewed by the Romans as the power over life and death and was vested in the proconsul. Here, Christ assumes this right. Thus, He reminds His Church that He alone is sovereign and supreme. He alone has all power!

There were two doctrinal errors that Christ addressed in this church. The *doctrine of Balaam* refers to the Old Testament story of the prophet Balaam's religious compromise with Balak, the king of Moab. The *doctrine of the Nicolaitans* is believed to have derived from Nicolas of Antioch, whose disciples insisted that Christian freedom meant "lawlessness." Like Balaam of old, they believed that a little idolatry or a little immorality or a little compromise of the truth couldn't really hurt anything. In fact, such compromise made Christianity all the more tolerable in a pagan city. But Jesus said that He *hated* such false doctrine (2:15).

Challenge. The Great Shepherd was concerned about the wayward condition of the flock at Pergamum. He was concerned that a little compromise would lead to the ultimate destruction of the church. In fact, the Greek term *nikolaos* means "destroyer of the people." The false doctrines of Balaam and the Nicolaitans said that Christian liberty allowed participation in worldly activities. They attempted to use Christian liberty to justify their personal compromise with sinful paganism.

Our Lord's letter emphasizes several things that are vital for any effective church:

1. *Love for the truth.* We cannot tolerate doctrinal error under the excuse that we must love everybody. First and foremost, we must love the truth and let it be the final authority in the church.

2. *Desire for holiness.* We cannot win a lost world with a worldly Christianity. Only godly believers who practice what they preach will win them to Christ. Integrity is the missing ingredient in modern religion. The unbelieving world will not listen to anyone who doesn't have it.

3. *Willingness to repent.* The Lord called upon this church to repent of their compromise. If He insisted they repent, how much more would He call upon us to do the same! To those who would repent, He promised three things: 1) hidden manna, 2) a white stone, 3) a new name. All three of these point to His high priestly role. The manna was hidden in the Ark of the Covenant (Ex. 16:32–34; Heb. 9:4). The white stone was the Urim on the high priest's vestment. And the "new" name was the self-revelation of Christ (cf. Rev. 3:12, "My new name").

In summarizing the situation at Pergamum, John Stott observes: "The emperor cult has long since vanished. But the 'false prophet' has not died. He lives again in every non-Christian religion and philosophy, and in every attempt to divert to others the honor that is due to Jesus Christ alone."[12]

4. Thyatira: Prosperous Church

The longest of the seven letters was written to the church in the smallest town. Thyatira had little political or religious significance. There was little threat of persecution for the believers here. But there was a more subtle temptation: social acceptance. Thyatira was a manufacturing center known for its cloth industry—weaving, dyeing, and sewing were the major sources of income (cf. Lydia of Thyatira whom Paul met in Philippi, Acts 16:14). It was a town dominated by trade guilds and powerful "designing women."

Edward Myers points out that the trade guilds were religious in nature. One could not make a living without being a member. Each one was dedicated to a particular deity. Feasts to these guild gods were lavish parties that everyone was expected to attend.[13] These included three basic elements: 1) a cup of wine, poured out in worship of the god; 2) a fellowship meal, which included excessive drinking; and 3) a sexual orgy following the meal. Christians were placed in the terrible situation of participation or rejection—which meant losing their jobs.

City. Thyatira was a defenseless city. It had no natural fortress and was generally under the military protection of Pergamum, some 30 miles to the east. The city was conquered by the Roman general Scipio Africanus, who defeated Antiochus III at Magnesia in 190 B.C. In 133 B.C. it became a Roman possession along with Pergamum. Its status as a commercial and manufacturing center was well attested in ancient literature.[14]

Religion in Thyatira was connected to material prosperity and participation in the trade guilds. Caesar was worshiped there as Apollo incarnate. But in general, religion seems to have taken a backseat to commercial enterprise in this city. Powerful women who lived in the lap of luxury dominated the trade guilds. The latest fashions were readily available from the many sewing and weaving looms. Wool workers, linen workers, dyers, and leather tanners were everywhere. The local population was mainly of Macedonian descent. While there was a small Jewish community there, it seems to have had little effect on the church.

Church. Our Lord's letter commends the church for its charity, service, faith, patience, and good works—qualities that were undoubtedly encouraged by strong Christian women who were part of the congregation. But there were also serious problems with this church. A powerful woman, symbolically called Jezebel (cf. 1 Kin. 16:31), had influence so great that she encouraged the believers to participate in the guild festivals—committing fornication and eating things sacrificed to idols (2:20).

Robert Thomas observes of this church, "Not only did the Christians lack zeal for godly discipline and correct doctrine; they also obliged those who erred in these ways and condoned their errors."[15] Just as Old Testament Jezebel, the pagan wife of King Ahab, led the Israelites astray, so this New Testament "Jezebel" was doing the same. Her compromise with the socially acceptable immorality of the times is described by the Savior as plunging into the "deep things of Satan" (2:24). Like the modern church today, the believers at Thyatira were more concerned about fashion than faith. They preferred social acceptance to spiritual integrity. They wanted to tolerate sin in the name of cultural accommodation.

Challenge. The bottom line of our Lord's appeal to the believers at Thyatira was ethical as well as doctrinal. He criticizes their practice more than their doctrine. It may well have been that the false prophetess was encouraging and tolerating secret sin, rather than promoting it publicly. Thus, the Lord reminds them that He has "eyes like a flame of fire" which penetrate the human heart and reveal its secret desires. In Acts 1:24 and 15:18, He is called *kardiognostes,* "the heart-knower." His divine insight sees beyond outward appearances and penetrates the inner hearts of people.

Christ threatens to cast this immoral woman into a bed of great tribulation (2:22). The call to repentance was issued and there was still time to repent, but the door of divine opportunity was about to close. Like careless and immoral believers today, those in Thyatira did not take seriously the coming of the Great Tribulation.

To the other believers in Thyatira, who had not fallen under "Jezebel's" spell, our Lord imposes no other burden (2:24). For them, He promises "authority over the nations" to rule with Him in His earthly kingdom (cf. Ps. 2:8–9). Secondly, He promises to send them the "morning star" (2:28), which in Revelation 22:16 is Christ Himself! The morning star is the one that shines brightest. It can still be seen even as the sun is beginning to rise. Instead of the "deep things of Satan," they have the heights of heaven!

Study Questions

1. Read Matthew 16:18. What key to the prophetic significance of Revelation 2 do you find in this verse?

2. Who are the angels (Greek, *angelos:* "messengers") of the seven churches?

3. What do the seven golden lampstands (1:20) represent?

4. If a church still has a lampstand (2:5), is it still a legitimate church?

5. Is it proper to hate false doctrine (cf. 2:6, 15)?

6. Who is ultimately behind the persecution of Christians (cf. 2:10)?

7. What is the significance of "Satan's seat" (2:13) being in Pergamum?

8. Can false doctrine ever be tolerated (cf. 2:14–15)?

9. What is the significance of the phrase "I know thy works" (2:2, 9, 13, 19)?

10. Can the message to these seven churches be applied to all churches in general (cf. 2:23)?

11. Will the true Church ever actually rule on earth with Christ (cf. 2:26–27)?

CHAPTER 3

Who's That Knocking At My Door?

Preview:
The letters to the seven churches conclude in this chapter. Each letter includes a personal assessment of the local church by Jesus Christ, the Lord of the Church. In the last letter, the Laodiceans are pictured as closing Him out of their church. Imagine the Lord of the Church knocking on the door of the church, begging us to let Him in!

The focus of our Lord's letters to the churches is both earthly and heavenly. They address the struggles of the churches on earth. But the view of the churches is seen from a heavenly perspective. The risen Christ is seen moving among the seven candlesticks, which symbolically represent the seven churches. The Savior is pictured in the Apocalypse as actively ministering to and caring for His Church on earth. New Testament scholar Bruce Metzger notes, "The literary structure of the seven letters discloses a certain uniform pattern. Each message is prefaced with an identification of the heavenly Christ."[1]

Revelation 2 introduces us to four of the seven letters: Ephesus, Smyrna, Pergamum, and Thyatira. Chapter 3 continues with the letters to Sardis, Philadelphia, and Laodicea. Since there were no chapter divisions in the original Greek manuscripts, the Greek text moves right along to include these three with the other four. The pattern (commission, character, commendation, condemnation, correction, call, challenge) is identical in all seven letters.

5. Sardis: Powerless Church

Have you ever attended a dead church? There is nothing worse than dead orthodoxy, dead traditionalism, or dead liberalism. The service is dull, lifeless, empty, and irrelevant. Everyone is bored and nodding off to sleep. No wonder our Lord said, "Wake up!" Sardis was a church that was ready to die. The light of the gospel was about to be extinguished. The power of the Spirit was about to fade. What is worse is that few people seemed to care.

There is nothing more tragic than watching a church die. Some die because *tradition* ("the way we've always done it") kills the spirit of innovation. Some die because *prejudice* ("we don't want them") keeps them from reaching a changing neighborhood. Others die because *complacency* replaces fervency. People "lose heart in doing good" (cf. Gal. 6:9) and just give up. But whatever else goes wrong, one thing especially will kill a church: Stop evangelizing!

Whenever a church stops preaching the gospel, it turns inward and self-destructs. When we get our eyes off the lost and focus on ourselves, we have lost our true spiritual vision. Churches that are not winning people to Christ are failing to obey the Great Commission (cf. Matt. 28:19–20). Without new converts, the church stagnates. When it stops growing, it starts to die.

City. Sardis was a commercial and industrial city at the junction of five roads. It had been the ancient capital of Lydia. But its greatest glory was in the past. In the sixth century B.C., it was one of the greatest cities in the world, ruled by the fabled King Croesus, whom the Greeks called *Midas*, known for his golden treasures. But twice in ancient times the city was caught off guard and captured despite its great fortress citadel and steep cliffs.

Cyrus the Great dethroned Croesus in 546 B.C., and Sardis became the western capital of the Persian Empire. In 499 B.C. the city was totally destroyed by the Greeks. In 334 B.C., Sardis surrendered to Alexander the Great without a battle. In 214 B.C. Antiochus the Great captured it. In A.D. 17 it was destroyed by an earthquake but was rebuilt by Tiberius Caesar, the Roman emperor.

Church. Like the city, the church, too, was in constant danger. Just as Sardis had fallen because of a lack of vigilance, so the church was in danger of falling as well. As the city had flourished and then decayed, so the church had done the same. No wonder they were told to "wake up" and "strengthen the things that remain" (3:2). Metzger notes, "Here are five staccato imperatives: Wake up! Strengthen! Remember! Obey! Repent!"[2]

Reading this letter we get the distinct impression there were only a few Christians left in Sardis (3:4). Times were changing and the church was being left behind. The Savior warned them to wake up and repent lest He "come like a thief" (cf. Matt. 24:43) and catch them unprepared. To those who wake up, he promises not to "erase [their names] from the book of life" (3:5). This is a *litotes*, a figure of speech in which an affirmation is expressed by the negative of a contrary statement. By a denial of the opposite ("I will not erase"), our Lord affirms emphatically that the overcomer's name will be retained in the book of life.[3]

Challenge. The solution to escaping this spiritual graveyard is found in our Lord's challenge to this church. Their nominal faith amounted to little more than spiritual death. Therefore, the Savior's appeal was to the *godly remnant* that remained, rather than to the dead unbelievers who dominated the church roles. John Stott observes: "The metaphor has changed from death to sleep. You cannot appeal to a dead man to wake up! But some church members (the remnant) were sleepy rather than dead, and the risen Jesus calls them to rouse themselves from their heavy slumbers and to be watchful."[4]

How was this believing remnant to "strengthen the things that remain"?

1. *Remember* how you were first converted to Christ. Get back to the basics of New Testament Christianity.

2. *Keep* the truth. It is the only anchor for your soul in changing times.

3. *Repent* of your apathy. Become vigilant and diligent about your walk with God.

If they would do that much, the Lord promised them "white raiment"— the symbol of righteousness and justice in the Apocalypse (cf. 2:17; 14:14; 19:11; 20:11). He also promised a secure and permanent place in the book of life (3:5). This is the "scroll of remembrance" where all the saved of all time are recorded. Your name may be written on every church register in town, but if it's not written in heaven, all hope is lost!

6. Philadelphia: Persevering Church

The church at Philadelphia was one of the strongest of the seven congregations. It was a church with missionary zeal and spiritual commitment. Outwardly, it was small and poor compared to the church at Sardis. But inwardly, it was a dynamic and faithful church. Observing the contrast between the two churches, Bruce Metzger writes, "The letter to Sardis contains almost unmitigated censure; the letter to Philadelphia is one of almost unqualified commendation."[5]

The city itself was the youngest of the seven. Attalus II Philadelphos, one of the kings of Pergamum, founded the city in circa 150 B.C. Attalus was known for his love and devotion to his brother, Eumenes. Hence the name of the town:

city of "brotherly love." Ironically, the Roman historian Strabo called it a "city full of earthquakes." A severe one in A.D. 17 devastated nearby Sardis and totally demolished Philadelphia. But the Romans rebuilt the city, and a congregation of Christian believers flourished there by the end of the first century.

City. Philadelphia was relatively small compared to the other cities of the Apocalypse. It sat in a lush valley in the heart of Asia Minor, near the Timolous Mountains. Its greatest distinction was that it was strategically located on the Roman road that ran from Rome to Troy, Pergamum, Sardis, and on to Philadelphia. Even in ancient times, Philadelphia was the "gateway to the East." Beyond lay the great central plateau of Asia Minor (modern Turkey).

Attalus originally had intended the new city to serve as a dissemination point for the Greek language and culture to penetrate the eastern provinces. So the Lord saw the city's strategic location as an opportunity to spread the gospel. Undoubtedly, many early Christians traveled through Philadelphia as they journeyed east and west from Jerusalem to Rome. As they went, they spread the gospel both to Europe and to Asia.

Church. The local congregation had stood firm in its faith despite persecution from the local Jewish synagogue (3:9). The reference to the "synagogue of Satan" is not meant to be anti-Semitic, since both the human and divine authors were Jewish. Rather, it reminds us that Satan is the source of all religious persecution. Despite this opposition, the church at Philadelphia is promised an open door of evangelistic and missionary opportunity.

The symbolic descriptions of this church are indeed vivid: a key, a door, and a pillar. Jesus is pictured as the one holding the "key of David"—an allusion to Hezekiah's steward Eliakim (2 Kgs. 18:17–18; Is. 22:21–22). He, too, held the key to the house of David. The phrases "who opens and no one will shut," and "who shuts and no one opens" (3:7) refer to the divine sovereignty of Jesus Christ.

Just as Eliakim had free access to King Hezekiah's palace, so Christ has free access to the heavenly palace. He alone can take us into the Father's house. Jesus said, "I am the way, and the truth, and the life: no one comes to the Father, but through Me" (John 14:6). Thus it is that access to the heavenly palace is through Jesus Christ and no other.

In a similar analogy, our Lord said, "Enter by the narrow gate; for the gate is wide, and the way is broad that leads to destruction, and many are those who enter by it. For the gate is small, and the way is narrow, that leads to life, and few are those who find it" (Matt. 7:13–14).

But thank God, Jesus came to give us the "keys of the kingdom" (Matt. 16:19) that we might use them to open the door of heaven to all who would enter by faith in Jesus Christ. John Stott observes, "The key of salvation is in the hand of Christ. . . . 'I have put before you an open door' (verse 8), he says. The tense is perfect, for he opened the door for all long ago, and it still stands open today."[6]

Challenge. The church at Philadelphia had only a "little power" (3:8), but our Lord promised to do great things through them. He promised to use their testimony to convert the Jews who opposed them (3:9). He also promised to keep them from the "hour of testing" which shall "come upon the whole world" (3:10). This is no mere local persecution to which He refers, but the Great Tribulation itself. It will affect the "whole world" and test those who "dwell upon the earth."

But the promise to the believer is that he will be kept "from" (Greek, *ek*, "out from") the time of judgment that is coming on the earth—the Great Tribulation. This does not refer to the Great White Throne Judgment (or the final judgment), which takes place in heaven. This is an "hour of testing" (Greek, *tēs horas tou peirasmou*), which takes place on the earth for a brief period of time—three and one-half years (cf. Rev. 12:14; 13:5).[7]

If indeed this is a promise that the Church will be removed in the rapture prior to the time of tribulation, then the promise to the church at Philadelphia is a promise to the Church universal. This indicates that the specific instructions and promises of our Lord to these local Churches are not limited to any particular era of church history. Rather, these instructions and promises are applicable to all the churches of all time.

The promises to those who are victorious (who "overcome") are fourfold:

1. *Pillar in the temple of God.* Just as massive pillars supported ancient temples, so the believers will be secure in their position in God's heavenly temple.

2. *Name of God.* God's name is a reflection of His character. Having His name written on us symbolizes having His character indelibly inscribed on our hearts and lives.

3. *Name of city of God.* The promise of the New Jerusalem reminds us that we are destined for the heavenly city where the Church will reign triumphant. Our "right of citizenship" has already been guaranteed.

4. *Christ's new name.* His "new name" indicates the full revelation of His character. The Scripture promises, "We know that, when He appears, we shall be like Him, because we shall see Him just as He is" (1 John 3:2).

Philadelphia, "the church of the open door," represents the ideal church in many ways. The *open door* symbolizes their great opportunity, the *key of*

David represents Christ's authority, the *pillar* of God's temple depicts our security, and the *names* reveal the assurance of our new nature and eternal destiny.

7. The Church at Laodicea

Laodicea is one of the most well known of the seven churches. It has often been identified with everything that is wrong in the church. The Puritans believed it typified the "lukewarm" state of the Church of England. Scofield saw it as the liberal, apostate church of the twentieth century. Some have viewed it as dead orthodoxy, while others are convinced it represents rampant liberalism.[8]

Caution should be exercised before we can come to any such conclusions. Remember, these were seven literal, local churches that actually existed in the first century. There is no indication in the text itself that they had any prophetic significance at all. At best we may draw parallels as to the kind of churches they might typify. On that basis, one could just as easily argue that Laodicea typifies the modern evangelical church: wealthy, prosperous, successful, and spiritually bankrupt!

City. Laodicea was the key city in southern Phrygia. It lay forty miles southeast of Philadelphia, near the great limestone cliffs in the Lycus River Valley. It was only ten miles from Colossae and was situated across the river from Hierapolis. The apostle Paul mentions all of these cities in his letter to the Colossians (cf. Col. 2:1; 4:13–15).

Laodicea was founded in circa 260 B.C. by Antiochus II and named for his wife, Laodice, whom he later divorced. The Romans took control of the city in 129 B.C. and made it a "free city." In time it became a large and prosperous city known for its famous hot springs health resort, a medical center that produced a well-known Phrygian eye salve which was in great demand, and a prosperous wool industry known for its black wool.

Edward Myers also notes: "Laodicea was a popular place for wealthy people to retire . . . making the city a famous banking center. The wealth of the city caused her to be proud and self-sufficient. . . . Pride, self-sufficiency and dependence upon material wealth were big factors in the Lord's denunciation of the Laodicean church."[9] Unfortunately, the material prosperity of the citizens produced a very materialistic church that our Lord sternly condemned for relying on its riches rather than on His righteousness.

Church. Christian tradition credits Epaphras of Colossae as the founder of the church at Laodicea. Philemon was also from this same general area. Thus, the churches at Laodicea and Colossae were strongly interconnected. Archaeologist Sir William Ramsay actually found an inscription to Laodicea referring to one

Marcus Sestius Philemon. While he may not be the biblical Philemon, the inscription certainly indicates the prominence of this name at Laodicea. The apostle Paul wrote a letter to the church at Laodicea (cf. Col. 4:16), which was apparently lost.[10]

The basic designation of the church as "lukewarm" is taken from the contrasting hot springs of nearby Hierapolis and the pure, cold waters of Colossae. By contrast, Laodicea was lukewarm. The phrase "I would that you were hot or cold" (3:15) refers to their usefulness or effectiveness. By contrast, the lukewarm spiritual condition of the church at Laodecia was virtually useless. Cold water and hot water have legitimate usages, but lukewarm water is often spit out of the mouth as distasteful. The Greek terms are striking in the original: boiling hot or icy cold. Our Lord would prefer us to boil or freeze rather than simmer down to a tasteless and nauseatingly insipid commitment.

Challenge. There are *no words of commendation* for the church at Laodicea. Their material prosperity wasn't even being used for God. Their self-sufficiency only kept them from reliance upon the total sufficiency of God. Thus, our Lord's letter to this church was one of stern rebuke. Stott observes that we read neither of heretics, evildoers, nor persecutors. He writes, "Perhaps none of the seven letters is more appropriate to the church at the end of the twentieth century than this. It describes vividly the respectable, nominal, rather sentimental, skin-deep religiosity which is so widespread among us today."[11]

In reality, the Laodiceans were "poor and blind and naked" (3:17). In language these commercially prosperous believers could readily understand, the glorified Savior urges them to do three things:

1. *Buy gold*. Christ alone can enrich their spiritual poverty with the "gold" of the gospel. This is the parity that can withstand the refining fires of hostile persecution or spiritual corruption. The language is reminiscent of Isaiah 55:1: "You who have no money come, buy."

2. *Put on white raiment*. This symbol is used throughout the Revelation to denote righteousness. It is indeed the robe of righteousness, which our Lord gives to those who are His own. Notice Revelation 19:8, where the Bride of Christ is arrayed in "fine linen, bright and clean: for the fine linen is the righteous acts of the saints."

3. *Anoint their eyes with eye salve*. In contrast to the famous Phrygian eye salve for which Laodicea was so well known, the Lord urges them to anoint their eyes with the eye salve of the truth so that they might see things as God sees them. Only thus can they perceive a spiritual world of which they have never dreamed.

Two additional observations need to be made about this church. The Lord says, "Those whom I love, I reprove and discipline; be zealous therefore, and repent" (3:19). Christ still loved this church and was concerned about its future. Laodicea still had one of the seven candlesticks. Therefore, this church cannot represent apostate Christendom, which has no candlestick! Nor could He say of apostates that He loved them, when He earlier stated that He hated false doctrine (cf. Rev. 2:6, 15). Whatever else was wrong at Laodicea, they were still a valid church—and there was hope if they would repent.

The Lord of the Church is pictured in verse 20 as standing at the door of the Laodicean church, knocking and seeking entrance. This is not a final summary statement for all the churches. Nor is it an evangelistic appeal to the unsaved. It is part of the letter to Laodicea. Here is the Lord of the Church pleading with this particular church not to close the door of their church to Him. Whenever we refuse to let Christ take His rightful place as Lord of the church, we, too, in essence close the church door in His face, leaving Him on the outside, seeking admission to that which is rightfully His.

Following His solemn admonitions of tough love to the church at Laodicea, our Lord changes His tone to one of tender affection and personal concern. "Behold, I stand at the door and knock," He reminds them. Then He adds, "If any one hears My voice and opens the door, I will come in to him, and will dine with him, and he with Me" (3:20). Metzger writes, "The image of eating with the Lord symbolizes the joy of fellowship. In the Near East the sharing of a common meal indicates the forming of a strong bond of affection and companionship."[12] The imagery undoubtedly points to the great marriage supper of the Lamb (Rev. 19:7–9).

The appeal to the church at Laodicea ends as do all seven letters: "He who has an ear, let him hear what the Spirit says to the churches" (3:22). In each case, the individual admonition to each particular church is applied to all the churches (plural). Therefore, we must realize that there are universal truths in each church's message that apply to all churches of all time.

J. Ramsey Michaels also points out that the messages to the seven churches cannot be isolated from the rest of the Apocalypse as a whole for three reasons:[13]

1. Christ's self-description in each letter follows the parallels to His self-revelation in chapter 1.

2. The promises given to those who "overcome" parallel the general promises given to the Church in chapters 19—22.

3. The general parallels between the seven letters and the prophecies of chapters 4—18 indicate a close relationship.

The Church is at the center of our Lord's concern throughout the book of Revelation. He appears in chapter 1 as Lord of the Church—walking among the seven symbolic candlesticks. He expresses His love for the Church by asking John to write the seven letters to the seven churches of Asia Minor. He takes the church home to the marriage supper, while He pours out His wrath on the unbelieving world (chaps. 4—19). Finally, He returns with the Church triumphantly at His side (19:11–16), defeats the satanic opposition, and establishes His kingdom on earth (chaps. 19—22).

In these letters to the seven churches we have our Lord's personal encouragement to keep the faith, suffer persecution, remain zealous, and seize the opportunity to spread the gospel. And when He calls us home, we will escape the Great Tribulation and suffer no more. We will join the Church triumphant, that great innumerable host of believers from every nation on earth, who shall stand before God's throne day and night worshiping Him. And He shall lead us to the fountains of living water that we may be refreshed forever and never thirst again. Hallelujah! What a day that will be!

Study Questions

1. Read Matthew 24:14. What key to the prophetic significance of Revelation 3 do you find in these verses?

2. What do the seven stars represent (cf. 3:1; 1:20)?

3. What does Christ mean by the expression "I will come like a thief" (cf. 3:3; Matt. 24:43)?

4. What is the significance of the believers' white robes (cf. 3:4, 18; 19:7–9)?

5. Is Christ actually threatening to blot out the names of true believers from the book of life in 3:5?

6. What event in the Old Testament is alluded to by the phrase "the key of David? (cf. 3:7; Is. 22:20–22)?

7. What is the phrase "synagogue of Satan" a reference to in Revelation 3:9?

8. To be kept "from the hour of testing (trial)" is probably a reference to what end-times event (3:10)?

9. What was the major spiritual problem with the Laodiceans (3:17)?

10. Because of their lack of zeal for the Lord, what word is used to describe the church in Laodicea (3:16)?

11. What door is Christ knocking at in Revelation 3:20?

SECTION III: PROBLEM

Seven-Sealed Scroll

Revelation 4—5

CHAPTER 4

God Is Still on the Throne

Preview:

The scene shifts from earth to heaven. John is summoned into the throne room of God Almighty. Everything and everyone is worshiping the Creator of the universe. John is overwhelmed by the majestic scene and stands transfixed by the elders, creatures, and angels who in unison worship the One on the throne.

The prophetic scene shifts dramatically at this point. The "vision of the exalted Christ" (chap. 1) and His "letters to the seven churches" (chaps. 2—3) are followed by the "vision of heaven" (chaps. 4—5). This is the key *turning point* in the Apocalypse. John is summoned into the throne room of heaven and views everything from this point on from a heavenly perspective. He will look behind the scenes at the divine transactions that determine the course of human events. He will look down the corridor of time, through the halls of history, and into the canyon of eternity.

G.R. Beasley-Murray writes, "It is evident that a new beginning in the book of Revelation is made at 4:1. A door in heaven is opened to enable the prophet to enter its portals and see what transpires in heaven, that he may understand what takes place on earth."[1]

This is the *key* to interpreting the Revelation. It provides us with a heavenly perspective on human events. And it reassures us that God is in control of it all. He is still on the throne! His sovereign will shall be done. His eternal purposes will be accomplished. And His ultimate triumph is certain.

The "vision of heaven" (chaps. 4—5) serves as the fulcrum of the Apocalypse. It is the pivot on which the entire book turns our attention from earth to heaven and from time to eternity. Yet, the vision is a self-contained unit of its own. It introduces us to the problem of the seven-sealed scroll and its dramatic solution. In the process, it assures us that God's eternal purpose for the world will come to pass without fail.

Chapters 4 and 5 contain a *double vision:* 1) God the Creator and 2) Christ the Redeemer. In chapter 4, all of heaven worships God the Father for creating the world. In chapter 5, all of heaven worships Christ, the Lamb of God, for redeeming the world from the curse of sin. Beasley-Murray observes, "A single motif binds together the double vision of Chapters 4—5, namely that the God of creation is the God of redemption, accomplishing His gracious will through the crucified and risen Christ."[2]

The Great Transition

The transition that occurs in these chapters is emphasized by the words *after this* or *after these things* (Greek, *meta* and *houtos*). It denotes a sequence of events that transpires at this point. These phrases occur ten times in the Revelation. It marks the beginning of a new vision (cf. also Rev. 7:9; 15:5; 18:1; 19:1) or a new series of events. Thomas writes, "It introduces a new section of the book as the scene now changes from a picture of the glorified Christ walking among the churches on earth to that of the Father in the court of heaven."[3]

The transition that occurs at 4:1 also shifts our focus into the *future.* John Walvoord states: "Chapters 4 and 5 are the introduction and background of the tremendous sweep of prophetic events predicted in the rest of the book."[4] As such, this shift in focus is one of the important clues to interpreting the prophetic events that are revealed in the succeeding chapters. It unlocks the chronological structure of the book.

This explains the absence of the Church from Revelation 4:1 to 19:7. The word *church* does not appear again until 22:16. From the opening of the seals until the marriage of the Bride, the chapters in between focus on the nation and people of Israel. She is the woman who delivers the male child (Christ) in 12:1–2. The 144,000 who are sealed during the tribulation are Jews from the twelve tribes of Israel (chap. 7). The temple of God (11:1–2) is in Jerusalem. The two witnesses (11:3–12) are Jewish believers. Jerusalem is the scene of the great earthquake (11:13). The "rest of her offspring" is Jews who are persecuted by the Antichrist (12:17).

The "Jewishness" of Revelation 4—19 is so strong that some critics have objected that the Apocalypse is little more than a "weakly Christianized Judaism."[5] In reality, the Christology of the Revelation is quite "advanced." The book constantly ascribes the attributes of God to Christ. The Savior is confessed as Alpha and Omega (22:13). He is the mediator of creation (3:14), redemption (5:9), and of the final kingdom (19:11). As in John 1:1, He is called the "Word of God" (19:13). He is also depicted as the Lamb of God (5:6). In the final vision of the book, the eternal state is pictured as jointly ruled by God and the Lamb as a unity. Beasley-Murray comments, "The Lamb remains the mediator of judgment and redemption, yet he is inseparable from the God who enacts his works of judgment and redemption through him."[6]

Let's Get a Better View

Transported to heaven: "Come up here" (4:1). John is about to be temporarily "raptured" to heaven "in the Spirit." He suddenly sees a door opened in heaven. The force of the original Greek text emphasizes that the door was already opened and that it remains open.[7] It is the third door mentioned in the Revelation:

1. Door of opportunity (3:8)
2. Door of the Church (3:20)
3. Door of heaven (4:1)

John is instantly transported "back to the future" to view the things which "must take place after these things" (4:1). This experience is a vision of the future. It is a "trance," not an actual rapture. The apostle's body remained on earth while his spirit ascended into heaven. This is not unlike the experience the apostle Paul describes in 2 Corinthians 12:1–4, of being "caught up" (Greek, *harpagenta*) into the third heaven. The concept of the rapture is clearly indicated by the root word, *harpazō* ("snatch away").

The call to "come up here" is similar to what believers will experience at the time of the rapture, when "the Lord Himself will descend from heaven with a shout, with the voice of the archangel, and with the trumpet of God; and the dead in Christ shall rise first. Then we who are alive and remain shall be caught up (Greek, *harpagēsometha*) together with them in the clouds to meet the Lord in the air" (1 Thess. 4:16–17).

The purpose of John's "translation" into heaven was to provide him with a divine perspective on what was presently occurring behind the scenes of the human dilemma and what would occur on earth in the future. The reference to "heaven" is in the singular, as are fifty-one of the fifty-two uses of the term in the Revelation. Here it refers to the dwelling place of God Almighty.

The invitation to "come up here" (Greek, *anaba*) is issued by the same voice of authority ("like the sound of a trumpet") that John heard from the glorified Christ in 1:10. The speaker further announces: "I will show you what must take place after these things." Therefore, Christ Himself issues the invitation and promises to reveal the future to the apostle.

Transfixed by the Throne: "One sitting on the throne" (4:2–11). The focal point of what John saw in chapter 4 is the One seated on the throne, not the throne itself. The throne merely symbolizes His great authority, power, and position. It is the One seated on the throne, God the Father, who is the focus of attention in this chapter.

John's description of the One seated on the throne is that of His Shekinah glory. John was overcome by the presence of the glory of God. He became transfixed on the indescribable occupant on the throne of the universe. He sees the One of whom he himself had said, "No man has seen God at any time" (John 1:18). Therefore, John's description is limited to that of His glorious appearance. Other than the references to Him sitting on the throne (4:2) and to His holding the scroll in His right hand (5:1), there are no other anthropomorphic descriptions of the Father.

John tells us that God was "like a jasper stone and a sardius in appearance" (4:3). The ancient jasper (Greek, *iaspidi*) was a translucent rock crystal, like a diamond. The sardius (Greek, *sardiō*) was a deep fiery red, like a carnelian. Together, they pictured fire and ice. Charles Feinberg observes that these stones were the first and last precious stones in the breastplate of the high priest (cf. Ex. 28:17–20).[8]

The emerald rainbow (Greek, iris) surrounds the throne of God. The term *throne* (Greek, *thronos*) is referred to thirteen times in chapter 4, and thirty-seven times in the entire book. The rainbow is reminiscent of God's covenant with nature (cf. Gen. 9:16). He promised Noah He would not destroy the world by water (floods), but He will destroy it one day by fire. The green color depicts life, and the circle depicts eternity. "Lightnings and thunderings" emanate from the throne (verse 5). It is the life source of the universe—the power plant of divine energy.

There were twenty-four elders seated on twenty-four lesser thrones surrounding the throne of God (verse 4). They are described as robed in white (righteousness) and wearing "golden crowns" (rewards). Together they depict the courtroom of heaven. Their number is significant since there were twenty-four courses (shifts) to the Old Testament Levitical priesthood (cf. 1 Chr. 24:7–19). The Church is also described as a "royal priesthood" (1 Pet. 2:5–9). We, like they, are "elders" in the economy of God.

Whom do the twenty-four elders represent? They are either the elders of Israel or the Church or a combination of both (twelve scribes and twelve apostles). Feinberg points out the fact that if they represent the Church, their position in heaven is evidence of their being raptured already.[9] He argues that they represent the raptured Church since they already have white robes and golden crowns, indicating the Judgment Seat of Christ has already taken place (cf. 2 Cor. 5:10).

David Jeremiah observes that there are five different *crowns* mentioned in the New Testament that are available to believers:[10]

1. Imperishable wreath (1 Cor. 9:25)

2. Crown of life (James 1:12)

3. Crown of exultation (1 Thess. 2:19–20)

4. Crown of glory (1 Pet. 5:1–4)

5. Crown of righteousness (2 Tim. 4:8)

In front of the throne are three symbolic *items:*

1. Seven lamps of fire

2. Crystal sea

3. Four living creatures

The seven lamps of fire depict the seven Spirits of God (cf. 1:4). The crystal sea represents the "great gulf" fixed between man and God (cf. Luke 16:26). It is also reminiscent of the bronze sea in Solomon's Temple (2 Chr. 4:2–6). The four living creatures are depicted as a lion, a calf, a man, and an eagle. Their description is taken from Ezekiel 1:10, where the prophet also saw these creatures of God. Some of the early Christian writers saw them as symbolizing the depiction of Christ in the four Gospels. But the fact that they have six wings and cry, "Holy, holy, holy," indicates they are the *seraphim* (see Is. 6:2–3). The angelic creatures are continually ablaze with the glory of God. They are burning incendiaries of praise.

The fact that they are described as being "full of eyes" (or "lights") indicates their divine knowledge and wisdom. They have access to the omniscient ("all-knowing') wisdom of God to carry out His commands and His judgments. The reader is assured that all of heaven operates under the infinite wisdom of God. His wisdom and grace shall indeed prevail. G.B. Caird writes, "There will be no triumph of God's sovereignty at the expense of His mercy."[11]

The declaration, "Holy, holy, holy," recognizes the triune nature of God. Just as Isaiah the prophet (6:3) heard this declaration in the throne room of heaven, so John the apostle hears it as well. This is but one of the numerous interconnections of the divine revelation of Old and New Testament Scripture, proving that the symbols of the Apocalypse are drawn from the biblical record.

Robert Coleman points out that the expressions of praise and worship in the Revelation are the *"songs of heaven."*[12] He finds fourteen of them in the pages of the Apocalypse, beginning with 4:8. God's holiness is thrice proclaimed and He is exalted as the One who was, and is, and is to come. Coleman views the angelic creatures as the guardians of the throne exclaiming, "Only God is great!" His nature is holy. His kingdom is divine. His rule is just. And His will shall be done. He alone is worthy of our worship.

The chapter ends with the elders (the redeemed) on their faces before God, casting down their golden crowns before Him and singing, "worthy art thou." The term *worthy* is the basis of our English word *worship*—to ascribe "worth-ship" or honor to someone greater than ourselves. The term *worthy* (Greek, *axios*) was used in biblical times to attribute praise when the emperor marched in a triumphal procession. For Christians to ascribe this term to God was their way of saying that He and He alone deserved their worship. No human emperor could compare nor dare compete with Him.

The crescendo of praise exalts God the Father as the Creator of the universe. He receives praise for His glory, honor, and power. The chapter closes with a hymn of praise to our Creator—the One on the throne. It reminds us that all the disasters that follow in this book may plunge the world into chaos, but never out of His control.

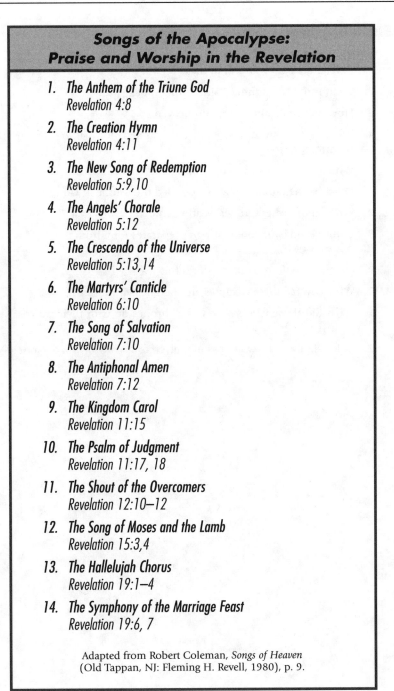

Songs of the Apocalypse:
Praise and Worship in the Revelation

1. **The Anthem of the Triune God**
   Revelation 4:8

2. **The Creation Hymn**
   Revelation 4:11

3. **The New Song of Redemption**
   Revelation 5:9,10

4. **The Angels' Chorale**
   Revelation 5:12

5. **The Crescendo of the Universe**
   Revelation 5:13,14

6. **The Martyrs' Canticle**
   Revelation 6:10

7. **The Song of Salvation**
   Revelation 7:10

8. **The Antiphonal Amen**
   Revelation 7:12

9. **The Kingdom Carol**
   Revelation 11:15

10. **The Psalm of Judgment**
    Revelation 11:17, 18

11. **The Shout of the Overcomers**
    Revelation 12:10–12

12. **The Song of Moses and the Lamb**
    Revelation 15:3,4

13. **The Hallelujah Chorus**
    Revelation 19:1–4

14. **The Symphony of the Marriage Feast**
    Revelation 19:6, 7

Adapted from Robert Coleman, *Songs of Heaven*
(Old Tappan, NJ: Fleming H. Revell, 1980), p. 9.

Study Questions

1. Read Isaiah 6:1–3. What key to the prophetic significance of Revelation 4 do you find in these verses?

2. What is the key turning point in the Apocalypse?

3. How did John gain access into heaven (4:1)?

4. What was John doing when his "translation" into heaven occurred (4:2)?

5. Who was depicted as a great shining light (4:2)?

6. Describe the rainbow that surrounded the throne of God (4:3).

7. Who sat on lesser thrones wearing golden crowns (4:4)?

8. In his vision, what body of water separates John from the throne of God (4:6)?

9. Describe the four living creatures (4:7).

10. What covered these creatures around and within (4:8)?

11. What did those who sat on lesser thrones do with their crowns (4:10)?

12. In Revelation 4:11, what reason is given for their worship of God?

CHAPTER 5

Worthy Is the Lamb!

Preview:

The seven-sealed scroll remains unopened until the Lamb of God (Jesus Christ) appears. In response to His appearance, all of heaven sings: "Worthy is the Lamb!" The expressions of praise and worship in this chapter emphasize the deity of Christ.

Jesus Christ is again the central figure of this chapter. He appears suddenly and dramatically at the center stage of heaven. He comes to claim His rightful inheritance from His Father's hand. He is the heir of the line of Jewish royalty—the "Root of David." He comes with divine authority to receive the title deed to the world and to enact the eternal purposes of God Almighty.

He explodes into the courtroom of heaven as the Lamb of God. Here the emphasis is upon His atonement for our sins. The symbolism is that of the Old Testament lamb slain for the sins of mankind. It is the same terminology John the Baptist used when he first saw the Messiah and proclaimed: "Behold, the Lamb of God who takes away the sin of the world!" (John 1:29).

As John the apostle turns to see Christ, he recognizes the Savior as having been "slain" (5:6). There in the midst of the throne, John sees the only man-made things that will ever enter heaven: the wounds of Christ! He and the other apostles had seen them before on the risen Christ in the upper room (John 20:20–27). But now, the apostle sees them in the glorified Christ in heaven. The nail prints and the spear mark are still there to remind us of God's eternal love.

Walter Scott writes, "The memories of Calvary are treasured in heaven. John the *baptist* first points out Jesus on earth as the 'Lamb of God.' John the *apostle* now beholds him in that same character on high. But how different the position! *There,* wounded and slain; *here,* the center of heaven's strength and glory, yet bearing in His Person the marks and scars of the cross."[1]

John's attention is initially focused on the **book** (Greek, *biblion,* "scroll") in the right hand of God Almighty. Since bound books as we know them today were developed much later, it is best to understand this document as a rolled papyrus scroll sealed with seven seals across the outer edge. It is possible that the seals were affixed throughout the scroll at the longitudinal ends so that it could be unrolled section by section. However, this arrangement of seals is virtually unknown in ancient documents.

Robert Thomas points out that four new scenes of the vision currently in progress are introduced by the phrase "and I saw" (Greek, *kai eidon*) in 5:1, 2, 6, 11. This adds to the continuous sense of movement one experiences while reading the Revelation. Thomas also observes, "The throne room described in chapter 4 functions as the setting of these scenes, the first of which introduces a scroll whose contents comprise essentially the remainder of the Apocalypse."[2]

The scroll itself is described (5:1) as having been written on the inside ("within") and on the back. Its description is very similar to that of an ancient will or testament. This would have been the general nature of wills, contracts, and official documents of John's time. Commentators vary in their opinions regarding the scroll. Some see it as the gospel, new covenant, book of life, decrees of God, or plan of redemption. Since the opening of the seals enacts the judgments of God on earth in order to bring about the return of Christ as King of the earth, it seems best to view the scroll as the title deed or divine contract to the world. As such, the scroll certainly contains the eternal decrees of God and expresses His divine will and counsel.

John weeps because no one is found "worthy" to open the seals of the scroll and fulfill God's plan for human history (5:3–4). *Worthiness,* as in 4:11, implies deity—worthy of our worship. Those falling short of this nature are described in three locations:

1. In heaven (angelic)

2. On the earth (human)

3. Under the earth (demonic)

At this point, one of the "elders" interrupts John to announce that the "Lion that is from the tribe of Judah" and the "Root of David" has prevailed to open the book (5:5). Therefore, he tells John, "stop weeping." Notice, John's crying indicates there are tears in heaven but they shall later be wiped away (Rev. 21:4). The symbolism of the "Lion that is from the tribe of Judah" comes from Genesis 49:9–10. The lion served as the symbol of Israel's messianic tribe. The "Root of David" (cf. Is. 11:1–10) reminds us that Jesus is both the *descendant* of David's royal line and the *source* of it.

Lamb of God

Hearing this startling announcement, John brushes his tears aside and turns to see the Deliverer. Bruce Metzger writes, "What follows is altogether unexpected. John looked to see the Lion, the king of beasts, and instead he sees a Lamb with the marks of slaughter upon it (5:6)!"[3]

The symbolism of the lamb emphasizes the ultimate triumph of the sacrificial death of Christ. The symbol of the lamb appears twenty-eight times in the Revelation. His death is the only atonement for sins that God the Father will accept. The issue is not whether your religion satisfies you, but whether it satisfies God! And God is only satisfied with the blood atonement of Jesus Christ, His Son. That sacrifice alone can pay the sinner's debt, satisfy the demands of divine justice, and set the sinner free.

His death is our triumph! He alone has overcome every obstacle by His death on the cross. Thus, He alone has the unchallenged right to approach the throne of God on our behalf, take the scroll from the hand of the Almighty, and effectuate the counsels of God. Indeed, the whole scope of the Revelation tells us that the Lamb that was slain shall become King of kings and Lord of lords.

In Jesus Christ alone the majesty and might of the lion and the meekness and sacrifice of the lamb are combined in one glorious Person. He is at the center of the universe, and all of heaven waits breathlessly as He approaches the throne of God. The Lamb who once stood silent, meek, and humble before His accusers, now marches boldly through the throngs of heaven. He who was rejected shall rule and reign in righteousness. He who was spit upon shall sit upon the throne of David. He who was crowned with thorns shall be crowned with the diadem of the Almighty.

God's Son approaches the Father's throne and all of heaven bows before Him. The nail-pierced, thorn-scarred, spear-marked Son of the Almighty comes with His wounds of love crying out for the redemption of mankind. He has come to claim the heathen for his inheritance (Ps. 2:8), and He will not be denied. His innocent blood, which flowed like a river of mercy at Calvary, has paved the way into the heavenly courtroom. The title deed is His, and His alone.

The Lamb of God reaches forth His nail-scarred hand to receive the scroll from the Eternal Father. Who can deny such love? Such sacrifice? Certainly not the God of the universe! For He Himself is love (1 John 4:16). In that one incredible moment, the love of the Father meets the love of the Son. The scroll is passed and the triumph is secured. The Lamb of God now holds the title deed to the universe. Hallelujah! What a triumph!

Walter Scott writes, "Now the self-same Lamb bearing in His person the marks of His passion is here seen as the object of heaven's worship. No voice is, nor can be silent when the slain Lamb appears."[4] What follows are the greatest hymns of triumph in all of Scripture. The heavenly hosts break into songs of praise and worship that clearly portray Christ as deity.

The picture of the Savior in 5:1–7 underscores the great transformation of *messianic expectation* in the New Testament. The Messiah did not come as a conquering hero, but as a wounded lamb. He did not come to destroy the enemies of Israel, but to love His enemies into submission to His kingdom. He did not come to condemn the world, but to save the world (John 3:17).

David Jeremiah observes, "Every one of the writers of the New Testament was horribly persecuted."[5] Matthew was beheaded. Mark was dragged to death by a team of wild horses. Luke was hanged in an olive tree. John was tortured and abandoned. Paul was beheaded. Peter and Jude were crucified. James was battered to death with a club. They all died for one Person and for one purpose: the Lamb of God. Each one had been captured by His love, His power, and His passion. They gave their lives willingly to perpetuate His gospel. And they are among the host of martyrs in heaven who now sing His glorious praise.

The Songs of Heaven

Robert Coleman has written a superb study on the songs of the Revelation, entitled *Songs of Heaven.*[6] He finds 14 such songs (a double seven) throughout the last book of the Bible. He calls attention to the fact that the heavenly choir bursts forth with a "new song of redemption" in this atmosphere of holy communion. He writes, "It is called 'a new song' because that which Christ has accomplished is wholly different and superior to the old covenant; nothing like it has ever existed before."[7]

This *new song* is one of praise and worship to Jesus Christ, the Lamb. It acknowledges that He is also "worthy" (Greek, *axios*) of our worship. The fact that the song of praise to the Lamb follows the song of praise to the Creator emphasizes the deity of both. Only that which is divine deserves our worship ("worth-ship"). There can be no doubt that this emphasis is intended to underscore the deity of Christ. He, like the Father, is "worthy" of our worship.

Those who deny that the Bible teaches the deity of Christ cannot escape the clear and powerful affirmation of this truth in Revelation 5:9–14. Let every Christ-denying heretic fall down and worship Him! All of the redeemed people of heaven sing: "Worthy art Thou to take the book, and to break its seals; for Thou wast slain, and didst purchase for God with Thy blood men from every tribe and tongue and people and nation" (5:9).

This is the song of redemption sung only by the saved. It is the expression of the "prayers of the saints" (5:8). No angel can sing this song. They can only bow down in wonder and amazement that the Son of God would become the Lamb of God who died for the sins of the world.[8] At the heart of this expression of worship is the blood of Christ shed for our sins.

Coleman notes, "Christ's worthiness in carrying out the divine purposes rests upon His sacrificial death, by which mankind was purchased for God. Without the offering up of His own life on Calvary, there could have been no redemption of the world, and Christ would have entered heaven alone."[9]

The "song of redemption" begins with the words, "Worthy art Thou." These are identical to the words of praise given to God the Father in Revelation 4:11. Beasley-Murray observes, "He who has taken the scroll and undertakes to put into effect its decrees carries out the divine functions of judgment and sovereignty, and so is to be acknowledged as divine."[10] The words of praise and worship that follow emphasize the divine nature of the Lamb who is worshiped in a manner equal to the Father.

The Church in Heaven

The worthiness of Christ is extolled because He alone is authorized to execute the judgments that will conclude the present age and usher in the kingdom of God on earth. The timing of these events is not clearly stated but must be understood as part of that which John was told in 4:1 were "what must take place after these things." We can only assume that this great enthronement ceremony takes place in heaven after the Rapture of the Church and before the judgments of the Tribulation.

The elders who are expressing these words of praise are representative of the whole Church because they are described as having been redeemed "from every tribe and tongue and people and nation" (5:9). Such a host cannot be limited to the Old Testament saints alone, although it may include them. What is clear is that this host must include the New Testament church, and that they are already in heaven prior to the judgments that are about to fall on the earth.

Leon Morris observes, "The universal scope of redemption receives mention with the piling up of expressions to show that the redeemed come not from any restricted group, but from all over the world."[11]

In the Olivet Discourse (Matt. 24—25), Jesus predicted that the end of the age would come when this "gospel of the kingdom shall be preached in the whole world for a witness to all the nations" (Matt. 24:14). We must assume, therefore, that this process has been completed by the time we get to Revelation 4—5.

While some have suggested that the "gospel of the kingdom" is different than the gospel of the Church Age, this is highly unlikely! The New Testament emphasizes that there is but one gospel and that any other gospel is a perversion of the "good news" (see Gal. 1:6–9). The task of world evangelization is part of our Lord's Great Commission (Matt. 28:19–20; Acts 1:8). The fact that it would take time to accomplish this task did not eliminate the sense of the imminent return of Christ that the early church expressed. Nor should it eliminate that same sense of imminency that we should experience either.

Jesus, however, did give a hint of the amount of time it would take to accomplish this task in the "Parable of the Talents," which was part of the Olivet Discourse. He symbolically refers to Himself in that parable as "a man about to go on a journey" (Matt. 25:14). The "journey" is a reference to His ascension back to the Father in heaven.

In the meantime, His servants (the Church) are to be busy multiplying the talents (resources) He has left them. Then our Lord said, "After a long time the master of those slaves came and settled accounts with them" (Matt. 25:19). The reference to "a long time" clearly indicates that it would, in fact, take some time to accomplish the assigned task. This is the only such indication anywhere in the New Testament of the length of time He might be gone. The concept of timing, however, may also be indicated by the term "delaying" in Matthew 25:5.

If we are correct in understanding the worship of the elders in heaven as representative of the Church in heaven, then we must assume the Rapture has already taken place. Why? Because the host of the redeemed from every nation are already there! Notice how they are described in Revelation 5:9–10:

1. Purchased

2. A kingdom and priests to our God

3. Will reign upon the earth

The angelic host of angels and creatures (seraphim) will join the elders in singing praise to the Lamb in 5:12. But the expression of praise in the "song of redemption" (5:9–10) is limited to the elders' expression of the "prayersof the saints" (5:8). This is specifically the song of the raptured Church in heaven. They are redeemed (saved) by Christ's blood. They are given the status of being "a kingdom and priests" (cf. 1 Pet. 2:9). Their position as "a kingdom and priests" is emphasized three times in the Revelation (1:6; 5:10; 20:6). And they will rule with Him "upon the earth" when He returns in triumph.[12]

Their praise is for their redemption, which is accomplished "with Thy blood" (5:9). Thus, the theology of the Revelation is clearly in line with the concept of blood atonement throughout the Bible. The author of Hebrews reminds us that it was "through His own blood, He [Christ] entered the holy place once for all, having obtained eternal redemption" (Heb. 9:12). He also reminds us that this is the blood of the New Testament (new covenant), adding, "And without shedding of blood there is no forgiveness [of sins]" (Heb. 9:22).

Beasley-Murray emphasizes the fact that the blood atonement is in keeping with the "passover theology" of John. He writes:

> The sacrifice of the Lamb led not simply to a general emancipation of men, but to the creation of a people for God. The redeemed become a kingdom and priests to our God. Inasmuch as the exaltation of the Lamb initiates the new age, the privilege of being kingly priests for God belongs to the emancipated people even now. Nevertheless, as the revelation of Christ and His kingdom takes place at His parousia, so the full exercise of their royal priesthood belongs to the time of His triumph.[13]

The redeemed Church of the Lord Jesus Christ shall reign with Him "upon the earth" (5:10). This expression emphasizes the coming earthly reign of the Millennial Kingdom (one thousand years) promised in Revelation 20:4. While the nature of this earthly kingdom is not described in detail in the Apocalypse, it is generally thought to encompass the fulfillment of the prophecies to Israel of a literal reign of the Messiah on earth (cf. Is. 51—66). During His rule on the throne of David in Jerusalem, He will be attended and assisted by His Bride—the Church. This is why the Church is pictured in Revelation 19:11–16 as returning in triumph with Christ prior to His thousand-year rule on the earth.

The Angelic Choir

Chapter 5 ends with myriads of angels joining the elders to praise the Lamb. Their innumerable host is described as "myriads of myriads, and thousands of thousands" (5:11). The best modern equivalent would be "millions." The angels are not redeemed because they are not fallen creatures. Therefore, they could not sing redemption's song. But now they join the redeemed in singing praise to the Lamb for who He is.

Angels play a prominent role in the Apocalypse.[14] An angel dispatched the message to John (1:1). Each of the seven churches is said to have an angel (1:20). An angel asked if someone was worthy to open the scroll (5:2). Angels are pictured as the proclaimers and executors of God's judgments in chapters 8, 9, 10, 12, 14, 15, 16, 17, 18, 19, 20. They are also told to seal the elect (7:1–4) and to assist in their prayers (8:3–5). In eternity, they unveil the New Jerusalem (21:10) and guard the gates of the city (21:12).

The expression "worthy is the Lamb" places the worship of Christ equal with that of God the Father. God is worshiped as Creator in chapter 4, and Christ is worshiped as Redeemer in chapter 5. The combined impact of these two chapters leaves no doubt as to the deity and divine nature of Christ. He is to be worshiped as equal in essence to the Father, while the Holy Spirit draws our attention to both because "he will not speak on His own initiative" (John 16:13).

The worship of the Lamb is based upon His sevenfold worth to receive:

1. Power (Greek, *dunamis*, "unlimited ability")

2. Riches (Greek, *ploutos*, "unconditional wealth"

3. Wisdom (Greek, *sophia*, "mental excellence")

4. Might (Greek, *iskus*, "superhuman power")

5. Honor (Greek, *timē*, "praise of character")

6. Glory (Greek, *doxa*, "majestic radiance")

7. Blessing (Greek, *eulogia*, "thanksgiving")

Each of these qualities is recognized in the Lamb Himself. They are also blessings that He bestows. But their emphasis here is on the qualities He possesses. They begin with a focus on His power and might (points 1–4) and move to the more usual sequence of doxologies: honor, glory, and blessing (points 5–7). These rapid-fire expressions of praise and worship leap from the lips of the angelic host with the spontaneous recognition of who He is and what He has done. These thrilling crescendos lead to the grand finale of praise.

The chapter ends with all of creation praising both God ("Him who sits on the throne") and the Lamb, equally ascribing "blessing and honor and glory and dominion" to both. These songs express an exuberance of praise and adoration for all that God has done through the Lamb. Leon Morris says it so well: "There cannot be the slightest doubt that the Lamb is to be reckoned with God and as God."[15]

The four "living creatures" add their final "Amen." And the twenty-four elders prostrate themselves in worship. What a picture! All of heaven is on its face before the Father and the Son. Praise resounds in crescendos, and worship exudes from every heart. The Lamb has taken possession of the title deed to the universe. He holds the divine contract in His nail-scarred hands. He stands ready to open the seals, pronounce the judgments, and take possession of His rightful kingdom on earth.

Study Questions

1. Read Philippians 2:9–11. What key to the prophetic significance of Revelation 5 do you find in these verses?

2. Describe the seven-sealed scroll (5:1).

3. What does it mean to be "worthy" to open the scroll (5:2)?

4. What was John's reaction when no one could open the scroll (5:4)?

5. How is Jesus first pictured in this chapter (5:5)?

6. In what distinctly different way is He pictured in Revelation 5:6?

7. What are the "seven horns" and "seven eyes" (5:6)?

8. What do the "golden bowls full of incense" represent (5:8)?

9. According to Revelation 5:9, why is Christ "worthy" of our worship?

10. Where will believers rule with Christ (5:10)?

11. Who is included in the final chorus of praise (5:11)?

SECTION IV: PROCESS

Seven Seals and Seven Trumpets

Revelation 6–11

CHAPTER 6

The Wrath of the Lamb

Preview:

The first six seals are opened on the scroll. These are described collectively as the "great day of their wrath." The seals unleash a series of terrible and cataclysmic catastrophes on the earth. Included in this chapter are the famous "four horsemen of the Apocalypse."

The process of God's judgments upon the world is unleashed by the opening of the seven seals. These result in a series of catastrophic events that express the "wrath of the Lamb." Each opening of a seal hurtles the world further along a course of ultimate disaster. Eventually, the opening of the seventh seal (8:1) results in the sounding of seven trumpets, which intensify the judgments even further.

Chapter 6 begins with the words "and I saw." In fact, every one of the first 16 verses of this chapter begins with the word *and* (Greek, *kai*). The constant development of the *kai*-meter in this chapter increases the reader's anticipation of what is going to happen next. The pace is so fast that by the end of the chapter the reader runs out of breath.

Bruce Metzger notes that "with the sixth chapter, the main action of the book may be said properly to begin."[1] Robert Thomas adds that this chapter marks "the commencement of the revelation proper, the first five chapters having been introductory."[2] In other words, the prophetic table has been set, and the main course is about to follow!

Jesus Himself is pictured as the Lord of the future. He stands in the throne room of heaven, opening the seals and setting in motion the events contained in the scroll. These unleash catastrophic judgments that result in the collapse of human governments and the pronouncement: "The kingdom of the world has become the kingdom of our Lord, and of His Christ; and He will reign forever and ever" (11:15).

A simple reading of chapters 6—11 leaves one with the impression that it is all over. Worldly kingdoms have fallen, Christ's kingdom has arrived, divine wrath has been dispensed, the judgment of the dead is at hand, and the temple of God in heaven is opened (see Rev. 11:15-19). So what is Revelation 12—22 all about? Why are there seven more bowls of judgment ("seven last plagues") yet to come? How does the fall of Babylon in chapters 17—18 relate to the fall of the "kingdom of the world"?

How Do We Interpret This Book?

The basic question is, How does one read the succession of events predicted in the Apocalypse? Some view these prophecies as a strict succession of events:

Seals ⟶ Trumpets ⟶ Bowls

Others view them as happening simultaneously. Various schemes have been proposed, but the most common seems to be:

Seals ⟶ Trumpets
+
Bowls

The trumpet judgments (8—11) and the bowl judgments (15—16) have several obvious similarities. Merrill Tenney has observed, "The seven bowls are a closely knit series following each other in rapid succession. They parallel the trumpets in their spheres of action, but they are more intense."[3] The similarities in the parallels are as follows:

While there are some differences in the two accounts (wormwood, locusts, kings of the east, Armageddon), there are far more similarities. Both accounts describe a succession of events that result from catastrophic wars:

1. Vegetation destroyed
2. Sea waters polluted
3. Fresh waters polluted
4. Air pollution
5. Demonic plagues
6. Armies of millions
7. Final victory of God

Trumpets	Bowls
1. "to the earth" (8:7)	1. "into the earth" (16:2)
2. "into the sea" (8:8)	2. "into the sea" (16:3)
3. "on the . . . rivers" (8:10)	3. "into the rivers" (16:4)
4. "sun . . . moon . . . stars" (8:12)	4. "upon the sun" (16:8)
5. "bottomless pit . . . torment" (9:1–5)	5. "upon the throne of the beast . . . pain" (16:10)
6. "river Euphrates" (9:14)	6. "river, the Euphrates" (16:12)
7. "loud voices in heaven" (11:15)	7. "loud voice . . . from the throne" (16:17)

New Testament scholar Bruce Metzger writes,

Following this complicated and repetitious pattern, John preserves unity in his work, interlocking the various parts together and at the same time developing his themes. The development, however, is not in a strictly logical fashion such as we are familiar with in Western writing; it is, rather, a product of the Semitic which runs through the whole picture again and again.[4]

This observation must make us consider the fact that the Revelation unfolds in a pattern. First it gives us the big picture. Then it fills in the details. We get the wide-angle view, followed by individual snapshots. For example, the "kingdom of the world" falls in 11:15, but the final collapse of Babylon does not come in detail until chapters 17—18. Armageddon appears in 16:16, but the actual final battle occurs in 19:11–21.

Therefore, we cannot simply slice up the Revelation into strictly sequential events. In some cases, these events overlap one another. Remember, the seven-sealed scroll was originally described as being written both on the inside and on the outside. The writing on the inside of such a scroll was usually *private* in nature. The writing on the outside of the scroll was *public* in nature. Norman Geisler has suggested that chapters 6—11 (seals and trumpets) are the external message to the unbelieving world ("Bad news, you lose") and chapters 14—19 are the internal message to the believers ("Good news, we win").[5]

Another interpretive question in this section has to do with the issue of divine sovereignty and human agency. In other words, who is doing what? Are these judgments directly from the hand of God (cosmic destruction)? Or, are they the result of human conflict (nuclear war)? While it is easy to speculate one way or another, we must let the text of Scripture speak for itself.

The seal judgments (chap. 6) result when Christ Himself breaks the seven seals. Yet, these involve people killing one another (6:4, 8). They also involve geological forces such as earthquakes (6:12) and cosmic forces such as the sun, moon, stars, and heavens (6:12–14). The trumpet judgments result from angelic pronouncements (cf. 8:7) and include cosmic and geological forces (8:7–12). They also seem to include demonic forces (locusts from the bottomless pit) and human armies and modern weapons (9:16–19). The bowl judgments follow the same pattern and include the same elements.

The Seven Seals
- *White horse: conquest*
- *Red horse: war*
- *Black horse: devastation*
- *Pale horse: death and hell*
- *Faithful martyrs: slain for Christ*
- *Great earthquake: planet shaken*
- *Seven trumpets: world on fire*

All of these judgments (seals, trumpets, bowls) include divine, demonic, human, and natural forces. Satan is pictured as spewing out his wrath on the earth (12:12). The beast and the False Prophet are pictured as his human agents (13:1–18; 19:19–21). At times the forces of evil are embodied in an individual (beast or Antichrist). At times they are an entire system of human government (Babylon). In other passages, the evil forces seem to be coming from hell itself (9:1–11). But time and time again our attention is refocused on the immediate factor: human armies bent on mass destruction. Thus we read of swords, weapons, armies, horsemen, flame-throwers, kings, battles, and Armageddon.

The *grand overview* of the Apocalypse presents every possible perspective on the catastrophic destruction that will come in the future. Nothing in previous human history compares to the intensity or extent of these disasters. The whole world is pictured as being at war, and the entire planet is about to be destroyed. Preterists who attempt to view these events as having already happened in the past have missed the whole point of the book altogether.

The overarching theology of the Apocalypse touches every possible element of the coming conflict:

Divine—God is in control of all forces.

Satanic—Satan tries to destroy mankind.

Demonic—Demons assist Satan's attempt.

Angelic—Angels announce the judgments of God.

Human—Armies are at war over the world.

Geologic—The planet is reeling from destruction.

Cosmic—The heavens are shaken and depart.

The Seven Seals

The opening of the seven seals initiates the messianic judgments that comprise the whole of Revelation 6—11 and 14—19. Beasley-Murray observes, "The conviction that judgments must fall prior to the coming of the kingdom of God is rooted in the teaching of the Old Testament prophets concerning the day of the Lord" (cf. Amos 5:18ff.; Is. 2:12ff.; Zech. 12:2ff.).[6]

These judgments also parallel the pattern predicted by Christ in Matthew 24—25 and Mark 13. Apocalyptic scholar R.H. Charles arranges the parallel patterns as follows:[7]

Mark 13:7-24	*Revelation 6*
1. Wars	*1. Wars*
2. International strife	*2. International strife*
3. Earthquakes	*3. Famine*
4. Famines	*4. Pestilence*
5. Persecutions	*5. Persecutions*
6. Shaking of the heavens	*6. Earthquakes and shaking of the heavens*

John omits Mark's reference to the fall of Jerusalem since it has already occurred. Instead, John draws on the symbolism of the four horsemen of Zechariah 1:8ff. and 6:1ff. The Old Testament prophet foretold of red, black, white, and bay (or "grisled") horses (Zech. 6:2-3) that represented the four spirits ("winds") of the heavens (6:5). In John's vision, the four horsemen of the Apocalypse represent various disasters that are forthcoming.

The Tribulation period commences with the opening of the seals. Thomas states, "The happenings enumerated follow the pattern of the Olivet Discourse (cf. Matt. 24—25; Mark 13; Luke 21) sometimes called the 'Little Apocalypse.' . . . The similarities are so close that some venture to call that discourse the main source of the seal judgments."[8] For our purposes, note that the predictions of the seal judgments are identical to Jesus' predictions of the coming judgments in the Olivet Discourse.

Thomas further notes that Jesus divided the time of judgment into two periods: "birth pangs" (Matt. 24:8) and the "great tribulation" (Matt. 24:21). He writes, "The former part closely parallels the first four seals in particular. So an important key in fixing the time of the seals in this message was given by Christ some sixty-five years earlier when He taught about the future time of trial on the earth."[9]

In dramatic fashion, Jesus Christ (the Lamb) opens the seals of the scroll. John suddenly hears the "voice of thunder," which is one of the four beasts ("creatures") saying, "Come" (Rev. 6:1). Interestingly, the term *thunder* (Greek, *brontē*) appears only outside the Apocalypse in John's Gospel (John 12:28–29) and in Mark 3:17, where John and James are called "Sons of Thunder."

Notice again that John records what he *sees* in these visions. Thus, we have an eyewitness account of the end of the world by the seer of Patmos. The Revelation itself is hastily written to keep pace with the incredible panorama of end-time events, which John witnesses from his heavenly vantage point.

Four Horsemen of the Apocalypse

The first four seals involve four riders and four horses. Following the typical pattern of the Revelation, they give us an overview of events to come. The details follow in the trumpet judgments. The order of events is always the big picture first, then the snapshots. The panorama always precedes the individual landscapes of prophetic detail in the Apocalypse.

Leon Morris observes that the first four seals form a unity (four horsemen). The two seals that follow deal with things in heaven (martyrs and cosmic disaster). The final seal doesn't come until 8:1, and it ushers in the seven trumpets.[10] Again, the pattern is the same: overview followed by details.

The *Seal Judgments* are as follows:

1. *White horse:* conquest

2. *Red horse:* bloodshed

3. *Black horse:* famine

4. *Pale horse:* death

5. *Martyrs:* "How long, O Lord?"

6. *Earthquake and heavens shaken:* "great day of His wrath"

7. *Seven trumpets:* silence, then disaster.

Galloping across the earth, the four horsemen appear suddenly on the horizon. Metzger observes, "Notice how brief and concise this account is.

Each of the four scenes is like a cameo, very small and compact. None of the four horsemen says a single word. Each rides forth in silence."[11] As each rides forth, the four heavenly creatures remark, "Come." Walter Scott writes, "So the living creatures, the executives of the throne, successively call on the human instruments of vengeance to execute their divinely-appointed task."[12]

These judgments are providential in character but are executed by human agencies. The picture in this chapter assures us that God is in control of the future. No judgment shall fall nor disaster occur without His divine permission. The massive catastrophes yet to come are part of the fulfillment of the divine will. The rulers of this world shall be brought to their knees before His omnipotent power.

1. *White horse:* Antichrist (6:2–3).

The rider carries a bow and is given a crown. He then sets forth on a career of military conquest. Many, including most of the Puritans, view this rider as Christ, since He also rides a white horse in 19:11ff. They view the conquest as the successful spread of the gospel. While this is possible, it is unlikely for several reasons: 1) The context of the four horses involves war and disaster; 2) The rider carries a bow (instrument of war), whereas Christ has no weapon but the "sword of his mouth" (19:15); 3) The rider is given a crown, whereas Christ already has many crowns (19:12); 4) The rider's crown is called a *stephanos*, "victor's wreath," whereas, Jesus wears the *diadema*, "royal crown" (19:12).

Since there is no point of similarity between Christ and this rider, other than the color of the horse, this must be an imposter—the Antichrist. He is called the "beast" in Revelation 13:1–18; 16:10–13; 17:3–14; 19:19–21; 20:10. Other biblical names include "man of lawlessness" (2 Thess. 2:3), "the son of perdition" (John 17:12), the king who does "as he pleases" (Dan. 11:36–45), and the "antichrist" (1 John 4:3). David Jeremiah calls him the "Dark Prince on a White Horse."[13]

2. *Red horse:* world war (6:4).

The rider on the red horse is associated with war and bloodshed. He takes "peace from the earth" with a "great sword" so that men slay one another. Notice, there is no mention of bloodshed with the first rider. Therefore, many assume that the Antichrist comes to power peacefully during the chaos that follows the Rapture of the Church. If this occurs early during the Tribulation, they see a turning point later when war erupts— perhaps after he breaks his covenant with Israel (cf. Dan. 9:26–27).

Leon Morris observes that the conquest initiated by the rider on the white horse eventually leads to the conflict related to the red horse. He writes, "Any nation that embarks on a career of conquest unleashes blood-shed and famine and destruction."[14] Thus, the four horsemen interrelate with one another. Each comes across the horizon of history like a wave over the ocean of humanity.

The red horse symbolizes bloodshed and war. The word translated "slay" means to "slaughter" or "butcher." The fiery-red color symbolizes the intensity of the destruction that shall take place. The fact that this horseman shall "take peace from the earth" indicates a world war of incredible magnitude. The twentieth century witnessed two such wars. ten million people died in World War I and 20 million died in World War II, including six million Jews. It is no secret that the world could not survive World War III with the potential of nuclear holocaust. Jack Van Impe notes that twenty-four "third world" nations are now developing long-range bal-listic missiles capable of delivering nuclear warheads.[15]

3. *Black horse:* famine (6:5–6).

Famine always follows the devastation of war. Food supplies are exhausted, and those who survive the conflict must now struggle to survive the aftermath of war. The "quart" represents a measure of about one liter, and a "denarius" (KJV, "penny") was a typical day's wages (cf. Matt. 20:2). These are famine prices but not starvation prices. The immediate results of war will be food shortages, especially for the poor. Things are bad, but they will get much worse. The end is not yet in view.

The "pair of scales" for measuring the weight and value of grain sym-bolizes the severity of this famine and its economic consequences. It may well be that one of the results of this famine will be the need for stricter control of the global economy (cf. Rev. 13:16–18). This may enhance the Antichrist's power over the world population by the imposition of his mark ("mark of the beast").

4. *Ashen horse:* death and hell (6:7–8).

The infamous ashen rider appears next on the horizon. The ashen (Greek, *clōros,* from which we derive *chlorine*) horse symbolizes the gaunt, colorless look of death. While the preceding riders each carried a symbol-ic emblem (bow, sword, balance), Death needs no such symbol. His name (Greek, *Thanatos,* "death") speaks for itself. Alongside, John says, "Hades (Greek, *hadēs*) was following with him." The picture is a gruesome one. Death rides roughshod over the world's population, while Hades personi-fied, walks alongside, gobbling up the carcasses.

The fourth seal emphasizes the power given to death and Hades over one-fourth of the earth's population to kill them with the elements of seals two, three, and four: sword, famine, and death. This interconnection makes it clear that all four seals and riders are related. One aspect leads to another and results in another. This is the general pattern of the Revelation throughout. Thus, conquest leads to war, which leads to famine, which results in death. Metzger states, "We have here all the appalling aftermath of war—famine, pestilence, and the final devastation when wild animals overrun what was once the habitat of people."[16]

The World at War

The destruction described in the first four seals is a preview of what is to come in the trumpet and bowl judgments. First, we have the wide-angle panorama, then the detailed snapshots follow. The seer is describing a vision of worldwide destruction that shall come at some distant time in the future, prior to the glorious return of Christ.

5. *Martyrs in heaven* (6:9–11).

The scene shifts back to heaven with the opening of the fifth seal. The souls of martyred believers "underneath the altar" cry out for vengeance. They are described as those "who had been slain because of the word of God, and because of the testimony which they had maintained" (v. 9). One of the interpretive issues in the Revelation is the question, Who are these martyrs? Are they Christians who have died throughout the years of church history? Or are these martyrs the Tribulation saints who have come to faith in Christ after the Rapture and been slain? The fact that they were "underneath the altar," the place where the blood of the sin offering was poured out, signifies the completion of their sacrifice (see Lev. 4:7).

There are no particulars given to explain the identity of the martyrs. However, chapter 7 serves as an interlude and introduces the 144,000 Jews and the great multitude of Gentiles that no man could number. In the same context, the four winds of heaven are told, "do not harm the earth" (7:3) until God has sealed the 144,000. A continuous reading of these chapters implies that these are converted during the time of the Tribulation.

It is certainly possible that the martyrs who cry out for vengeance could represent all the Christian martyrs of all time who have taken their rightful place in heaven. Their cries may well be intensified as they see new converts being slaughtered during the Tribulation because they are told that other "brethren" will still be killed as they were (6:11).

Walter Scott reminds us that if the Church has indeed been removed at the Rapture prior to the Tribulation, the salt of the earth and the light of the world are gone! While people may still come to faith in Christ during the Tribulation, it will not be an easy process. There will be no Church on earth to preserve it from judgment or to testify to it of truth.

Scott writes, "The Lord at present, by the power of the Holy Spirit on earth, bridles the passions of men, but let the presence and power of the Spirit be withdrawn, and the world's enmity to Christ and those who are His shall burst out in fierce and bitter persecution even unto death."[17] In other words, all hell will break loose on the earth after the Rapture of the Church. The unregenerate nations of the world will unleash a bloodbath on anyone claiming the name of Christ.

6. *Universal devastation* (6:12–17).

The final seal mentioned in this chapter is opened and the planet is shaken to its very core. Disorder reigns supreme; the powers of nature and human government collapse. Chaos ensues, and people call upon the rocks and mountains to "fall on us." In this awful moment of divine retribution, there is no repentance by the ungodly. They call upon the powers of nature to deliver them but they will not call upon God.

A "great earthquake" rocks the planet. The sun is darkened, the stars fall, and the heavens (atmosphere) splits apart "like a scroll." These passages clearly indicate some sort of nuclear or cosmic disaster, which causes the entire planet to be shaken so that the sun, moon and stars appear to be moving, and the atmosphere "is split apart like a scroll when it is rolled up" (v. 14). John's description is very similar to that in 2 Peter 3:10. In both passages, the "heavens" refer to earth's atmosphere, not the dwelling place of God (which, of course, remains undamaged). But the planet is totally devastated, and universal terror reigns supreme in the hearts of unregenerate men.

What is all of this? Our text says it is the "wrath of the Lamb; for the great day of their wrath has come: and who is able to stand?" (vv. 16–17). Some limit the wrath to the sixth seal and onwards. Some divide the first four or five seals into the first half of the Tribulation, and seal six initiates the last half, or the Great Tribulation. However, there is nothing in the text itself to indicate this. The reference to the "wrath of the Lamb" could just as easily be a summary statement covering His opening of all six seals.

The opening of each seal has led to a progression of events that intensifies the divine judgment ("wrath of the Lamb"). That intensity culminates in international wars, planetary devastation, and what certainly appear to be the consequences of nuclear holocaust. Despite the human instruments who cause this devastation, the catastrophe itself is called the "great day of the

Lord." Amos predicted it would be a day of darkness (Amos 5:18). Isaiah said it would "make the earth tremble" (Is. 2:19, 21) and make the earth empty and waste, distorting its surface and scattering its inhabitants (Is. 24:1).

With the opening of the first six seals, the process of judgment begins. The world is at war and the future of the planet is in jeopardy. But behind the scenes, one thing remains clear: God is still in control. Jesus Christ is in charge of the opening of the seals, and the sovereign will of heaven prevails despite the inhumanity of a depraved and corrupt society.

Study Questions

1. Read Isaiah 24:1; 18–20. What key to the prophetic significance of Revelation 6 do you find in these verses?

3. Who is the rider on the white horse (6:2)?

4. What did the rider on the red horse use to took peace from the earth (6:4)?

5. Which rider carries a pair of scales and symbolized famine (6:5)?

6. What name is given to the rider on the ashen horse (6:8)?

7. Who is "following with" the rider on the ashen horse (6:8)?

7. What portion of the population of the earth will die because of the devastation brought by the first four seals (6:8)?

8. Why have the martyrs "underneath the altar" died (6:9)?

9. What is going to occur while the martyrs "underneath the altar . . . rest for a little while longer" (6:11).

10. What resulted from the opening of the sixth seal (6:12)?

11. What name is given to all these judgments (6:16)?

CHAPTER 7

From Tribulation to Jubilation

Preview:

Two great hosts of people appear on the prophetic horizon. The first are 144,000 Jewish converts. The second are a "great multitude" of Gentiles from every nation. Together they make up the redeemed saints of the Tribulation period, who have given their lives for the cause of Christ.

We move next to an interlude in the progression of the seven seals. It appears between the sixth and seventh seals. John the Revelator stops to describe two great hosts of people who will be saved "out of the great tribulation" (7:14). These are divided between converted Jews and converted Gentiles.

John Walvoord writes, "The question has often been asked, Will anyone be saved after the Rapture? The Scriptures clearly indicate that a great multitude of both Jews and Gentiles will trust in the Lord after the Church is caught up to glory."[1] Later, two "witnesses" are introduced who are instrumental in the conversion of the Jews (Rev. 11:3–12).

The chapter begins with the four winds of earth being held back so that an angel with the seal of God can seal His servants (7:1–3). Robert Thomas observes that this interlude (or parenthesis) is an integral part of the vision of the seals because it answers the question, "Who is able to stand?" (6:17). The implied answer is, "Those who have the seal of God."

The seal (Greek, *sphragis*) was usually a signet ring by which a king gave official validity to various documents. It was used both to authenticate and protect. The passage does not identify the nature of the seal, but Revelation 14:1 suggests it is the name of God (cf. Is. 44:5). The term *seal* used here is the same in the original as the term for the seven seals on the scroll. It is quite different from the "mark" (Greek, *charagma*) of the beast in Revelation 13:16–17. That term implies more of a brand or tattoo, which were often used in pagan religions.

The symbolism of a seal of protection upon the elect is similar to that used in Ezekiel 9:4, where a man is told to set a mark on the foreheads of the righteous. This is a protective measure in light of the impending doom that is coming. In the Revelation passage, a fifth angel comes from the east and cries out to the other four angels not to unleash their destruction until they have "marked" or "sealed" the servants of God.

Who Is Who in This Chapter?

How one interprets the Revelation as a whole will determine how he or she views the two companies of people mentioned in chapter 7. Dispensationalists (who are pretribulational in their view of eschatology) see two distinct groups of people: Jews on earth and Gentiles in heaven. Nondispensationalists are forced by their own hermeneutics to view these two companies as the same people.[2] They generally hold that the 144,000 Jews from the twelve tribes of Israel symbolize the new Israel—the Christian Church. They also believe that the great host that comes out of "great tribulation" is representative of the Church as well in its long, historic struggle on earth.

One of the unique and complex features of biblical prophecy is that different hermeneutical models may interpret it. *Eschatology* is the theological term for the study of the "end times." It comes from the Greek word *eschatos*, meaning "last" or "last things." Thus, it is used as a broad designation for biblical prophecy.

Within the Christian Church there have been a variety of approaches to the study of eschatology. More liberal Protestants refuse to consider it at all, preferring to dismiss prophecy as hopelessly confusing or generally irrelevant. But among evangelicals, prophecy has always been taken seriously. Jesus Christ Himself predicted His return to earth, as well as several significant end-time events (Matt. 24—25).

The issue at stake among evangelicals has generally involved *how* one interprets prophecy. Three main schools of thought have been proposed. While most evangelicals are premillennialists in their view of eschatology, amillennial and postmillennial opinions also exist.[3]

Postmillennial. This school of thought believes that the Millennium (one thousand years of Rev. 20:1–3) is to be interpreted symbolically as synonymous with the Church Age. Satan's power is viewed as being "bound" by the power of the gospel. Postmillennialists believe that during this "millennium" (Church Age) the Church is called upon to conquer unbelief, convert the masses, and govern society by the mandate of biblical law. Only after Christianity succeeds on earth will Christ return and announce that His kingdom has been realized. Postmillennial advocates have included Catholics, Puritans, charismatics, and dominionists who urge believers to take dominion over the earth and its political governments in order to actualize the kingdom of God on earth.

Amillennial. This approach sees no millennium of any kind on the earth. Rather, amillennialists tend to view so-called millennial prophecies as being fulfilled in eternity. References to the "thousand years" are interpreted symbolically. In this scheme the Church Age ends with the return of Christ to judge the world and usher in eternity. God's promises to Israel are viewed as having been fulfilled in the Church (the new Israel of the new covenant); therefore, amillennialists see no specific future for national Israel. They view the Church Age as the era of conflict between the forces of good and evil, which culminates with the return of Christ.

Premillennial. This view holds that Christ will return at the end of the Church Age in order to set up His kingdom on earth for a literal one thousand years. Most also believe there will be a Great Tribulation period on earth prior to the return of Christ. Among premillennialists are those who believe the Church will go through the Tribulation (postribulationists), those who believe the Church will be raptured prior to the Tribulation (pretribulationists) and even a few who believe the Church will be raptured in the middle of the Tribulation (midtribulationists). Despite these differences in regard to the Rapture of the Church, premillennialists generally believe in the future restoration of the state of Israel and the eventual conversion of the Jews to Christianity.

With these distinctions in mind, notice several things about the two groups of people in Revelation 7.

144,000 servants of God. These are described as Jews from "every tribe of the sons of Israel" (7:4). The number seems to be literal, but it could also be symbolic of totality (i.e., national conversion of the Jews). There is no indication in the text that they are to be viewed as the New Testament church or Gentile Christians. They are said to be living on earth and need to be sealed in order to be protected from the judgments that are coming on the earth. When we consider the symbolism of the "woman" (Israel) and the "rest of her offspring" (converted Jews) in 12:1–17, it is clear that the 144,000 are literal Israelites. In fact, Revelation 7:5–8 specifically lists the fact that 12,000 come from each of the twelve tribes of Israel:

Judah	12,000	Simeon	12,000
Reuben	12,000	Levi	12,000
Gad	12,000	Issachar	12,000
Asher	12,000	Zebulun	12,000
Naphtali	12,000	Joseph	12,000
Manasseh	12,000	Benjamin	12,000

The actual listing of each tribe would be irrelevant if they were not intended to represent the specific people of Israel. The specification of the tribes is consistent only with a literal interpretation of those tribes. John Walvoord writes, "The fact that the twelve tribes of Israel are singled out for special reference in the Tribulation time is another evidence that the term 'Israel' as used in the Bible is invariably a reference to the descendants of Jacob who was first given the name, Israel."[4]

There is one notable omission from the list of tribes, and that is the tribe of Dan. Dan is missing because the tribe apostatized, forsook its God-given territory, and turned to idolatry (Judg. 18:14–31). Jacob originally had twelve sons, including Dan and Joseph. Dan apostatized, while Joseph received the double-portion "blessing" of his father (Gen. 49:1–22) through his two sons.

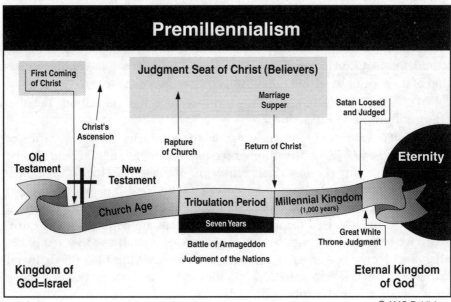

© AMG Publishers

Manasseh is mentioned here but not Ephraim. These both were the sons of Joseph; therefore, the name Joseph stands in place of Ephraim.

There are nineteen arrangements of the twelve sons/tribes of Israel in the Old Testament that differ from each other, and Revelation 7:5–8 differs from all of them. John's list begins with Judah, the tribe of the Messiah. The exclusion of Dan (the apostate tribe) parallels the twelve disciples and the exclusion of Judas Iscariot (apostate disciple) and his replacement by Matthias (Acts 1:16–26). The parallel is so obvious that it cannot be dismissed as merely coincidental.

Innumerable Multitude from all Nations. Having listed 144,000 Jews (12,000 from each of the twelve tribes), John says, "After these things . . ." (Greek, *meta tauta*). This is John's typical literary expression to move the reader on to the next event, or, in this case, the next group. The innumerable multitude is not just Jews from the twelve tribes of Israel. They are a host of people from every nation (Gentiles and Jews) and are so great in number they cannot humanly be counted.

John specifically identifies this group as coming from every nation (Greek, *ethnos*, "ethnic" group), tribes (Greek, *phulē*, "family" group), people (Greek, *laos*, "people" group), and tongue (Greek, *glōssa*, "language" group). The partitive *ek* ("from") means only some from every one of these groups will be represented. That this is a body of redeemed people is obvious from the fact that they stand before the Lamb in white robes (righteousness), waving palm branches (victory).

The text itself tells us who they are: "These are the ones who come out of the great tribulation" (7:14). They are also pictured as already standing before the throne of God, serving Him day and night in the heavenly temple (7:15). This innumerable multitude is a group of saved people, mostly Gentiles, who are already in heaven praising God. There is no specific reference to their having been martyred to get there. The fact that one of the elders (representing the Church) asks who they are (7:13) implies they are not Church Age saints.

This multitude represents the Tribulation period believers who have come to faith in Christ. Non-pretribulationalists say this is the church of Jesus Christ, persecuted, martyred, and betrayed down through the centuries of church history. To hold this position, they must view the Great Tribulation as the entire Church Age.

Pretribulationalists believe, as the text says, that these are people who have been saved on earth during the Tribulation period (first six seals) and "come out of" (Greek, *ek*, "from") the Great Tribulation (seventh seal and following). In other words, they have apparently died during the first half of the tribulation period and have been taken from the earth prior to the Great Tribulation.

Divine Wrath and Great Tribulation

The fact that "God shall wipe every tear from their eyes" (7:17) indicates that these believers have suffered greatly on earth. The Great Tribulation (Greek, *tēs thlipseōs tēs megalēs*) refers to that eschatological period of God's wrath. It is not merely the persecution or "troubles" of John's own time, but a time of future global retribution, called in Revelation 3:10 the "hour of testing," and in 6:16, "the wrath of the Lamb."

Understanding the nature of these judgments is crucial to one's interpretation of the Apocalypse. If the judgments of the Tribulation period are something less than divine wrath, one might better argue for the Church remaining on earth during the Tribulation. But there are two glaring contradictions to that viewpoint: 1) This is divine wrath; 2) The multitude is already in heaven, but the Tribulation judgments are not yet finished.

The Church is pictured in Revelation 19:7–10 as the Bride of Christ. She is in heaven at the marriage supper of the Lamb. She is also preparing to return to earth with Him in His ultimate triumph (19:11–16). She is the object of His love, not His wrath. She may be disciplined, corrected, or rebuked in the days of her earthly sojourn (Rev. 3:19). But she is *never* the object of His wrath! He cannot pour out divine wrath on the Church because the Father poured out divine wrath on Jesus Christ on the cross. He already took the punishment of divine wrath for us (cf. Is. 53:1–12; 2 Cor. 5:17–21; Heb. 9:24–28; 10:5–25). He is our perfect substitute. He paid the price in full. "There is therefore now no condemnation for those who are in Christ Jesus" (Rom. 8:1).

These two pictures are clearly portrayed in the New Testament:

Divine Wrath ──────▶ Jesus Christ the Lamb of God ──────▶ Sinner is saved/Eternal Life

Divine Wrath ──────▶ Unbelieving World ──────▶ Tribulation Period/Eternal Torment

There is no logical way to explain how these judgments, the wrath of the Lamb, would ever be allowed to fall on His Bride. He wouldn't be much of a husband if He beat her up and then took her to the wedding reception! I believe that the Church, the Bride of Christ, will have already been raptured home to glory.

Can Anybody Be Saved During the Tribulation?

There will be people converted during the Tribulation period. While the witness of the Church and its restraining force in society is missing, the omnipresent Holy Spirit will still convict men of sin, righteousness, and judgment (John 16:7–11). It is true that many will believe what is false and be deceived by "a deluding influence" (2 Thess. 2:10–12). Nevertheless, we see both Jewish and

Gentile converts believing in Jesus as their Savior in Revelation 7. No wonder they "cry out" (literally, "keep on crying"), "Salvation to our God" (Rev. 7:10).

Paul Benware of the Philadelphia Biblical University writes:

> One of the major purposes of the Tribulation is to save people. Mankind's apathy and unconcern about spiritual matters will be swept away during the Tribulation when the world is startled by supernatural signs and shaken by cataclysmic events. In that setting many will turn to Jesus Christ for salvation. The 144,000 will probably come to faith during this time, along with multitudes of others, as evidenced by the large numbers who will be martyred for their faith (cf. Rev. 6:9–11; 17:6). The Holy Spirit will be very active during the days of the Tribulation, since it is He who regenerates people, giving them eternal life (cf. John 3:5–8; Titus 3:5). The Holy Spirit is not removed from the world at the Rapture event, as some have taught. It is His ministry of restraining sin that is removed. But the omnipresent Spirit is present on the earth saving millions of people."[5]

John Walvoord, chancellor emeritus of Dallas Theological Seminary, adds:

> Chapter 7 of the book of Revelation serves as a review of the situation described in the previous chapters and emphasizes two important facts. First, God is going to judge Israel in the period of great trial, and 12,000 from each tribe, totaling 144,000, will be protected and sealed from the judgments which will fall upon the world in general. Second, a great multitude of Gentiles will also be saved, but many of these will be martyred, and a multitude of the martyred dead are found in heaven rejoicing in the presence of the Lamb and representing every tongue and nation. It is an indication that even in the tragic closing hours prior to the second coming of Christ to the earth, countless souls will find Christ as Savior and be saved by His grace.[6]

The response in heaven is overwhelming (7:12). The angels, creatures, and elders fall before the throne on their faces and worship God with a sevenfold *doxology of praise* which begins and ends with *Amen* and connects each element with "and" (Greek, *kai*).

1. Blessing
2. Glory
3. Wisdom
4. Thanksgiving
5. Honor
6. Power
7. Might

The list is almost identical with the sevenfold praise of the Lamb in Revelation 5:12, with *thanksgiving* (Greek, *eucharistia*) replacing *riches*. It is recorded as a spontaneous response, but it follows the pattern of symbolic numbers in the Apocalypse—seven representing completeness.

Thus, this chapter ends with all of heaven on its face before God. His sovereignty is extolled in His redemption of Israel and the Gentiles alike, just as it was extolled in His divine act of creation (4:11). What a powerful and beautiful picture! God is the One who saves people:

1. Before the Law (Abraham and the patriarchs)
2. Under the Law (Old Testament believers)
3. During the Church Age (New Testament church)
4. During the Tribulation period (Tribulation saints)
5. During the Millennial Kingdom (kingdom saints)

Salvation is a free gift of God's grace. It is secured for all believers from every age by the sacrificial and substitutionary death of Christ on the cross. It was there that He bore our sins and endured the wrath of God against us. In those awful moments, suspended between heaven and earth, the cup of divine judgment fell upon Him. He who knew no sin was made sin for us, that we might receive the righteousness of God as a free gift (2 Cor. 5:17–21). In His death on the cross, He triumphed over sin, death, and hell. No wonder He shouted, "It is finished!"

Study Questions

1. Read Romans 11:25–27. What key to the prophetic significance of Revelation 7 do you find in these verses?

2. How many angels held the winds of the earth (7:1)?

3. What does the angel who ascended from the rising of the sun have with him (7:2)?

4. Why does this angel halt the destruction caused by the angels who are holding the winds (7:3)?

5. What is the total number of those from the tribes of Israel who are sealed (7:4)?

6. Of this total, how many represent each of the twelve tribes (7:5–8)?

7. From which nation does the "great multitude" come (7:9)?

8. The praise of the elders and angels includes how many elements (7:12)?

9. Who asks about the identity of the multitude (7:13)?

10. What does this multitude come out from (7:14)?

11. What is the guarantee or emblem of their salvation (7:14)?

CHAPTER 8

The World at War

Preview:

The seven trumpets begin to sound and terrible calamities follow. These judgments are so severe that the global conflagration they ignite nearly destroys the whole planet. The whole world is at war and all life is in danger of extinction.

In a desert expanse fifty miles from Alamogordo, New Mexico, the first atomic bomb was exploded at 5:20 A.M., July 16, 1945. Then, less than three weeks later, President Harry Truman gave the orders to drop an atomic bomb on Hiroshima, Japan, at 8:15 A.M. on August 6. It leveled two-thirds of the city of 350,000 people in one of the most incredible decimations in human history.

By 1949, the Soviet Union had also developed the atomic bomb, and the Cold War was under way. Then, on November 1, 1952, the United States tested the first hydrogen bomb on a small atoll in the Pacific Ocean. The explosion was so devastating that it blew the one-mile island of Elugelab right out of the Pacific, leaving a 175-foot-deep hole in its place in the ocean floor! A frightening new era of apocalyptic proportions had dawned.

Sir Winston Churchill said that in the twentieth century, "War began to enter into its kingdom as the potential destroyer of the human race." Today the vast coalition of nations and the modern weapons of warfare are such that the enterprise of slaughter can be, as Churchill put it, "executed on a scale and with a perseverance never before imagined."[1]

The Center for Defense Information estimates that the United States alone has an arsenal of over 35,000 nuclear weapons and is capable of producing them at the rate of three per day. Each of these bombs carries the equivalent of 460 million tons of TNT—35,000 times *greater* than the atomic bomb that killed 70,000 people at Hiroshima in 1945.

Russia's 100-megaton H-bombs are each capable of creating an all-consuming firestorm 170 miles in diameter. Just twenty of these "super bombs" could destroy seventy-five percent of the population of the United States in less than one hour! American retaliation includes enough nuclear warheads to wipe out 400 million people in the Soviet Union and China within thirty minutes' time.[2]

Today the United States, Great Britain, France, Russia, China, India, and Pakistan already have atomic weapons. Israel, South Africa, and Germany likely have the bomb as well. And how soon till almost any well-funded dictator or terrorist leader in the oil-rich Middle East will have nuclear warheads at his disposal? As the clock ticks on, it is only a matter of time until the inevitable disaster strikes.

A World Gone Mad

Since 1945, when the atomic bomb was dropped on Hiroshima, Japan, mankind has lived with the threat of nuclear annihilation. The "baby boomers"—those born in the population boom after World War II—could just as easily be called the generation of the bomb. Many psychologists believe that people in this generation do not think like any generation that has ever preceded them because they have to live with the reality of their own vulnerability every day.

Educator Arthur Levine has described the current mentality as, "Going first class on the Titanic!"[3] In his study sponsored by the Carnegie Foundation for the Advancement of Teaching, Levine found that today's students are self-centered, individualistic "escapists" who want little responsibility for solving society's problems, but who want society to provide them with the opportunity to fulfill their pleasures. They have given up noble causes because they have given up any real hope of solving the world's problems. They see themselves on a hopeless voyage destined to disaster. Unable to turn the ship around, they simply clamor for the first-class seats so they can enjoy the ride until the inevitable strikes.

It should not surprise us, therefore, that people today will spare almost no expense for elaborate vacations, expensive trips, and romantic cruises. They are trying to pretend everything is all right, even though they know it isn't.

While the desire for peace clings to the deepest crevice of the human heart, the prospects for global destruction are far greater than the prospects for global peace. Undoubtedly, men will continue to strive for peaceful solutions. But beyond the attempts at peace is the final holocaust.

The Final Blast

The Bible predicts the final devastation in "one hour" (Rev. 18:10) of the prophetic "Babylon," the symbolic name for the kingdom of the Antichrist. The Bible says, "All your riches and splendor have vanished, never to be recovered" (Rev. 18:14 NIV). Even the merchants and sailors will not come near this land, but will "stand far off, terrified at her torment," and crying out, "In one hour such great wealth has been brought to ruin!" (Rev. 18:15, 17 NIV).

The apostle Peter provides an even more vivid description of the final blast that shall devastate this planet when he warns, "But the day of the Lord will come like a thief. The heavens will disappear with a roar; the elements will be destroyed by fire, and the earth and everything in it will be laid bare" (2 Pet. 3:10 NIV).

John Phillips notes that Peter's prophecy of a great end-times conflagration of the earth and its atmosphere uses precise terminology that accurately describes a nuclear explosion. Liddell and Scott's *Lexicon* define the *elements* (Greek, *stoicheia*) as "the components into which matter is divided" (or atoms), and the term *dissolved* (Greek, *luō*) comes from the basic Greek word meaning to "loose" that which is bound (as in nuclear fission). The term *great noise* (Greek, *rhoizēdon*) is found nowhere else in the New Testament and signifies "a rushing sound as of roaring flames." The term *fervent heat* is derived from the Greek medical term *kausoō*, denoting a fever. But Peter's use of it in application to inanimate objects is the only such known usage anywhere in Greek literature. Thus, Phillips concludes, "Peter described in accurate terms the untying of the atom and the resulting rushing, fiery destruction which follows it."[4]

The Seven Trumpets

John's description of the trumpet judgments (Rev. 8:2—11:19) sounds very similar to a global holocaust. The entire planet will be affected by massive destruction, loss of life, and human suffering. The chaos that results will destabilize both the global economy and the world government predicted in chapter 13.

The seventh seal of the scroll is finally opened in Revelation 8:1. The imagery that follows, including the half hour of silence, follows the liturgy of the Jewish temple services.[5] After the sacrificial lamb was slain, the altar of incense was prepared. Two of the priests would go into the holy place and take the burnt coals and ashes from the golden altar and relight the lamps of the golden lampstand. One priest filled the golden censer with incense, while the other placed burning coals from the altar into a golden bowl. Deep silence fell over the temple during this solemn ceremony.

The picture here in the Revelation is very similar. There is silence for one half hour after the opening of the seventh seal. It is the silence of solemn worship. But it was also the holy hush before the ungodly storm—one last gasp before all hell breaks loose. The final seal is opened, and now the entire scroll is exposed. We have seen glimpses of what is to come (overview). Now we will witness with John the final devastations (details).

Seven Trumpets
1. Rain of fire: vegetation destroyed
2. Fireball: oceans polluted
3. Falling star: fresh waters polluted
4. Sun darkened: air pollution
5. Demonic plagues: suffering and torment
6. Great army of east: 200 million men
7. Divine wrath: heaven opened

The angel offers the "prayers of all the saints (believers)" from the golden censer (8:3). Then he filled the censer with fire from the altar and "threw it to the earth" (8:5). This initiates the conflagration that is about to engulf the planet. Bruce Metzger writes, "Then—bang! Catastrophic consequences follow. Seven angels, one after another, blow their trumpets, announcing hailstorm with fire and blood descending, volcanic eruption, blood in the sea, blight in the land . . . climaxed by an enormous plague of demonic locusts."[6]

The "seven angels" standing before God are given seven trumpets to sound these various judgments. Their imagery may have been taken from the Jewish apocryphal tradition where seven angels (Raphael, Uriel, Raguel, Michael, Sariel, Gabriel, and Remiel) appear in Tobit 12:15 and Enoch 20. John leaves them unnamed but notes that each one sounds a warning of ominous destruction. With the sounding of each trumpet, the destruction becomes more pervasive.

Graham Scroggie correctly notes that the seven trumpets do not *follow* the seventh seal but they *are* the seventh seal.[7] As the final seal is opened, the seven trumpets sound in rapid succession—so much so that the destruction of the vegetation and pollution of the salt and fresh waters and the atmosphere (first four trumpets) may well happen simultaneously.

These trumpets may be associated with nuclear or chemical warfare. The devastation that they predict was unknown and unfathomable in the ancient world. These destructions are certainly beyond anything known to the people of John's day, which makes the Apocalypse all the more fascinating. There is no way John could have merely imagined these great catastrophes had he not seen them by divine permission in these visions. The cataclysmic destruction he pictures certainly sounds like the devastating effects of nuclear war.

A *limited nuclear exchange* between the modern superpowers would kill an estimated one billion people and seriously injure another five hundred million. The immediate results would include:

Radiation poisoning

Environmental destruction

Uncontrollable fires

Massive food shortages

Air and water pollution

Soil contamination

Unparalleled human suffering

Long-term results would mean the decivilization of the earth. Human culture would be thrown back into primitive survival tactics. Roving bands of lawless raiders would become the only means of survival in contaminated areas. Whole populations would likely be wiped out in North America, Europe, or the Middle East. Africa, Australia, South America, and parts of Asia might be the only survivors left on the planet.

John the revelator paints a picture of global conflagration. He sees the vegetation burned up, a mountain of fire (fireball) falling into the sea, stars falling from heaven and the darkening of the sun by a thickened atmosphere. It is no wonder that he hears an angel flying through heaven shouting, "Woe, woe, woe, to those who dwell on earth" (8:13).

1. *First Trumpet:* hail and fire (v. 7).

The results of this destruction are so vast that one-third of all the trees and all the grass on the entire planet burn up. Such a massive destruction of vegetation would result in food shortages and a limited air supply. John provides no explanation of how this will occur. One gets the impression that he watched this destruction in utter amazement.

The very fact that the Bible predicts a massive global conflagration at the end of human history, coupled with the fact that we live in a time when such a catastrophe is humanly possible, ought to be a wake-up call to everyone on the planet!

John Phillips writes, "Truly the dawning of the atomic age is of great prophetic significance. . . . We have lived on the edge of a potential holocaust for so long we find it difficult to believe that we are on the brink of the Rapture of the Church and the subsequent unleashing of apocalyptical doom."[8] Ironically, even the seer's description of "hail and fire" fits the description of a nuclear explosion of fire and ice.

2. *Second Trumpet:* Fireball into the sea (vv. 8–9).

Next, John describes a large fireball ("great mountain burning with fire") falling into the sea, polluting one-third of the oceans and destroying one-third of the ships. The reference to the "ships" seems to imply military targets, but no other details are given. The parallel second bowl judgment is also poured out on the sea but results in the destruction of all sea life (Rev. 16:3).

Again, a destruction of such massive proportions was unknown in the first century. The greatest devastation John could possibly have been familiar with was the eruption of Mount Vesuvius in A.D. 79. It completely destroyed and buried the city of Pompeii with molten lava and even destroyed a few ships in the Gulf of Naples. But what the revelator describes here goes far beyond that and looks forward to a time of unprecedented catastrophe.

3. *Third trumpet:* pollution of fresh waters (vv. 10–11).

The devastation of the seawaters is followed by the pollution of the fresh waters. The "rivers" and "springs" of water are polluted by a falling star called "Wormwood." Leon Morris notes that "wormwood" was a bitter substance, but was not poisonous.[9] It is most likely that John merely uses this term to describe the bitter pollution of radioactive fallout following a nuclear explosion.

It is obvious in the passages that describe the trumpet and bowl judgments that John struggles, even though inspired, to find first-century words to describe these future events—the likes of which he has never seen before. Terms like "mountain of fire" or "falling star" certainly come close to a description of nuclear fireballs.

4. *Fourth trumpet:* air pollution (v. 12).

The fourth trumpet sounds and the air becomes polluted (perhaps with nuclear fallout). The sun, moon, and stars are "darkened" for one-third of the day. While this may refer to an eclipse, it seems more likely that it refers to some cosmic destruction of the atmosphere. The sun, moon, and stars are obscured by particles in the air.

In the judgment of the fourth bowl (16:8–9), the sun "scorched" people as a result of this pollution. The implication is that the ozone layer of the atmosphere has been severely damaged and people are suffering from radiation poisoning. However one interprets this destruction, it is obvious that the air pollution is life threatening.

The chapter ends with an eagle (some texts read "angel") flying through heaven crying with a loud voice: "Woe, woe, woe to those who dwell on earth" (v. 13). *Woe* is a prophetic pronouncement of doom (cf. Is. 6:5). The triple *woe* is given here in connection with the three trumpets that are still to sound. As bad as the first four trumpets have been, the last three will be far worse!

The first four trumpets resulted in human devastation brought about by war and the forces of nature. But the last three trumpets involve supernatural forces—angels and demons. These last three trumpets take us behind the scenes of the human conflict to see the ultimate spiritual war being fought for the control of the earth.

The extent of these judgments affects the whole world. If the Church were still on earth during this time, she would be caught right in the middle of this great global disaster. Even non-dispensationalist Leon Morris admits, "The trumpet judgments do not concern the Church as such. They are God's judgments on the world."[10] But if the Church were still in the world, she could hardly escape such worldwide devastation. There is no mention of the Church in these chapters because she has already gone home to glory in the Rapture.

Study Questions

1. Read Joel 2. What key to the prophetic significance of Revelation 8 do you find in these verses?

2. What is the result of the opening of the seventh seal (8:1)?

3. What two things go up before God in Revelation 8:4?

4. What will fall to earth after the first trumpet (8:7)?

5. What is destroyed as a result of the first trumpet (8:7)?

6. What is thrown into the sea as a result of the second trumpet (8:8)?

7. What portion of the ships and sea creatures are destroyed by the second trumpet judgment (8:9)?

8. What is the name of the star that falls after the third trumpet (8:10–11)?

9. What is polluted as a result of this falling star (8:10–11)?

10. How does the fourth trumpet result in the blackening of the sun, moon, and stars (8:12)?

11. What is the significance of the three "woes" pronounced in Revelation 8:13?

CHAPTER 9

Demons Unleashed

Preview:

The fifth and sixth trumpets announce an unprecedented crisis: A demonic oppression followed by a military invasion that includes an incredible display of modern weaponry and military technology. The result: one-third of the world is wiped out!

Satan is determined to destroy this planet. The Bible describes Satan as the "father of lies" (John 8:44 NIV). He is pictured as the ultimate deceiver. His name means "accuser," and he is depicted as the accuser of God and His people (Rev. 12:10). He is opposed to God and seeks to alienate men from the truth. He misled the fallen angels (Rev. 12:4), and he tempts men and women to sin against God's laws (Gen. 3:1–13). He denies and rejects the truth of God and deceives those who perish without God (2 Thess. 2:10). Ultimately, he inspires the very spirit of Antichrist (1 John 2:18–23).

The term *angel* (Greek, *angelos*) means "messenger." God's angels are His divine messengers (Heb. 1:14; Rev. 1:1). By contrast, Satan is pictured in Scripture as a fallen angel, the leader of a band of other fallen angels, who deceives the whole world (Rev. 12:9). He is the ultimate power behind the Antichrist and the False Prophet (Rev. 13:4). Thus, the messengers (angels) of deceit are Satan-inspired false prophets whose messages are the very spirit of Antichrist (1 John 2:18).[1]

The late A.T. Pierson, the Bible teacher for Charles Spurgeon's Metropolitan Tabernacle in London, wrote, "Evil spirits acquire their greatest powers from their subtilty. They are masters of the art of deception, and aim to counterfeit that which is good rather than suggest what is obviously and wholly evil."[2]

Satan's oldest trick is *self-deception.* When he tempted Eve in the garden, he appealed to her selfish desire to be like God. It was the same desire that had led to his fall in the first place. And there is something selfish enough in all of us to be vulnerable to it as well. C.S. Lewis said, "What Satan put into the heads of our remote ancestors was the idea that they could 'be like gods' . . . and out of that hopeless attempt has come nearly all that we can call human history . . . the long terrible story of man trying to find something other than God which will make him happy."[3]

Satan was once called Lucifer, "son of the dawn" (Is. 14:12), but he was cast from his lofty position in heaven, along with the angelic hosts that rebelled with him. The Bible calls this rebellion the "mystery of lawlessness" (2 Thess. 2:7). Satan and his angels willfully and deliberately sinned against God. Jude 6 says they "did not keep their own domain, but abandoned their proper abode." Second Peter 2:4 adds, "God did not spare angels when they sinned, but cast them into hell and committed them to pits of darkness, reserved for judgment."

Prior to his fall from heaven, Satan was called "star of the morning," and he "drew the third part of the stars of heaven" with him (Rev. 12:4). Billy Graham writes, "Thus, the greatest catastrophe in the history of the universal creation was Lucifer's defiance of God and the consequent fall of perhaps one-third of the angels who joined him in his wickedness."[4]

Rebel with a Cause

Satan is the epitome of selfishness. He was created for the purpose of glorifying God, but he has always desired to displace God and rule the universe himself. The Bible describes his selfishness when it expresses his five "I wills": "I will ascend to heaven; I will raise my throne above the stars of God, and I will sit on the mount of assembly. . . . I will ascend above the heights of the clouds; I will make myself like the Most High" (Is. 14:13–14).

The "diabolical mastermind," as Hal Lindsay calls *Satan,* has a three-fold title:[5]

1. Ruler of this world (John 12:31)

2. Prince of the power of the air (Eph. 2:2)

3. God of this world (2 Cor. 4:4)

These titles make it clear that Satan is the unseen ruler behind the human rulers of the ungodly world. He is the inspiration for every tyrant who has ever used his power to kill, persecute, and suppress decent people. He is also the god of all those who reject the true and living God. Whether they realize it or not, they are following the enemy of mankind. The Bible says, "The whole world lies in the power of the evil one" (1 John 5:19). In reality, all men are under Satan's rule until they come into the kingdom of Christ by faith in Him.

Billy Graham has said, "Satan and his demons are known by the discord they promote, the wars they start, the hatred they engender, the murders they initiate, their opposition to God and His commandments. They are dedicated to the spirit of destruction."[6] The spiritual warfare between the forces of God and the forces of Satan is an ongoing conflict. The prophet Daniel gives us an inside (behind-the-scenes) look at this conflict (10:11–14), as does John the revelator.

David Jeremiah says, "Demons are Satan's servants, and are committed to his scheme to thwart the plan of God. . . . They are ruled by Satan himself, and they share in his dirty work."[7] Thus, it should not surprise us to find a demonic horde of evil spirits tormenting mankind in the Last Days. Satan has deceived this world into thinking that he is interested in its betterment and improvement, when he is really hell-bent on its destruction!

D-Day on Planet Earth

A dramatic shift occurs in Revelation 9. The scene is preceded by three ominous "woes" pronounced by an angel in 8:13. These set the stage for the last three trumpets that are about to sound. The first four trumpets leave the earth a devastated mess. But the last three trumpets finish it off and bring it to ruin.

Suddenly, a "star" (perhaps an angel) falls (literally, "descends") from heaven and is given the key to the bottomless pit (Greek, *abussos*). Seven of the nine biblical usages of *abyss* occur in the Revelation. It is the prison house of fallen angels and demonic spirits—the same place where Satan is later bound for one thousand years (Rev. 20:1–3). The angel is not likely a fallen angel, but one of God's angels. Robert Mounce comments, "The star-angel is simply one of the many divine agents who throughout the book of Revelation are pictured as carrying out the will of God."[8]

Notice, the angel is given the key to the pit. The key is a divine possession and would not be entrusted to a demon. The passage clearly portrays the sovereign authority of God over the forces of evil. By unlocking the pit, God allows the demonic horde of "locusts" to attack the unrepentant people of earth. The imagery of this attack is taken from Joel 1:15—2:11, where the devastation of a plague of locusts symbolizes the coming destruction of the day of the Lord.

Bruce Metzger notes, "As in the sequence of the seals, so in the sequence of the trumpets the fifth and sixth are described at greater length than the first four. When the fifth angel blows his trumpet, a plague of demonic locusts is released from the bottomless pit."⁹

The description of what follows is incredible. It defies the vocabulary of the first century, so John uses his descriptive terms as best he can muster them. The "locusts" are described as flying, stinging "like a scorpion," having faces like men, hair like women, breastplates of iron and "stings" in their tails. These are not hippies on motorcycles! They are either demonic hordes, human armies, or radiation-poisoned and mutated creatures.

5. *Fifth trumpet:* demonic invasion (9:1–12).

The plagues of locusts described in the Apocalypse represents a demonic invasion of planet earth. The creatures are depicted as having been imprisoned in the abyss. They are released by divine permission and torment unbelievers—those who do not have the "seal of God" (9:4). Whether these demonic creatures inhabit human bodies is not fully clear. The reference to the "appearance of the locusts" (9:7) seems to indicate some kind of weaponry.

The "locusts" are personalized as a military-like force led by one called *Abaddon* (Hebrew, "destroyer"). To make sure his readers understand, John adds the Greek equivalent: *Apollyon*. Both names carry the same designation: "one who destroys." He is symbolically depicted as the leader of the fallen angels in the bottomless pit.

Robert Thomas comments: "Another idea has been that he is Satan, but the fact that Satan is 'the prince of demons' (Matt. 12:24) does not necessarily make him king over the demons confined in the abyss. His domain is the heavenly places, not the lower parts of the earth (cf. Eph. 6:12). Nowhere does Satan have a connection with the abyss until being cast into it later (cf. Rev. 20:1–3)."¹⁰

The description of the "locusts" and their functions cannot be limited to natural insects. They must be symbolic of demons or demon-inspired combatants. These creatures do not eat the vegetation of earth (9:4). Instead, they torment earth's population for five months (9:5). Their "sting" is depicted as that of a scorpion. The passage is filled with *comparative* references:

1. "Smoke . . . *like* the smoke of a great furnace" (v. 2)

2. "Power . . . *as* the scorpions of the earth" (v. 3)

3. "Torment . . . *like* the torment of a scorpion" (v. 5)

4. "Appearance . . . *like* horses prepared for battle" (v. 7)

5. "On their heads, *as* it were, crowns *like* gold" (v. 7)

6. "Faces . . . *like* the faces of men" (v. 7)

7. "Hair *like* the hair of women" (v. 8)

8. "Teeth . . . *like* the teeth of lions" (v. 8)

9. "Breastplates *like* breastplates of iron" (v. 9)

10. "Sound of their wings . . . *like* the sound of chariots" (v. 9)

11. "Tails *like* scorpions" (v. 10)

Everything about this passage encourages us to look for a symbolic, rather than literal meaning. Modern explanations of nerve gas, laser beams, chemical warfare, etc., change with the times. However, two things are clear: Demons from the bottomless pit are involved, and some kind of modern warfare is implied. Whatever these things are, they fly, make noise, are armored, and "sting" people without killing them. Some type of neutralizing "ray" may be intended. One thing is certain: John had never seen anything like this before!

6. *Sixth trumpet:* the deadly attack (9:13–21).

The second "woe" is introduced and the sixth angel sounds his trumpet. Immediately, a voice speaks to the angel from the "four horns of the golden altar which is before God" in heaven (v. 13). This is the same voice as the angel of the altar in 8:3. This connects him with the requests of the saints that emanate from the heavenly altar. The triple use of the article (Greek, *tou*) indicates specificity: *the* altar, *the* golden one, *the* one before God (v. 13).

The voice instructs the angel with the sixth trumpet to release the "four angels who are bound at the great river Euphrates" (v. 14). Since they are bound, they must be fallen angels or demons. Their release is by divine permission only and is intended to allow them to function as agents of God's wrath.

The Euphrates River originates in the mountains of Armenia, south of Russia, and flows southeast until it joins the Tigris in lower Babylon. Together, the two rivers cover an eighteen hundred mile waterway through the deserts of Iraq. In biblical times, the Euphrates formed the border between Israel and her enemies, Babylon and Assyria. In New Testament times, the Euphrates formed the frontier between the Roman and Parthian empires.

In the meantime, the four angels prepared for a great conflict that will "kill a third of mankind" (v. 15). Added to the fourth part of the world population that has already perished (cf. Revelation 6:8), this would add up to nearly half the population of the world. The Greek text refers to "hour" and "day" and "month" and "year" (v. 15). Thomas notes, "One article governing all four nouns shows that duration is not in view, but that the occasion of each one of the time designations is one and the same: the appointed hour occurs on the appointed day in the appointed month in the appointed year. The four angels await the signal that this hour has arrived."[11]

This judgment, like all the others, may be carried out by men and angels, but not without the permission of God. It comes on His precise timetable, which is under His sovereign control. The fraction one-third represents an increase in intensity over the previous judgments. The number of the invading army is almost beyond calculation: 200 million. This army is as large as the entire populations of America or Russia.

While some prefer to view this invading horde as demons, I believe they are an actual army. The battles that follow involve killing men, and the attackers are described as men (vv. 16–18). The weapons with "breastplates the color of fire" could well be modern weapons. These "breastplates the color of fire" and the "fire and smoke and brimstone" that shot out of both ends of these vehicles certainly sound like tanks, airplanes, or some modern weaponry.

If John really saw the future, including the great end-times wars, he would have witnessed things he could hardly understand, let alone describe. Tanks, guns, flame-throwers, and laser beams all fit these possible designations. While the horde of demons is unleashed to torture and afflict men, the horde of soldiers is unleashed to attack them as well.

The Last Jihad

There is nothing in this passage to indicate who the invaders may be. A parallel verse (16:12) in the bowl judgments refers to the "kings of the east" crossing the Euphrates River in a similar maneuver. While some have suggested these are the Chinese, there is nothing in either passage that actually says that. The Euphrates River served as the eastern boundary of the Promised Land (cf. Gen. 15:18; Deut. 1:7; Josh. 1:4). It was also the eastern boundary of the Roman Empire. Beyond lay the Parthian kingdoms (equivalent today to Iran, Afghanistan, Pakistan, parts of India, and southern Russia).

It is certainly possible that China or Japan could be involved in an invasion of Israel in the End Times. But the text itself does not require that interpretation. It is much more likely that this invasion involves an alliance of the non-Arab Muslim nations led by Iran and the Muslim republics from the former Soviet Union. Sixty million Muslims live in these republics alone. A combined army of the entire Muslim world would stretch from North Africa to Kazakhstan (on the fringes of Mongolia). Given the right cause (like a last great *jihad* to overthrow the rebuilding of the Jewish temple) and the right leader, who could unite the warring Muslim factions, such an army could easily contain two hundred million soldiers.

The beliefs and prejudices of Islam are deeply entrenched. It is often pictured as a religion of fanatics, warmongers, and terrorists. While this is not a fair picture of Islam on the whole, it is certainly true of a radical element within the Muslim faith. It is this element that constantly calls for justice, revenge, and so-called "holy wars." Many Muslims believe in spreading their faith by the sword and killing the "infidels" who reject it. Tragically, this often leads to international "gang war."

Ironically, *jihad* means "struggle" and refers to the struggle of the soul against evil. But when it is applied to religious war in the name of God, *jihad* becomes an ugly and frightening concept that condones terrorism and mass murder in the name of religion. The "Islamic Curtain" cuts off the Arab world from outside influences. "Behind that wall of prejudice," writes Dave Hunt, "any religion except Islam is forbidden."[12] Converts to Christianity are often persecuted, imprisoned, or executed.

Tim LaHaye observes that it is the unrepentant that suffer during these judgments. He writes; "We find that about fifty percent of the world's unregenerate population will have died. It would seem then that God is ridding the earth of those who will never receive Him. These people could not possibly populate the Millennial Kingdom and therefore must be purged from the earth."[13]

Repentance is always a prerequisite to faith. Those who will not repent will not believe. The Bible clearly teaches that repentance and faith are both essential elements of the gospel message (cf. Acts 20:21; 26:20). The great tragedy of the unregenerate population of the Tribulation period is that they cannot believe because they will not repent.

Study Questions

1. Read Isaiah 13:6–11. What key to the prophetic significance of Revelation 9 do you find in these verses?

2. Who is given the key to the bottomless pit (9:1)?

3. What comes up out of the bottomless pit when it is first opened (9:2)?

4. What are the creatures that emerged from the pit called (9:3)?

5. What is the sting of these creatures compared to (9:3, 10)?

6. What is the only thing that can keep someone safe from this torment (9:4)?

7. How long are these creatures allowed to torment mankind (9:5)?

8. What is the name of the leader of these creatures (9:11)?

9. Where are the four angels that are released at the sixth trumpet (9:14)?

10. What percentage of earth's population is killed by the huge army described in Revelation 9:15–16?

11. What did those who were not killed refuse to do (9:20)?

CHAPTER 10

Can It Get Any Worse?

Preview:

This chapter serves as an interlude between the sixth and seventh trumpets. It includes the ominous seven thunders, which are sealed up and kept secret. The sounding of the seventh trumpet is delayed until John can take the "little book," devour it, and prophesy again.

Time is running out for the people of earth! By the end of the six trumpet judgments, half the population of the planet has been wiped out. The interlude that comes next (chaps. 10—11) sets the stage for the seventh and final trumpet. It is so dramatic that it results in the total collapse of the world system that has aligned itself against God.

Bruce Metzger writes, "The purpose of the interlude in each of the seven cycles is largely dramatic. With the completion of the sixth in each series we hold our breath in anticipation of the end. But this dramatic writer does not allow the end to come with such rapidity. Each time he makes us wait before we see the seventh of the series. . . . The effect is tantalizing."[1]

There was an interlude between the sixth and seventh seals consisting of the vision of the 144,000 (7:1-8) and the vision of the heavenly multitude (7:9-17). Now, between the sixth and seventh trumpets, there is an interlude that includes the vision of the little book (10:1-11) and the two witnesses (11:1-13). Robert Mounce observes, "There will be no corresponding interlude between the sixth and seventh bowl judgments (the final series yet to come) because at that time all warning and preliminary judgment will be over. When the bowls of divine wrath are poured out, the consummation will have been irrevocably set into motion."[2]

The sequence of events in the interlude heightens and intensifies our anticipation of what is coming next. Every verse in the tenth chapter begins with *kai* ("and") or *alla* ("but," v. 7). These conjunctions keep the pace moving forward in anticipation of whatever will happen next. The reader of the Revelation is left breathless time and time again by this amazing and rapid sweep of movement through time.

Robert Thomas observes that this interlude (chaps. 10—11) contains two preliminary elements that prepare the way for the seventh trumpet: announcement of the end of delay, the measurement of the temple and its worshipers. He writes, "This section is parenthetical to the sequential movement of the trumpet judgments. It contains no reference to the judgment of the earth-dwellers but consoles believers by reiterating God's role as the sovereign over earthly affairs. . . . The interlude prepares for the final trumpet blast by reviewing developments leading up to that moment, particularly those related to the city of Jerusalem."[3]

The Mighty Angel

The new vision begins with the words "and I saw," distinguishing it from the greater vision of the seven trumpets. What John saw was "another strong angel" carrying a "little book" (Greek, *biblaridion*, the diminutive of *biblarion*, which is the diminutive of *biblion*). The term "little scroll" (*biblaridion*) is very rare in the New Testament and only appears in this chapter (v. 2, 9–10). This fact alone certainly distinguishes it from the seven-sealed scroll in chapter 5.

The other interpretive issue in this chapter deals with the identity of the "strong angel" (10:1). Some have suggested this is Christ because of his majestic appearance. However, Christ never appears as an angel in the Apocalypse. In fact, Tim LaHaye notes that "we will look in vain for a presentation of Him as an angel after the incarnation."[4]

The glorious description of this angel is certainly stunning. He is clothed with a cloud, with a rainbow upon his head, his face glowed like the sun, and his feet were like pillars of fire (10:1). He is distinguished from the mighty angel in 5:2 by the term *another* (Greek, *allon*, "another of the same kind"). This distinction also eliminates the idea that Christ is this angel, since He is not of the "same kind." This angel also swears by God, lifting his hand to heaven (10:5–6)—something Christ would not need to do.

Angels play a prominent role in the Apocalypse. They are mentioned sixty-six times. They are involved in serving, worshiping, and praising God, announcing messages, delivering judgments, and battling evil forces. In 18:1, another powerful angel appears, pronouncing doom on Babylon. These angelic beings are the servants of God Almighty.

Seven Thunders

The mighty angel descends from heaven to earth and cries with a loud voice (10:3). In response, "seven thunders" speak an ominous message that John hears but is not allowed to record. The "loud voice" of the angel's cry is also unrecorded, unless it is the same as his statement in 10:6. The context implies a cry of judgment. "With a loud voice" (Greek, *phonē megalē*) indicates the loud volume of the cry. The comparison to a lion's roar is similar to the description of God's voice in Hosea 11:10 and Amos 3:8.

The "seven thunders" may be taken from Psalm 29:3–9, where the "God of glory thunders." The sevenfold description of *God's voice* is:

1. Over many waters
2. Powerful
3. Majestic
4. Breaks the cedars
5. Hews out flames of fire
6. Shakes the wilderness
7. Makes the deer to calve

In John 12:28–29, the voice of the Father speaks from heaven like thunder. John and James, his brother, were actually nicknamed the "Sons of Thunder" (Mark 3:17). The seven peals of thunder mentioned here are certainly typical of John's experiences with God. But there is something ominous about these "thunders," and he is told not to record their messages. This seems to indicate that they spoke of great physical judgment on the earth. The fact that God chose not to reveal their content is an act of mercy. We already know enough about the future to be concerned. If we knew what the thunders said, we probably would be scared to death!

John was told to "seal up" the utterances of the seven thunders and "do not write them" (10:4). Any attempt to guess their meaning is presumptuous and unjustified. Just as Daniel (12:9) was told to seal up his prophecies until the "end time," so we must wait on God's timing to reveal the seven thunders in the future. This entire experience is similar to that of the apostle Paul in 2 Corinthians 12:4, where he is commanded not to tell all that he heard in heaven.

The angel's major declaration was that "there shall be delay no longer" (10:6). "Delay" (Greek, *chronos*) refers to the movement of time (as in a chronology). The angel is answering the cry of martyrs in heaven (6:9–12) who were told to rest awhile until other martyrs joined them. Now, there will be no delay. The end has come!

Robert Mounce comments,

Now nothing stands in the way of the final dramatic period of human history. From this point on God will not intervene to give man further opportunity to repent. Restraint is to be removed and the Antichrist is to be revealed (cf. 2 Thess. 2:3ff). The forces of God will meet in final confrontation. This is the "time of trouble, such as never has been, [KJV]" foretold by Daniel (12:1) and repeated in the synoptic apocalypse (Mark 13:19 and parallels). It is the darkness before the dawn—the awesome period of Satan's wrath (12:12, 17). The appointed delay is over, and the period of the end is irrevocably set into motion.[5]

Mystery of God

The trumpet blast of the seventh angel indicates that the "mystery of God" is "finished" (Greek, *telesthē*, "fulfilled" or "completed"). The mystery "will have been fulfilled" is the force of the aorist indicative verb. John does not use the future indicative, but the proleptic aorist in anticipation of these days being in the past. Even his grammar indicates that he wrote of this event as it was actually occurring before his very eyes.

The expression "the mystery of God" (Greek, *mystērion*) refers to God's revealed purposes in bringing His kingdom to full fruition. Though this kingdom has been hidden from unbelievers, it will be fully revealed in the judgments that will follow. Thomas believes, "The mystery of God consists of the heretofore unrevealed details unfolded in the chapters from here to the end."[6]

The "mystery" also refers to the uniqueness of Jesus Christ in relation to the kingdom of God. In Colossians 1:26–27, He is the "mystery which has been hidden from the past ages and generations," but now is revealed "in you." The indwelling of the believer by Christ through the Holy Spirit is the mystery that is the "hope of glory." In Him are "hid all the treasures of wisdom and knowledge" (Col. 2:3). Other New Testament "mysteries" include the final destiny of Israel (Rom. 11:25), the transformation at the resurrection of believers (1 Cor. 15:51–52), and the mystery of lawlessness (2 Thess. 2:7).

The "mystery" in Revelation 10:7 is said to have been declared to His "servants the prophets." This indicates that the "mystery" in view here has something to do with the completion of the hope of the gospel. The Old Testament prophets declared that the Lamb of God was coming to atone for the sins of the world (Is. 53). The New Testament prophets declared that He had already come and called men to faith in Him. The task of the Old Testament prophets pointed ahead to the first coming of Christ. The task of New Testament prophets was to point back to Christ's atonement and to point ahead to His triumphant return.

Messianic Prophecies	
1. Born of a woman (Gen. 3:15)	17. Stumbling stone to the Jews (Ps. 118:22)
2. Born of a virgin (Is. 7:14)	18. Light to the Gentiles (Is. 42:6–7)
3. Son of God (Ps. 2:7)	19. Betrayed for 30 pieces of silver (Zech. 11:12)
4. Seed of Abraham (Gen, 12:2–3)	20. Forsaken by His own followers (Zech. 13:7)
5. Seed of Isaac (Gen. 17:19)	21. Beaten and spit upon (Is. 50:6)
6. Son of Jacob (Num. 24:17)	22. Publicly mocked (Ps. 22:7–8)
7. Tribe of Judah (Gen. 49:10)	23. Cast lots for His garments (Ps. 22:7–8)
8. Line of David (Is. 9:6–7)	24. Crucified (Ps. 22: 16; Zech. 12:10)
9. Born at Bethlehem (Mic. 5:2)	25. Executed with criminals (Is. 53:12)
10. Prophet (Deut. 18:18)	26. Buried with the rich (Is. 53:9)
11. Priest (Ps. 110:4)	27. Rise from the dead (Ps. 16:10)
12. King (Is. 9:7)	28. Ascends back to heaven (Ps. 16:10)
13. Anointed with the Spirit (Is. 11:2)	29. Seated at the right hand of God (Ps. 110:1)
14. Ministry in Galilee (Is. 9:1)	30. Coming again (Zech. 14:4)
15. Miracles (Is. 35:5–6)	
16. Enters the temple (Mal. 3:1)	

The Little Book

The "strong angel" is pictured holding a "little book" (scroll) in his hand when the chapter opens. As noted earlier, the designation *biblaridion* distinguishes this scroll from the one in chapter 5. This is not the seven-sealed scroll that is the title deed to the universe. Rather, it is a smaller document that John is now told to "eat" (10:9).

Metzger notes that eating the scroll is a way of saying that he is to read it and devour its message, even as we speak of "devouring a good book." He observes that the "little scroll" is a "special message" from God to John.[7] The scroll is sweet in his mouth but bitter in his stomach. Having assimilated the scroll, John is to make its message known by prophesying again "before many peoples, and nations, and tongues, and kings" (10:11). This may imply that he would eventually be recalled from Patmos and released or that the Apocalypse itself would be widely read in many nations.

The actual identity of the "little scroll" has had several suggestions: the Word of God, the gospel, the book of Revelation itself, the specific prophecies of chapters 12—22, chapter 11, or a message of judgment against unbelief in general. The "little scroll" itself is never specifically mentioned again in the Revelation. It is possible that the imagery is taken from Numbers 5:12–31, where the priest is told to write the oath of cursing on a scroll, blot it out with bitter water, and make the accused drink the water to determine his or her innocence or guilt.

The eating of the scroll is similar to the experiences of the prophets Jeremiah and Ezekiel. "Thy words were found, and I ate them," Jeremiah wrote (15:16). When he earlier had objected to his prophetic call, the Lord assured him, "Behold, I have put My words in your mouth" (1:9). God also promised, "I making My words in your mouth fire, and this people wood, and it will consume them" (5:14). To Ezekiel (3:1–3), the Lord said, "Eat this scroll, and go, speak to the house of Israel."

For every prophet, including John, there was a bittersweet message. It was sweet (Greek, *glukas*) to the believer because it offered hope. But it was bitter (Greek, *pikros*) to the unbeliever because it pronounced judgment. In this whole experience we see the humanity of the prophets. Theirs is a bittersweet ministry. They are not just purveyors of doom and gloom. They are real men whose hearts ache over those who reject so great a salvation.

The amazing feature in this passage is John's commission to "prophesy again" (10:11). Mounce writes, "There is a sense of divine compulsion in the charge given to John. He *must* prophesy again. . . . John's mission is to lay bare the forces of the supernatural world, which are at work behind the activities of men and nations. His prophecy is the culmination of all previous prophecies in that it leads on to the final destruction of evil and the inauguration of the eternal state."[8]

John sees further down the corridor of time than any of his contemporaries. Like Isaiah he sees all the way to the "new heavens" and the "new earth" (66:22). Whatever the "little scroll" represents, it indicates that John is still called to proclaim the message of God and the gospel of Jesus Christ while there is still time. Though John saw the future, he still lived in the present. The entire incident reminds him that he still has a vital ministry to his own and succeeding generations.

Mounce adds an important thought about the structure and progression of the Apocalypse. He says, "The drama has now moved to that moment immediately preceding the final scene. From this point on the Apocalypse becomes a multi-dimensional presentation of the final triumph of God over evil."[9]

One thing is very clear and that is that the next chapter brings us to a dramatic conclusion. It includes a terrible earthquake, the collapse of earthly kingdoms, the usurpation of power by God, the announcement of the coming judgment, and the opening of the temple of God in heaven. How one views the chronological development of the book will determine how he views the events in this climactic chapter. But first, there appear two key "witnesses" on the prophetic horizon.

Study Questions

1. Read Colossians 1:25–27. What key to the prophetic significance of Revelation 10 do you find in these verses?

2. Who comes down from heaven "clothed with a cloud" (10:1)?

3. What is he holding in his hand (10:2)?

4. When he cries out, who answers him (10:3)?

5. What is John told to do with the message they uttered (10:4)?

6. To what does the phrase "there shall be delay no longer" refer (10:6)?

7. What will be finished as soon as the seventh angel sounds (10:7)?

8. What was John instructed to do with the scroll (10:8–9)?

9. After doing as he was instructed, how did John describe the scroll (10:9)?

10. What was John assured that he would do again (10:11)?

CHAPTER 11

Hell on Earth!

Preview:

The invasion of Jerusalem by the Gentiles is accompanied by the rise of the two witnesses. The scene shifts to the earthly Jerusalem, which is the center stage of the coming conflict with the beast. The witnesses are martyred and then miraculously resurrected.

As if things were not bad enough, all hell breaks loose in this chapter. Satan's opposition to the two witnesses reaches a dramatic climax in their execution, resurrection, and ascension into heaven. Then a cataclysmic earthquake results in the collapse of the major world powers. All the forces of heaven and hell are engaged in the great end-times drama.

Time remains suspended between the sixth and seventh trumpets as John the revelator tells us about measuring the temple, the invasion of the Gentiles, the appearance of the two witnesses, and the rise of the beast out of the bottomless pit to oppose them. The spiritual conflict intensifies with human, natural, and cosmic forces in collision with God's final purposes for planet earth.

Virtually every commentator makes reference to the difficulties encountered in interpreting this chapter. John Walvoord states, "The guiding lines which govern the exposition to follow regard this chapter as a legitimate prophetic utterance in which the terms are taken normally."[1] The "great city . . . where also their Lord was crucified" is Jerusalem. The two witnesses are two individual evangelists. The earthquake is a real earthquake. The "beast" from the "abyss" is the same beast as the one described in 13:1–10: the Antichrist. The temple is the Jewish temple in Jerusalem.

One's eschatological viewpoint will inevitably determine how he or she interprets the various elements in this chapter. If the second temple (Herod's Temple) had already been destroyed twenty-five years prior to the writing of the Apocalypse, then this must be a third temple yet to be rebuilt by the Jews in Jerusalem in the future. A similar reference is made by Paul in 2 Thessalonians 2:3-4, where the "man of lawlessness [the Antichrist] . . . takes his seat in the temple of God" claiming to be God.

This chapter is also important in that it introduces the first references to the time elements in the Revelation. The Gentiles trample the holy city underfoot for 42 months (11:2). The two witnesses prophesy for 1,260 days (11:3). The beast is given power to rule 42 months (13:5). The woman (Israel) flees from persecution for 1,260 days (12:6), or "a time and times and half a time" (12:14). All of these calculations add up to three and one-half years. There is no clear reference in the Apocalypse to a seven-year Tribulation. This is generally assumed by paralleling the Tribulation to the seventieth week of Daniel 9:24-27. The three and one-half years then represent the last half of the Tribulation, or the Great Tribulation.

Jewish Focus of the Vision

Charles Feinberg has shown that reference to the temple, altar, court, and holy city (11:1-2) "alerts the reader that events continue on Jewish grounds."[2] The confusion that one finds in nondispensational commentaries comes from their attempts to read the Church into this chapter. Bruce Metzger admits, "What follows in chapter 11 has been generally acknowledged to be one of the most perplexing sections of the entire book. There is presented here an almost bewildering interweaving of symbols suggested by Old Testament history and prophecy."[3]

The confusion is the result of trying to force the Church into this vision. That is because it is the Jewish people and state that are in view here! What else is one to make of references to the temple, the altar, the descriptive ministries of Moses and Elijah, the wild olive trees and the lampstand of Zechariah, the plagues upon Pharaoh, the tyrant predicted by Daniel, and Sodom, Egypt, and Jerusalem?

All other approaches to this chapter fall into a hopeless quagmire. Beasley-Murray attempts to say that John has adopted a Jewish model to represent the Church.[4] Thus, the twelve tribes (7:1-8) equal the whole Church throughout the world. The temple and its worshipers equal the whole Church in all lands. The two witnesses become the evangelistic mandate of the Church. The problems with this approach are numerous. If the Church is meant by "Israel," what is meant by "Jerusalem"? If the two witnesses symbolize the ministry of the churches, why are they killing people with fire out of their mouths (11:5)? If the 1,260 days are not literal, what in the world do they symbolize? If the witnesses are killed and raptured to heaven (11:7–12), does that mean all true Christians will be martyred?

There is no doubt in my mind that the extensive Jewish symbolism in this chapter is intended to refer to the Jews in Jerusalem in the Last Days. The prophecy gives us a parenthetical glimpse into the persecution of believing Jews of the Tribulation period who have been converted to Christ by the ministry of the two witnesses and the 144,000 male virgins (14:3–5). The only way this chapter or any other chapter in the Revelation makes sense is to clearly separate that which refers to Israel and that which refers to the Church. All attempts to mix the two have led to hopeless disagreement and confusion.

Will the Temple Be Rebuilt?

The Jewish people have always loved the temple. As soon as David conquered Jerusalem, he desired to build a temple to Jehovah. While he raised the funds and collected the materials, it was his son Solomon who actually built the first temple in ca. 950 B.C. That temple stood until 586 B.C., when Nebuchadnezzar, the king of Babylon, destroyed it. After the Babylonian captivity, some of the Jews returned to Jerusalem and built the second temple under the leadership of Zerubbabel in 520–515 B.C. That temple was later remodeled and expanded by Herod the Great in 20 B.C. The second temple stood until A.D. 70, when the Romans demolished it.[5]

It has been nearly two thousand years since there has been a Jewish temple on Mt. Moriah. Since A.D. 691 the Muslim shrine, the Dome of the Rock, has stood on the site of the ancient Jewish temples. Ever since the Jewish people began returning to the Promised Land, there has been talk of building a third temple. There is presently a Temple Institute in Jerusalem that is dedicated to reconstructing the instruments of worship for the new temple. However, as long as the Dome of the Rock stands on Mt. Moriah, it is unlikely the new temple will be built there.

Both John (Rev. 11:1–2) and Paul (2 Thess. 2:3–4) indicate there will be a future temple in Jerusalem. We can only speculate at this time how that might come to pass. The Muslims revere the Dome of the Rock as a holy shrine to commemorate the place where Muhammad supposedly ascended into heaven. There is no way they will ever willingly give up this place. It is sacred to Islam. The only reasonable options would seem to be that it is destroyed by warfare, terrorism, or a natural disaster, like an earthquake. Only then could the Jews presume to rebuild the temple on that spot. But such an attempt would certainly be met with armed resistance throughout the Muslim world.

Prophecy scholars Thomas Ice and Randall Price have recently said,

> We believe that the current interest in rebuilding the temple, the first of its kind in the last 1,400 years, is of significant merit. . . . Something momentous is happening in the Middle East today that will soon affect the destiny of our entire planet. . . . This event is the rebuilding of the Jewish temple in Jerusalem. . . . While we do not suggest that the temple is being built today, nor that it can be built today, we are convinced that there is a ground swell of expectation in Israel . . . that a temple will be rebuilt tomorrow.[6]

John is told to take a "measuring rod" (a papyrus reed) and "measure the temple" (11:1). This symbolic act is similar to that done by the prophets Zechariah and Ezekiel. There are actually seven times in the narrative of the Apocalypse where John is invited to participate in the action (cf. 1:12; 5:4; 7:14; 10:9–11; 11:1–2; 19:10; 22:8). Yet no actual measurement is recorded here. Instead, John's measuring of the temple (Greek, *naos*) implies divine protection for the "sanctuary," despite an invasion of Gentile forces into Jerusalem. Since Daniel 9:26–27 indicates the Antichrist ("the prince who is to come") will make a covenant with Israel for seven years ("one week"), many believe this agreement will include a provision of protection for the temple against a Muslim invasion.

The Gentile Occupation of Jerusalem

The second verse in this chapter indicates that the Gentiles will occupy the holy city (Jerusalem) and "tread [it] under foot" for 42 months. All of the time indicators in this chapter (42 months and 1,260 days) add up to three and one-half years, marking the duration of the Great Tribulation. All attempts at taking 42 and 1,260 as symbolic numbers have proved futile. Until someone can come up with a better explanation (and no one has), it seems best to take these time indicators to mean literally three and one-half years. This time frame is very reasonable given what has already preceded in the Revelation.

A probable scenario would look something like the chart on the opposite page:

Seven Years of Tribulation (Daniel's Seventieth Week)

Rise of the Antichrist	→	War and Conflicts Erupt	→	Treaty with Israel	→	Temple will be Rebuilt	→	Invasion of Jerusalem

---

In the meantime, two witnesses appear on the scene. They prophesy (or "preach") the gospel of Jesus Christ to the Jews in Jerusalem. Their ministries sound a lot like Moses (Law) and Elijah (prophets). They have supernatural power to smite the earth with plagues (Moses) and to call down fire from heaven (Elijah). However, early Christian tradition saw them as Enoch and Elijah (cf. Tertullian, Irenaeus, and Hippolytus). The imagery of the "two olive trees" and "two lampstands," however, is taken from Zechariah (4:2–6, 11–14), where they represent Joshua the priest and Zerubbabel the prince. They were leading figures in helping reestablish Israel religiously and politically after the Babylonian captivity.

It is apparent that John uses both symbols (Moses and Elijah, Joshua and Zerubbabel) to depict these two future *witnesses*. Notice several details about them:

1. They are unnamed (we do not know their identity).

2. They will have a future ministry ("I will grant" and "they will prophesy").

3. Their ministry will be limited to 1,260 days (11:3).

4. They are clothed in sackcloth (11:3).

5. They will be killed by the beast and resurrected after three and one-half days (11:7–11).

Attempts to parallel the experience of the two witnesses to the Church or to Israel and the Church (God's two people) have proved unsatisfactory. In fact, no two commentators agree on how such symbolism should be applied. Some suggestions even border on being ludicrous. Mounce goes to great length to make "the great city . . . where also their Lord was crucified" equal Rome.[7] Leon Morris goes so far as to say it is "every city and no city. It is civilized man in organized community."[8]

Live from the Middle East

One of the objections often raised against viewing the two witnesses as two literal prophets is that the whole world (people, kindreds, tongues, and nations) will "look at their dead bodies for three and a half days" lying in the street (v. 9). The unbelieving world will rejoice in their martyrdom and send gifts to one another (v. 10). Their deaths will result in a worldwide holiday festivity.

Previous generations could not imagine how this could literally happen. Today, we know exactly how it could happen: live satellite television transmission. We can see televised pictures instantly all over the planet because of satellite communications. It happens every night on the national news! That fact alone ought to get our attention about how close we are to the end. A camera crew could easily film the deaths of these two witnesses and then continue to show televised updates throughout the next three and a half days. Televised pictures can be transmitted in seconds from Jerusalem to New York, Tokyo, London, Moscow, and the entire world.

Next, an even more shocking televised event: the resurrection of the witnesses! The Bible says, "The breath of life from God came into them, and they stood on their feet; and great fear fell upon those who were beholding them" (11:11). As if that were not stunning enough, the two witnesses next ascend up into heaven (11:12). The "loud voice" speaks from heaven, "Come up here." It is the same invitation that John himself received in 4:1.

The ascension of the witnesses was followed "in that hour" by a great earthquake that rocked the city. One-tenth of the city (buildings?) fell, and seven thousand people were killed. This incident was so powerful that the remnant of the people in the city were afraid and "gave glory to the God of heaven" (11:13). This is the first and only reference in the Apocalypse to people repenting as a result of a natural disaster. This time, no one shakes his fist in the face of God. They have seen too much to deny the hand of God.

Commentators are divided on whether "giving glory to God" is tantamount to repentance. Yet, elsewhere in the Revelation that is exactly what it represents (cf. 4:8; 16:9; 19:7). Robert Thomas notes that "'Giving glory to God' has a positive spiritual connotation elsewhere in the O.T. and in the N.T. too (cf. Josh. 7:19; 1 Sam. 6:5; Isa. 42:12; Jer. 13:16; Luke 17:18; John 9:24; Acts 12:23; Rom. 4:20; 1 Pet. 2:12)."[9]

At this point, John adds, "The second woe is past; behold, the third woe is coming quickly" (11:14). This connects us all the way back to 8:13, where the *three woes* were introduced. Thus, the progression has been:

1. First woe = fifth trumpet (9:1–12)

2. Second woe = sixth trumpet + interlude (9:13—11:14)

3. Third woe = seventh trumpet (11:15–19)

All of this dramatic buildup leaves the reader breathless. The insertion of the explanation of the "woes" at this point has an incredible shock effect on the reader. It's saying "In case you forgot, that was just the second woe!" The third woe is still to come in the seventh trumpet.

7. *Seventh trumpet* (11:15–19).

From this point on, everything follows in rapid succession. These five verses (15–19) are among the most dramatic verses in the entire Bible. They are so powerful that George Frideric Handel took the words of verse 15, "and He will reign forever and ever," as the closing chorus of his great oratorio, *The Messiah*.

The crescendo of worship that is expressed by the angelic choirs in this section is the most dramatic and climactic in the entire Apocalypse. It is the fulfillment of all the prophetic promises of the coming kingdom of God on earth. Daniel foresaw the day when "the God of heaven will set up a kingdom . . . it will itself endure forever" (Dan. 2:44). He also predicted: "One like a Son of Man was coming . . . and to Him was given dominion, Glory, and a kingdom . . . then the sovereignty, the dominion, and the greatness of all the kingdoms . . . will be given to the people of the saints of the Highest One; His kingdom will be an everlasting kingdom" (Dan, 7:13–14, 27).

One cannot read these verses without realizing that we have come to some great conclusion. It is all over except the shouting! William Barclay observes that the remainder of the chapter is a "summary of all that is still to come."[10] Mounce adds, "The declaration of triumph by the heavenly hosts (v. 15) and the anthem of praise by the worshiping elders (vv. 17–18) introduce the great themes of the following chapters. The extensive use of the aorist tense conveys a sense of absolute certainty about the events yet to come."[11]

The twenty-four elders (symbolic of the Church in heaven) are again on their faces before God as they were in 7:11, when we last saw them. They are praising God because He has taken power and has reigned (v. 17). The judgment of the nations has come (v. 18). And the heavenly temple is opened, revealing the Ark of the Covenant. Heaven is opened. The earth is judged. The kingdoms of this world have fallen. The Lord and His Christ (Messiah) have prevailed, and they shall reign forever and ever (v. 15).

It doesn't get any better than this! There is no greater statement of triumph in all the Revelation, with the possible exception of 19:11–16, where Christ actually returns to earth to reign and rule. We cannot overlook the significance of what happens with the *seventh trumpet:*

1. Christ takes possession of the kingdoms of this world.
2. He reigns and rules forever.
3. God's wrath has come upon the earth.
4. The nations will be judged.
5. The saints will be rewarded.
6. The temple of God in heaven is opened.
7. The Ark of the Covenant is revealed.

What started as hell on earth has become heaven revealed. The judgments of the seals and trumpets have sent the earth reeling and brought the people of Jerusalem to their knees. The climax is more than just the end of the first half of the Tribulation. It points all the way to the end of it! The reader is left with two basic choices. This is either the end of the reading of the outside of the scroll and the reading of the inside is about to begin, with the bowls repeating the trumpets. Or else, it is both the climactic conclusion of the seven trumpets and the overview of all that is yet to come in the details that follow.

The typical pattern of the Apocalypse is to give us the big picture followed by the snapshots. First the panorama, then the close-ups. I believe that is what we have in 11:15–19. We must take seriously the proclamation of final triumph in these verses. They look all the way down the canyon of eternity to the final victory at the end of the Tribulation. At the same time, they give us the overview of what is coming in detail in the chapters ahead.

Study Questions

1. Read Daniel 7:13–14, 18. What key to the prophetic significance of Revelation 11 do you find in these verses?

2. What was John given to measure the temple of God (11:1)?

3. Who was allowed to "tread under foot the holy city" for forty-two months (11:2)?

4. Who is raised up to prophesy for 1,260 days (11:3)?

5. What are they able to call down from heaven by the power God gives them (11:5)?

6. Who will ascend out of the bottomless pit to kill the witnesses (11:7)?

7. In what city will their dead bodies lay in the street (11:8)?

8. What will become of them after three and one-half days (11:11–12)?

9. What causes a tenth of the city to fall (11:13)?

10. When the seventh trumpet sounds, what will the kingdoms of this world become (11:15)?

11. What does John see within the temple of God in heaven (11:19)?

SECTION V: PLAYERS

Seven Key Figures in the End-Times Drama

Revelation 12—13

CHAPTER 12

War in Heaven?

Preview:

Right in the middle of the book of Revelation is a "scorecard." It lists the seven symbolic players in the great end-times drama. The identity of these figures is crucial to the interpretation of the whole book. The "woman" who brings forth the "male child" is especially significant.

"You can't tell the players without a scorecard!" we often say. The same is true in the book of Revelation. Seven symbolic "players" are introduced in chapters 12—13. Their identities are crucial to the interpretation of the entire book. Who they are and what they represent determine how we view what is happening in the Apocalypse.

The symbolic "scorecard" sits right in the middle of the Revelation just like a scorecard in the middle of a baseball or basketball playbook. We can fill it in just like we would fill in the scorecard, telling us who is playing each position in the game. In this case, the scorecard lists the major participants in the great end-times drama.

The twelfth chapter opens by stating that a "great sign" (Greek, *mega sēmeion*) has appeared in the heavens. Robert Mounce calls it the "great spectacle which points to the consummation."[1] Robert Thomas adds, "The seventh trumpet has opened the way for a revelation of the seven bowl judgments, but for that revelation to be meaningful, a sketch of the hidden forces behind this great climax of history and of the personages that play a part in that climax is necessary."[2]

END-TIMES SCORECARD: The Seven Symbolic Players in the Great End-Times Drama	
Woman 12:1–2, 6, 13–16	Israel
Dragon 12:3–4, 9, 12–13	Satan
Male child 12:2, 5	Christ
Michael 12:7–12	Archangel
Rest of her offspring 12:17	Seed of Woman (saved Israel)
Beast of the sea 13:1–10	Antichrist
Beast of the earth 13:11–18	False Prophet

It is clear that we have here something new and different. The style of the narration changes drastically. We suddenly move behind the scenes to see the "secret maneuvers that lie behind the visible conflict."[3] It is obvious the author intends to define the players in his apocalyptic pageant. The lifelong struggle between God and Satan that has gone on for centuries comes to its ultimate climax with "war in heaven" (12:7).

Thomas views this section as a part of the larger vision of the seven bowl judgments, linking chapters 12—18. Walvoord views 12—13 as a "parenthetical section" in which "the great actors of the tribulation time are introduced."[4] My own preference is closer to Walvoord's view in this regard. The list of the "seven significant signs" ends abruptly after the thirteenth chapter, and we move to a completely different parenthesis in chapter 14, introducing the Son of Man as He begins to head the "wine press of the wrath of God" (14:19), which paves the way for the bowl judgments introduced in chapter 15.

It is important to observe again that nondispensationalists are often at a loss to explain the mixing of Jewish and Christian symbols in these chapters.

Because they do not distinguish between Israel and the Church in the future, they often admit confusion at this point. Bruce Metzger acknowledges, "Because of the unusual kinds of imagery that are combined here, it is not surprising that many readers find this chapter to be one of the most bizarre in the book."[5]

Who's Who in the End Times?

Two key factors must be determined in order to interpret the apocalyptic scorecard: 1) Who's who? 2) What time is it? The timing factor is as important as the identity factor. Are the seven symbolic players involved in past, present, or future conflict? The time of this conflict will determine how one interprets the conflict itself. The other key is deciding who the symbols represent. This determination alone eliminates several false assumptions.

For example, if the woman symbolizes Israel, then the drama takes on a decidedly Jewish flavor. If, however, the woman symbolizes the Church, then the "rest of her offspring" must be Church saints who are suffering persecution during the Great Tribulation. This one identity alone distinguishes between a pretribulational or posttribulational view of the book.

Consider also the timing elements. If the war in heaven is past tense, when did it occur? At the time of Satan's fall? When Christ ascended triumphantly after His resurrection? Or is Satan's final expulsion yet to come? If we interpret it in the past, what are we to make of the phrase, "he has only a short time" (12:12)? This is later defined as "a time and times, and half a time" (12:14). This is generally taken to mean the three and one-half years of the Great Tribulation. How can this then apply to the whole Church Age?

While several explanations have been proposed, only two make much sense. Either the prophecy focuses on Israel in the Tribulation period, or it mixes Jewish and Christian symbolism by extending Israel to refer to the Church. This "extension eschatology" is the only way nondispensationalists can make any sense at all out of the Apocalypse.

Douglass Moo admits, "If a radical disfunction between Israel and the Church is assumed, a certain presumption against the posttribulational position exists."[6] John Walvoord also acknowledges, "If the term Church includes saints of all ages, then it is self-evident that the Church will go through the Tribulation, as all agree that there will be saints in this time of trouble."[7]

Paul Benware adds, "It is clear, then, that a person's view of the nature of the Church and Israel plays an important role in the position taken on the Rapture and the Tribulation. Having two distinct groups of God's people speaks to the idea of two distinct programs. That which applies to one group may not (and probably would not) apply to the other."[8]

Can We Make a Positive Identification?

It is obvious that John the revelator wrote these two chapters to help us identify the major players in the apocalyptic drama. He certainly did not intend their identities to be a mystery. In fact, he even went so far as to make their identities obvious. He tells us, for example, that the great Dragon is Satan (12:9). He also tells us clearly that Satan's time is short, for he has been cast to the earth.

We must remember that these chapters belong to the entire section of the Revelation that deals with "what must take place after these things" (4:1). Everything in chapters 4—22 falls into that category. It was part of John's vision of the future. Certainly, the allusion to the birth of Christ and His ascension into heaven (12:5) refers to a past event, but it does so in the context of a future prophecy related to the persecution of the woman.

When we let the author define symbols for us, their meanings become obvious. They all have their roots in the Old Testament. These are not a series of bizarre symbols taken from pagan mythology, as some have suggested. Rather, these are basic biblical themes that are clear in Scripture. John the apostle was steeped in Old Testament knowledge and tradition and that was the basis of his symbolic language. Even the author's use of the term *sign* (Greek, *sēmeion*) parallels the frequent use of this term for Jesus' miracles in John's Gospel.[9]

John uses these two chapters to take us behind the scenes of the great eschatological drama. His symbols are drawn from the Bible itself. And they point to the future conflict that is coming on the scene of human history. In these seven symbolic signs, we see the future that yet shall be. And, in them, we also see the role each important character will play in the final conflict between Christ and the Antichrist. As Armageddon looms on the horizon, the key players of the apocalyptic drama assume their prophetic positions. The end is almost here!

The Key Players

The seven symbolic signs in Revelation 12 and 13 help us identify the key players in the biblical end game. Their identities hold the keys to interpreting the entire Revelation and its prophecies of future events. Each symbol is drawn from the Old Testament Scriptures.

  1. *Woman: Israel* (Rev. 12:1–2, 13–16).
     A woman appears who was "clothed with the sun, and the moon under her feet, and on her head a crown of twelve stars (12:1)! The identi-

ty of this woman is the most critical issue in properly interpreting the Apocalypse. The woman symbolizes the nation and people of Israel. The imagery is taken from Joseph's dream in Genesis 37:9–11, where the sun and moon and twelve stars represent the patriarchs of Israel and the twelve tribes. The figure of Israel as a travailing woman is prevalent in the Old Testament (cf. Is. 26:17–18; Jer. 4:31; 13:21; Mic. 4:10; 5:3).

The woman is not the Church! The woman is depicted here as giving birth to the Messiah (the "male child"). The Church did not give birth to Christ. Rather, Christ gave birth to the Church. Despite the fact that the Reformers and Puritans pictured the woman as the true Church in contrast to the "harlot," she is not the Church at all. Nor is she to be viewed only as Mary the mother of Christ. Even Mounce admits, "The woman is not Mary the mother of Jesus, but the messianic community, the ideal Israel."[10]

The woman has the "crown of twelve stars," symbolizing the twelve tribes of Israel. Next, she is pictured as being "with child . . . being in labor and in pain to give birth" (12:2). The imagery pictures the long and difficult national struggle of the people of Israel and the perpetuity of the messianic line. The "male child" that she delivers is obviously Jesus Christ. He is the one who is pictured in the Revelation as destined to "rule all the nations with a rod of iron" (12:5).

This woman has to symbolize Israel because Christ was born of the seed of Israel (cf. Gen. 49:8–10; Matt. 1:1–16). Later in this chapter, the woman, the mother of Christ, is persecuted and driven into the wilderness for 1,260 days or three and one-half years (Rev. 12:6, 14) and suffers great tribulation— the "time of Jacob's [Israel's] distress" (Jer. 30:7). Amillennialists who see no future for national Israel are forced to view the woman as the Church, but she is not. She is the mother of Christ (Israel), not the Bride of Christ (Church).

2. *Dragon: Satan* (Rev. 12:3–4, 9, 12–13).

The "great red dragon having seven heads and ten horns" appears next. He is identified in 12:9 as "the serpent of old who is called the devil and Satan." Therefore, there can be no debate over his identity. He is called the "accuser of our brethren . . . who accuses them before our God day and night" (12:10). This description is reminiscent of Satan's activities in the book of Job. He is also described as the one who tried to devour the male child as soon as he was born.

The whole passage reminds us of the great spiritual warfare going on behind the scenes of human history. While King Herod attempted to kill the baby Jesus soon after His birth, it was actually Satan who provoked the murderous intent (Matt. 2:16–18). The crucifixion of Christ may also be in view here as well. Even then, Satan is pictured as the evil one provoking the crowd to shout, "Crucify Him!"

The Dragon is called "great" (Greek, *mega*) and red (Greek, *purros*). This is no ordinary monster, but the monster of monsters! The gigantic red Dragon is depicted by the same color as the red horse in Revelation 6:4. Thomas notes, "*Purros*, occurring elsewhere in the N.T. only at 6:4, adds to the expression of the Dragon's terrible appearance and fierce and cruel nature. Red is the color of blood and harmonizes with his murderous intentions to kill the offspring of the woman."[11]

The Dragon is said to have drawn "a third of the stars of heaven" and cast them to the earth (12:4). This is generally taken to mean that approximately one-third of all the angels fell with him and are now demons (fallen angels). The Dragon's seven heads, ten horns, and ten crowns are images drawn from Daniel 7:7–8, 20–24. These indicate that Satan himself is the ultimate power behind the final kingdom of the Antichrist.

   3. **Male child:** *Christ* (Rev. 12:2, 5).

   The "male child" who was destined to "rule all the nations" is Jesus Christ. He is the Messiah, the Promised One of the Father. His being "caught up" (Greek, *harpazō*, "snatch away") refers to His ascension back into heaven. The Greek verb meaning "caught up" is also used of Philip being "snatched away" after dealing with the Ethiopian eunuch (Acts 8:39), of Paul being "caught up" into the third heaven (2 Cor. 12:2–4), and of the Rapture of the Church itself (1 Thess. 4:17).

   The imagery for the "male child" is taken from Psalm 2, where the messianic Son receives the nations for His inheritance from the Father. He is pictured there as the Lord's "Anointed" (Ps. 2:2). He is the King whom God will set on Zion (Ps. 2:6). God says of Him: "Thou art My Son, Today I have begotten thee. Ask of Me, and I shall give the nations as thine inheritance. . . . Thou shalt break them with a rod of iron" (Ps. 2:7–9).

   John the revelator does little else with the symbol of the "male child." He does not need any further elaboration. It is obvious that the child is Christ. Metzger remarks, "Here the gospel story is surprisingly condensed, but enough is said to accomplish John's purpose. He has shown the deadly enmity of the Adversary, his defeat, and the exaltation of Christ to the place of supreme and universal power."[12]

   4. **Michael:** *the archangel* (Rev. 12:7–12).

   In this spectacular section of the prophecy, we are told that Michael and his angels will cast Satan out of heaven. Lucifer (Satan) has already "fallen" from his lofty position, but he still has access to the throne of God (see Job

1:6–12; 2:1–7). But now Satan is permanently cast out of heaven forever. He becomes angry because he realizes "he has only a short time" (12:12), so he vents his anger on the woman (Israel), who had given birth to the child.

Again, one's interpretation of this passage affects his or her view of the entire book. If the casting out of Satan is viewed as a *past* event, then it must coincide with his fall after Creation or his defeat by the death and resurrection of Christ. If it is viewed as a *future* event, then it must happen during the Great Tribulation. In favor of the future viewpoint is the fact that the time Satan is on earth after being cast out is three and one-half years ("times"). This also correlates with the 1,260 days the woman (Israel) is persecuted and driven into the wilderness (12:6).

The defeat of Satan pictured here must be yet in the future. He is pictured as the "accuser of our brethren" (12:10). They in turn are described as believers who overcame him by the "blood of the Lamb" and the "word of their testimony." Heaven is shown rejoicing at Satan's demise, and his time is "short" (12:12). If this war in heaven were in the past, the casting out of Satan would not allow time for him to accuse the believers. The 1,260 days (three and one-half years) and "short time" would be completely irrelevant. It has been nearly two thousand years since the crucifixion and resurrection of Christ.

Michael the archangel (see Jude 9) is referred to in Daniel 10:13 as one of the "chief princes," and in Daniel 12:1 as the "great prince" who assists the children of Israel in the Last Days. Daniel presents him coming to Israel's rescue during the "time of distress" that will come in the future. Daniel's prophecy alone eliminates the idea that the "war in heaven" in the Apocalypse happened in the past. Daniel clearly dates the final conflict at the "time of the end" (Dan. 12:1–4).

Satan loses the war with Michael and his angels. Having been permanently cast out of any access to heaven, Satan in his "great wrath" turns on the woman—converted Israel during the Great Tribulation. The earth becomes the scene of double wrath. The wrath of the Lamb is being sounded by the seven trumpets and poured out in the seven bowls. Now, Satan's wrath is added against the people of God left on earth after the Rapture —the "rest" of the woman's seed.

5. *Rest of her offspring: saved Israel* (12:17).

When Satan is thwarted in his attempts to destroy national Israel, he will turn against the "rest (remnant) of her offspring" that has the "testimony of Jesus." These are converted Jews who have come to faith in Jesus as their Messiah. They will be persecuted severely by the two "beasts" that are forthcoming in chapter 13.

This is the only explanation that makes proper sense of the text and maintains the distinction between Israel and the Church. If the "rest of her offspring" are Church Age believers, how are we to distinguish between them and the woman if the woman is also the Church? Only by viewing the woman as Israel and the "rest of her offspring" as converted Jews of the Great Tribulation does this section make any sense at all. By chapter 14, we again see the 144,000 Jews with Christ, the Lamb of God. The entire context from chapters 12—14 is Jewish.

The persecution of the Jews (anti-Semitism) has always been Satan's desire. He has always hated the line of the Messiah. He has tried time and again to destroy that line by attacking the Jewish people. He motivated Pharaoh to put them in bondage in Egypt. He tried to destroy them in the Exodus and in the wilderness. He tried to eliminate Israel's true king, David, by motivating Saul to kill him. He tried to destroy the Davidic line by sending them into captivity to Babylon. He urged Israel's enemies to resist the rebuilding of the walls of Jerusalem by Nehemiah after they returned. He provoked Herod to try to kill the incarnate Son of God. He even tried to tempt Jesus to kill Himself by casting Himself off the pinnacle of the temple. But every effort failed, and so will Satan's final grand scheme to rule the world by a satanic trinity.

Study Questions

1. Read Daniel 12:1. What key to the prophetic significance of Revelation 12 do you find in these verses?

2. What great thing appears in heaven (12:1)?

3. Who is prepared to deliver a male child (12:1–2)?

4. Who has seven heads and ten horns (12:3)?

5. What portion of the world is the male child destined to rule (12:5)?

6. To what place does the woman flee for 1,260 days (12:6)?

7. Who fights against Satan and his angels in the war in heaven (12:7)?

8. What is the true identity of the Dragon (12:9)?

9. What relationship does Satan have to the brethren (12:10)?

10. What simple fact causes Satan to be full of wrath (12:12)?

11. When he becomes enraged at the woman, who does Satan make war against (12:17)?

CHAPTER 13

Rise of the Antichrist

Preview:

Two beasts rise on the prophetic scene. The first is the beast out of the sea, symbolizing the Antichrist. The second is the beast out of the earth, symbolizing the False Prophet. These two diabolical characters are empowered by Satan himself and with him form the satanic trinity. They are evil and deception personified. Together they will control the entire world in the Last Days—economically, politically, and religiously.

The great conflict of the End Times pits the unholy trinity (Satan, Antichrist, False Prophet) against the holy Trinity (Father, Son, Holy Spirit). In particular, the two beasts called up by Satan become a threat to the survival of the whole world. The first arises from the sea—a grotesque seven-headed monster with ten horns. The second arises from the earth—less terrifying, but much more deceptive. Mounce writes, "Together with the dragon the two beasts constitute an unholy trinity of malicious evil."[1]

In commenting on the unholy alliance of Satan and his cohorts, Beasley-Murray observes several important parallels: "If Satan seeks to be recognized as God, the Antichrist is presented as the Christ of Satan."[2] He then suggests several points of comparison:

Christ	Antichrist
Many diadems (19:12)	Ten diadems (13:1)
Worthy name (19:11–16)	Blasphemous names (13:1)
Causes men to worship God (1:6)	Causes men to worship Satan (13:4)
Power and throne of God (12:5)	Power and throne of Satan (13:2)
Died but lives again (1:18)	Fatal wound is healed (13:3)

A similar parallel can be suggested between the False Prophet and the Holy Spirit:

Holy Spirit	False Prophet
Points men to Christ (John 15:26)	Points men to Antichrist (13:12, 14)
Instrument of divine revelation (John 16:13)	Instrument of satanic revelation (13:11)
Seals believers to God (1 John 3:24)	Marks unbelievers with the number of Antichrist (13:16)
Builds body of Christ (John 7:37–39)	Builds the empire of Antichrist (13:17)
Enlightens mankind with truth (John 14:17, 26)	Deceives mankind by miracles (13:13–15)

The symbolism of this chapter has no clear biblical antecedent, though some have suggested the Hebrew concepts of *Leviathan* (sea monster) and *Behemoth* (land monster). The closest biblical parallel to John's vision is Daniel's vision of the four beasts that came up out of the sea (Dan. 7:3). Certainly, lion, bear, leopard, and monster (dragon) parallel Daniel's vision of the four coming world empires: Babylon, Media-Persia, Greece, and Rome. John seems to use descriptive qualities of all four creatures to epitomize the final empire of the Last Days. This kingdom of the Antichrist is the culmination of all the evils of the human governments of all time.

The Great Sea Monster

The uniqueness of John's vision is his portrayal of the first beast as a giant sea monster. We should remember that John was on an island in the Aegean Sea when he received this vision. The Aegean sits between Greece to the west and Asia Minor (modern Turkey) to the east. The Aegean itself is a part of the "Great Sea" (Mediterranean), which the Romans called *mare nostram* ("our sea") because of their domination of the Mediterranean basin.

The monster from the sea is a very fitting symbol for the Roman Empire. From John's perspective, Rome lay across the waters of the Mediterranean to the west. It was separated from the eastern part of the empire by water at the Hellespont as well as between Greece and Asia Minor near the Black Sea. Technically, there was no direct land connection between Europe and Asia at that point.

The beast itself is described as having seven heads (one with a "fatal wound"), ten horns, and ten crowns. The ten horns are similar to the ten horns on Daniel's fourth beast (Dan. 7:7). They represent ten kings (or kingdoms), as they do in Revelation 17:12. The seven heads of the beast certainly parallel the seven heads of the Dragon (Rev. 12:3) that gives his power and authority to the beast. It is also possible that John pictures the seven heads by tabulating three beasts with one head each and one with four heads, for a total of seven in Daniel's prophecy (cf. Dan. 7:3–7).

The ultimate question is, Who is the beast of John's vision? At first, it is very clear that he intends his readers to interpret it as the Roman Empire. Though he obscures it under the symbolic name "Babylon," he plainly tells us the "seven heads are seven mountains" on which the city sits (Rev. 17:9). This is obviously intended to identify Rome, the city of seven hills. All attempts to explain this away in favor of a literal Babylon in Iraq are difficult to support. When the author defines his own symbol, we have to take him seriously! Otherwise, we could just as easily say he really did not refer to the Dragon as Satan or the male child as Christ.

When Will It Happen?

The only question left is the timing of the prophecy. Is John talking about the Roman Empire of the first century, or does he foresee a Roman Empire of the future? Remember, this chapter belongs to the section (chaps. 4—22) of "what must take place after these things" (4:1). John will ultimately tell us of the final conflict at Armageddon (16:16), of the fall of the "great city" which reigns over the kings of the earth (17:18), of the triumphal return of Christ (19:11–16), and of the defeat of the beast and the False Prophet (19:19–21) and the binding of Satan (20:1-3).

There are only three legitimate *options* for the reasonable interpreter:

1. *John predicted Rome would fall, and it did.* Therefore, the beast and False Prophet are already in the lake of fire. Satan is bound in the abyss, and Christ is now ruling in His Millennial Kingdom. Preterists actually believe this!

2. *John correctly predicted the fall of Rome but missed the timing on the rest of the prophecy.* Therefore, everything else is irrelevant. Heaven will come someday, but nobody really knows when. Liberal theologians have taught this view for over a century now!

3. *John envisions a revived Roman (European) Empire of the Last Days that is only now beginning to take shape.* The specific details in the prophecy about the mark of the beast (13:17–18), the final judgments

(15:1), Armageddon (16:16), the fall of "Babylon" (17—18), the return of Christ (19:11–16), and the final defeat of the beast and the False Prophet are yet in the future.

What is the determining factor in how we should interpret the timing of the prophecy? The answer is simple: the return of Christ! Jesus has *not* returned to earth. Human governments have *not* collapsed. Satan is *not* bound. And we are *not* in the Millennial Kingdom. Any suggestion that we are is ridiculous! Satan is alive and well on planet earth. He is still the "prince of the power of the air" (Eph. 2:2). In the meantime, he still wanders about as a "roaring lion, seeking someone to devour" (1 Pet. 5:8)—all pretense to the contrary not withstanding!

Here Comes the Beast

The Bible predicts the rise of a counterfeit messiah in the Last Days. While many of his titles and descriptions emphasize the diabolical character of his rule, we must remember that he is ultimately a deceiver who promises to bring world peace. Jesus reminds us, "I have come in My Father's name, and you do not receive me; if another shall come in his own name, you will receive him" (John 5:43).

Dave Hunt points out, "Many prophecy students have this picture of the Antichrist as some obviously evil ogre who will directly oppose Christ. However, the meaning of antichrist also means 'in place of.' Thus the Antichrist will rise to power brilliantly. He will oppose the Messiah by pretending to be Him."[3]

The *biblical titles for the Antichrist* include the following designations:

- *Wicked one (Ps. 10:2—4)*
- *Little horn (Dan. 7:8)*
- *Prince who is to come (Dan. 9:26)*
- *Despicable person (Dan. 11:21)*
- *Willful king (Dan. 11:36)*
- *Man of lawlessness (2 Thess. 2:3)*
- *Son of destruction (2 Thess. 2:3)*
- *Lawless one (2 Thess. 2:8)*
- *Antichrist (1 John 2:22)*
- *Beast (Rev. 13:1)*

The *career of the Antichrist* is outlined in various biblical passages (Ezek. 28:1–10; Dan. 7:7–8, 20–26; 8:23–25; 9:26–27; 11:36–45; 2 Thess. 2:3–10; Rev. 13:1–10; 17:8–14). A basic survey of those passages reveals the following concepts:

1. He will appear in the latter days after the Rapture of the Church (2 Thess. 2:2–7).

2. He is the epitome of all Gentile world powers (Rev. 13:1–3).

3. He will gain control of Europe ("revived" Roman Empire) and rule a confederacy of Western nations (Dan. 7:7–9; 9:26; Rev. 13:1).

4. He will also gain economic and political control of the entire world in a vast global system (Rev. 13:8, 16–18).

5. He gains power by promising world peace (Dan. 8:25).

6. His personal intelligence, persuasiveness, and power will deceive the nations (Dan. 7:8–20; 8:23; 11:36).

7. He will sign a peace treaty with Israel to guarantee their protection (Dan. 9:27).

8. He later breaks the treaty and demands that he be worshiped as God (Dan. 11:36–37; 2 Thess. 2:4).

9. He becomes the adversary of Israel and persecutes the Jews during the Great Tribulation (Dan. 7:21–25; 8:24).

10. He receives his power and authority from Satan himself (Dan. 8:25; 2 Thess. 2:9–19).[4]

The term *antichrist* (Greek, *antichristos*) appears only in the epistles of John (1 John 2:18, 22; 4:3; 2 John 7). Throughout the Revelation, he is called the "beast." In his epistles, John was mainly concerned with the manifestation of the spirit of the Antichrist, which was already present in the churches in the manifestation of false doctrine. In the Revelation, he foresees the embodiment of false religion in a person whom he calls the "beast."

Another biblical term that may be applied to this great leader is "false Christ" (Greek, *pseudochristos*). Jesus Himself used this designation for him in Matthew 24:24 and Mark 13:22. In commenting on the distinction of these terms, Greek scholar Richard Trench said, "The distinction, then, is plain . . . *antichristos* (antichrist) denies that there is a Christ . . . *pseudochristos* (false Christ) affirms himself to be Christ."[5] In fact, it is that very affirmation that is the ultimate denial of the true Christ!

6. *Beast of the Sea:* Antichrist (Rev. 13:1–10).

The eschatological monster from the sea represents the epitome and culmination of the Gentile powers of all time. Thus, he is the embodiment of the lion, bear, leopard, and monster of Daniel's vision of the four beasts (Dan. 7). As in Daniel's prophecy of the fourth beast, he is described as having seven heads and ten horns.

Most commentators understand the beast of the sea to be the Antichrist. Whether he is a specific person, a political system, or both, is a matter of debate. Since he is associated with the same symbols given to Rome (seven heads and ten horns), it is generally assumed that he represents the revived Roman Empire of the Last Days. The characteristics of the beast are the same as those of the "little horn" of Daniel 7:8. He is arrogant, egotistical, powerful, and ruthless. And he will bring the final abomination upon Jerusalem.

The beast is said to "blaspheme God" and make "war against the saints." He receives "worship" from unbelievers and establishes the final apostate church on earth. The apostle Paul calls him the "man of lawlessness" and the "son of destruction" (2 Thess. 2:3). He exalts himself above all that is called God and sits in the temple demanding to be worshiped as God. Yet, Mounce notes, "The twice-repeated 'it was given to him' stresses the subordinate role of the beast. He is the Dragon's instrument for revenge and operates at his bidding. Yet . . . even this unholy alliance is under the control of the One in whom resides all authority and might."[6]

John pictures himself standing on the beach as the beast rises out of the sea. The sea is probably meant to be literal, though Revelation 17:15 uses it as a symbol for the great mass of humanity. Revelation 11:7 and 17:8, however, picture the beast ascending from the abyss. Thus, all these figures may be used somewhat interchangeably. But the contrast between the beast of the *sea* and the beast of the *earth* seems to favor taking the sea to be literal.

The term *beast* (Greek, *thērion*) indicates a ferocious beast or monster. The beast itself may well refer to Rome (17:9, city on seven hills) or the Roman Empire (Dan. 7:7). It is also clear that the beast represents an individual: the false Christ of the End Times. He has a mouth speaking blasphemies. He is wounded to death but recovers. He makes war "with the saints" (13:7). His number is the number of a man: 666 (13:18). And his power is limited to 42 months (13:5).

A thorough study of the Apocalypse reveals that the beast is both an individual leader and a political system. He is a king who is also emblematic of the kingdom he rules. Both he and that kingdom collectively are the beast of the Revelation. Even his symbolic number (666) does not equate perfectly with any historical figure, though both pagan Rome and papal Rome have been suggested. The earliest candidate was Nero, but in order to make the computation work, the calculation required using a Hebrew transliteration of the Greek form of the Latin name. Even that method required adding an *n* (*Neron Caesar*) to add up to 666. "Nero Caesar" in Latin adds up only to 616. We must also remember that John's readers did not know Hebrew for the most part.

Irenaeus, who had close ties to John, claimed the number stood for the "Latin Empire," basing the calculation on the Greek alphabet, since John wrote the Revelation in Greek. Others have suggested that "666" merely stands for the creation of man on the sixth day to the third power. In other words, the Antichrist will be the ultimate man—a super man. Six, the number of man, falls short of seven, the number of divine perfection. Despite all of his greatest efforts, the Antichrist will fall short in the end. Many believe his identity will not be known nor can it be calculated until he appears on the scene in the future.

John Hagee writes, "In Revelation 13:18, John made it possible for the world to identify the Antichrist. This cryptic puzzle is not intended to point a finger at some unknown person. It is, however, intended to confirm to the world someone already suspected as being the Antichrist." Hagee then wisely adds, "This information about how to identify the Antichrist is of no practical value to the Church since we will be watching from heaven by the time he is revealed."[7]

One thing is certain: No one now knows who he is! Twentieth-century candidates for the Antichrist have included Kaiser Wilhelm, Benito Mussolini, Adolph Hitler, Joseph Stalin, John F. Kennedy, Henry Kissinger, Juan Carlos, Mikhail Gorbachev, Ronald Reagan, and Saddam Hussein. It is a waste of time to try to guess who he is. You won't know until after the Rapture, and then it will be too late!

One of the greatest problems with interpreting biblical prophecy is the tendency to view the future through the eyes of the present. Once we go beyond what the biblical text actually says, everything else is sheer speculation. The apostle Paul reminds us that the day of Christ will not come until the "man of lawlessness be revealed" (2 Thess. 2:3). That will occur after the Church has been taken to glory. While it is true that the "mystery of lawlessness" is already at work (2 Thess. 2:7), the divine Restrainer, the Holy Spirit, holds back his ultimate arrival until the body of Christ is complete.

7. ***Beast of the Earth:*** False Prophet (Rev. 13:11–18).

This creature is distinct from the beast of the sea in that he calls attention to the first beast and persuades the world to worship the Antichrist. He even sets up an "image" of the first beast and "deceives those who dwell on the earth" (Rev. 13:14). He is pictured as having power to make fire "come down out of heaven" (13:13). He also gives "breath" to the image of the beast and uses his power to pervert true religion (13:15).

The second beast looks like a lamb (a possible parody of The Lamb—Jesus Christ), but he talks like a dragon (the power and authority of Satan). He also exercises all the authority of the first beast. This second beast is later called the "false prophet" (16:13; 19:20; 20:10). Thus, he is pictured as a false religious leader, in contrast to the more political nature of the first beast.

Attempts to identify the False Prophet have included the priests of the Caesar-cult, the Roman pope, and Muhammad, the prophet of Islam. Jesus Himself warned of the coming of false prophets (Matt. 24:24; Mark 13:22) in the Olivet Discourse, picturing a "worldwide anti-God system sponsored by Satan [that] manifests itself in periodic human antichrists" and finally culminates in one ultimate false prophet of the future.[8]

Beyond what we read in the Apocalypse, there is little else in Scripture to identify the False Prophet. Jonathan Edwards and the Puritans were convinced it was Muhammad because such a large percentage of the global population is under Muslim control. However, the connection of the first beast with Rome (possibly Europe) would tend to mitigate against that view. It is most likely that the False Prophet is a Satan-inspired leader of apostate Christendom, be it Catholic, Orthodox, or Protestant. It will not matter after the Rapture. The true Church will have been removed, and all that remains will be apostate.

Our attention is also drawn to the False Prophet's ability to heal the deadly "sword wound" of the beast (13:14), or at least of one of his "heads" (13:3). This miraculous healing calls attention to the supposed power and authority of the False Prophet. So does his ability to give life to the image and his authority to kill those who refuse to worship it.

The speculative possibilities here are endless. Is this "image" some kind of televised image? Can this telecast accommodate two-way communication (interactive television)? Is the "image" a projected holographic image that actually appears to be three-dimensional? There is no way we can be sure at this point in time. But the fact that such technology is now being developed ought to get our attention. Jack Van Impe calls the Antichrist the "global charmer" and writes, "I believe that the Antichrist will enslave and control earth's billions through a sophisticated computer fashioned in his likeness."[9]

Our passage specifically states several facts about the *False Prophet*:

1. He causes men to worship the image of the beast (vv. 12–15).

2. He can do great wonders and miracles (v. 13).

3. He calls down fire out of heaven (v. 13).

4. He deceives the whole world by his miracles (v. 14).

5. He gives breath to the image of the beast (v. 15).

6. He causes men to receive the mark of the beast (v. 16).

We also learn from this passage that the world of the Last Days will involve three interconnected elements: 1) global economy, 2) world government, and 3) world religion. Ironically, the entire system is driven by the global economy. The Antichrist does not have to conquer the world by force. He only needs to control the communications systems that make it run.

Peter Lalonde writes, "It is breathtaking to realize that what we are witnessing today in the emergence of the 'New World Order' may well be a fulfillment of Revelation 13! In the world's rejection of the true Prince of Peace and in their rush to build their own earthly kingdom, the Antichrist's government is being fashioned for him!"[10]

Study Questions

1. Read 2 Thessalonians 2:8–10. What key to the prophetic significance of Revelation 13 do you find in these verses?

2. Out of what place does John see the first beast rise (13:1)?

3. What are its seven heads (13:1) later compared to (cf. 17:9)?

4. Who empowers this creature (13:2)?

5. For how long will the beast be given the power to rule (13:5)?

6. Against whom does the beast (Antichrist) make war (13:7)?

7. Out of what place does the second beast come up (13:11)?

8. Though he has two horns like a lamb, how does he speak (13:11)?

9. Who will cause the whole earth to worship the first beast (13:12)?

10. What will the second beast use to deceive the people (13:14)?

11. What does the second beast force everyone to receive on his or her right hand or forehead (13:16)?

SECTION VI: PLAGUES

Seven Bowls of Final Judgment

Revelation 14—20

CHAPTER 14

Wine Press of the Wrath of God

Preview:

Having identified the key players in the eschatological end game, John now reintroduces the drama itself. The everlasting gospel is proclaimed and the fall of "Babylon" is announced. The Son of man appears to judge the world and to tread the wine press of the wrath of God.

The last half of the Apocalypse opens with chapter 14. We move now to the reading of the inside of the scroll (cf. 5:1). Chapters 6—11 announced the prophetic message to the world in general: "Bad news, you lose!" Now the message focuses on the people of God: "Good news, we win!"

As the scene opens, we see the 144,000 standing on Mount Zion with the Lamb. Following the typical pattern of the Revelation, this chapter provides the overview of what follows in chapters 15—19. The chapter opens with the 144,000 and proceeds to four climactic announcements: 1) the everlasting gospel, 2) the fall of Babylon, 3) the judgment of the lost, and 4) the blessedness of the saved. John's perspective in this overview takes us all the way to Armageddon (vv. 19-20) and the judgments that follow (v. 11).

The Greek phrase *kai eidon* ("and I looked" or "and I saw") introduces each of the three scenes in chapter 14 (14:1, 6, 14). The whole chapter is proleptic and surveys the final states of blessing and judgment that are to come in the future. The 144,000 appear secure with the Lamb on Mount Zion and with the Father's name (seal) in their foreheads. This is in direct contrast to the followers of the beast who have his mark in their foreheads.

Several suggestions have been proposed to identify the **144,000**. It is obvious by their specific number that they are the same group as in 7:3-8.

To suggest otherwise is to confuse the symbolic reference to the Jewish people. What is different in this passage is that they are more precisely defined as male "virgins" (Greek, *parthenoi*) who are "purchased from among men as first fruits to God and to the Lamb" (14:4).

God seals this group unto salvation. Thomas notes, "The sealing they received protects them only from the wrath of God, not from the wrath of the Dragon and the beast (cf. 12:2)."[1] They do not experience the impact of God's wrath in the seal, trumpet, and bowl judgments. But they are part of the "rest" of the woman's offspring and are persecuted by Satan and the Antichrist. Thomas pictures them as already having been martyred for their faith and says, "They are the vanguard who bear the brunt of the struggle against the beast and pay the price with their own lives."[2]

The passage referring to the 144,000 (14:1–5) does not specifically refer to them being killed. This can only be found in 14:13: "Blessed are the dead who die in the Lord from now on!" This does not necessarily apply to all 144,000. They are basically described as:

1. Purchased and sealed to God (vv. 1, 3)

2. Morally pure male virgins (v. 4)

3. Followers of the Lamb (v. 4)

4. Speakers of the truth (v. 5)

5. Blameless (v. 5)

Chapter 7 refers to them as the "bond-servants of our God" (7:3), and this passage calls them the "purchased" (14:3–4). They are never specifically called "witnesses"—the claims of the Jehovah's Witnesses notwithstanding. Nor are they specially called "preachers" as many evangelicals assume. Who are they then, the 144,000? These are the saved Jews of the Tribulation period. Their identity is clearly Jewish in their connection to the 12 tribes of Israel (7:4–8) and to Mount Zion (14:1). The 144,000 may represent the whole nation or a specific group (male virgins) within the whole nation. Whether the number 144,000 is literal or symbolic of the national conversion of Israel, one thing is clear: These are the Jews saved out of the Great Tribulation.

Now Hear This!

Three angels fly across the sky, one after another, making dramatic and climactic announcements. These are followed by a fourth announcement from heaven itself. Each of these is a proleptic remark. Each serves as a summary statement (preview) of what is to follow.

1. "Fear God and give Him glory . . . and worship Him" (14:6–7).

The first angel flies across the horizon with the everlasting gospel to preach to all nations. The gospel (Greek, *euangelisai*, "good news") is the same gospel as is always declared in the New Testament. To try to make it anything else is to miss the point altogether! Paul said, "But though we, or an angel from heaven, should preach to you a gospel contrary to that which we have preached to you, let him be accursed" (Gal. 1:8).

Even H.B. Swete's remark that the angel's message is "pure theism . . . an appeal to the conscience of untaught heathendom" misses the point here.[3] The idea emphasized in the passage is that salvation is still possible during the Great Tribulation by believing the gospel. The very fact that it is called the "gospel" presumes the message of the death, burial, and resurrection of Christ (cf. 1 Cor. 15:3–4). That it is to be preached to "all the nations" follows the pattern of the Great Commission (cf. Matt. 28:19–20). To "fear" God and "give him glory" is an idiom for repentance. And to "worship" God the Creator certainly implies a believing response to the gospel.

The introduction of the angel's message is intended to remind us one last time that the gospel is the only message of salvation for all time right up to the moment of final judgment. This is the only reference to the gospel in the Revelation. The terms "gospel" and "good news" appear in one hundred other verses in the New Testament (fifteen times in the Gospels, six in Acts, five in the general epistles, and seventy-four in Paul's epistles). That the gospel is referred to one last time in the last book of the New Testament is certainly fitting and necessary. To attempt to call it something else or something other than the "good news" of salvation is both tragic and heretical!

2. "Fallen, fallen, is Babylon the great" (14:8).

A second angel follows the first one, presumably flying through heaven as well. He announces in advance the fall of Babylon, which will be described in detail in chapters 17—18. It is described as "great" six times in the Apocalypse (14:8; 16:19; 17:5; 18:2, 10, 21). This is the title Nebuchadnezzar, in his pride and arrogance, gave to the literal Old Testament Babylon (cf. Dan. 4:30).

One of the great interpretive questions of the Revelation has to do with *Babylon.* Is it the literal Babylon on the Euphrates—Israel's ancient enemy? Or is the term *Babylon* used symbolically in the Revelation for Rome? Evangelicals, especially dispensationalists, are divided over this point. Those favoring a literal Babylon point out the references to the Euphrates and its proximity to Babylon. However, the passages that refer to the Euphrates (Rev. 9:14; 16:12) do not mention Babylon. Rather, they speak of the "kings from the east" and the army of 200 million.

Another line of argument for a literal Babylon is taken from the predictions of its destruction in Isaiah 13 and 47, Jeremiah 50—51, and Zechariah 5.[4] These prophets predicted that Babylon would fall, be destroyed, and remain uninhabited. Proponents argue that ancient Babylon, which has been in ruins for centuries in fulfillment of these prophecies, will be rebuilt on a grand scale and become the political and economic center of the planet and the capital of the Antichrist—all within the first half of the Tribulation!

First, this line of argumentation *overliteralizes* the Old Testament prophecies. Archaeological and historical records clearly attest the conquest and destruction of ancient Babylon. The city fell in one night to Cyrus the Persian in 539 B.C. Later, in 482 B.C., the Persian king Xerxes (the Ahasuerus who married Esther) totally demolished Babylon and burned it. Attempts to rebuild Babylon by Alexander the Great (331 B.C.) and Antiochus IV Epiphanes (173 B.C.) both failed. By 24 B.C., Strabo described Babylon as "empty" and "desolate." In A.D. 116, the Roman emperor Trajan stopped there and reported he found nothing but ruins.[5] Left behind was the largest mound of ruins in the ancient world. Thus, the name "Babylon," once associated with greatness and splendor, came to refer to great ruins to the people of John's day when the Revelation was written.

Second, the view that overliteralizes "Babylon" in the Revelation passages misses the obvious *symbolism* that is intended there. Even Robert Thomas admits, "The writer is very clear to point out when he intends a figurative meaning."[6] That is exactly what John the revelator does in 17:5–9! He plainly tells us that the "Babylon" of the Apocalypse is a symbolic name for Rome. He calls it "mystery, Babylon" (17:5). It is drunk with the blood of the "witnesses of Jesus" (17:6). Its seven heads are "seven mountains" on which the city sits (17:9)—an obvious reference to Rome. Finally, he calls it "the great city, which reigns over the kings of the earth" (17:18). How much more clearly can he state it?

David Reagan observes, "The city is referred to metaphorically as Babylon because at the time of the Antichrist's reign, it will represent the epitome of the occultic spiritual evil that originated in Babylon and has always been associated with its name."[7] Two thousand years of church history verify that apocalyptic "Babylon" is Rome. It is either pagan Rome, papal Rome, or a future revived Rome—but it is Rome!

The argument that modern Iraq will rebuild Babylon to its original greatness is ludicrous. Muslims have no interest in pagan sites. Babylon has no religious meaning to them. Besides, it would take decades for such a city to be rebuilt to prominence and become the political and economic capital of the world. It is totally contradictory to hold to both the rebuilding of Babylon, given its current status, and to the imminent return of Christ. If we have to wait for Babylon to be rebuilt, there is no doctrine of imminency!

The "Babylon" of the Apocalypse is already in place. The technology currently exists to drive the global economy of the Western world. The United States and Europe are the political, social, and economic hub of the entire planet. The new "globalism" is already promoting a one-world economy, government, and religion. The "spirit of antichrist" is already operating in the world and will produce both a system that is "antichrist" and an individual who will control that system: the Antichrist.

3. "The wrath of God . . . mixed in full strength" (14:9–11).

A third angel flies across the prophetic landscape announcing the doom of all who follow the beast and receive his mark. Just as "Babylon" made all nations to drink of the "wine of . . . her immorality" (v. 8), so God will make the beast worshipers drink of the "wine of the wrath of God" (v. 10). His final judgments are pictured as "mixed in full strength" (undiluted or not watered-down) into the "cup of His anger."

This cup represents the cup of God's wrath. It is probably this same "cup" that Jesus agonized over in the Garden of Gethsemane (Matt. 26:39–42). When it was poured on Him on the cross, He endured the wrath of God against our sins and on our behalf. Thus, "he made Him who knew no sin to be sin on our behalf, that we might become the righteousness of God in Him" (2 Cor. 5:21). This is why Jesus cried, "My God, My God, why hast Thou forsaken Me?" (Matt. 27:46). In that awful moment on the cross, He took the wrath of God for us.

The cup of wrath represents the final and irrevocable judgment of God against the unbelieving and the unrighteous. This final judgment will be without mercy. Thomas says, "To imbibe of this cup is tantamount to eternal torment in fire and brimstone."[8] The references to "fire and brimstone," "the smoke of their torment," and "no rest day and night" (vv. 10–11) point ahead to the lake of fire (cf. 19:20; 20:10; 21:8).

The Revelation never hesitates to emphasize and point out the reality of eternal punishment. The "torment" of the unbelievers is real and conscious and lasts day and night forever! This clearly explains that the "second death" in the lake of fire is eternal punishment, not annihilation. The future tense verbs used here in the Greek text ("he will drink," "he will be tormented") predict the lasting anguish and punishment of the lost. And the endless trail of smoke reminds us they are there forever.

4. "Blessed are the dead who die in the Lord" (14:12–13).

The messages of the three angels are followed by a comment about the "perseverance of the saints" and a voice from heaven commanding John to write. It is difficult to tell who speaks in verse 12, but it appears to be a spontaneous and unsolicited remark by John himself, although it could be part of the third angel's message. The comment involves a threefold observation regarding:

1. The perseverance of the saints
2. Those who keep the commandments of God
3. Those who have their faith in Jesus

All three qualities belong to the Tribulation saints who must endure and persevere despite the threat of martyrdom. This is made clear by the reference to "the dead who die in the Lord" in verse 13. Despite their martyrdom, they have three enduring promises:

1. They die in the Lord.
2. They rest from their labors.
3. Their deeds follow with them.

Each of these promises emphasizes the security of the martyred believers. Their deaths are not in vain, and they shall be rewarded on the other side. " 'Yes,' says the Spirit," adds the approval and assurance of the Holy Spirit Himself to these promises. Believers can face death because what awaits them in heaven is far better than anything on earth.

The Grapes of Wrath

A white cloud catches John's eye next. It is the messianic cloud associated with the return of Christ (cf. Dan. 7:13–14; Matt. 24:30; 26:64; Acts 1:9–11). The reference to "a son of man" with a golden crown assures us this is the Christ. Here, Jesus is pictured as the Judge of the unbelieving world. He is the "Grim Reaper" at the final judgment (cf. Matt. 25:31–46).

The imagery of the harvest and the vintage is taken from Joel 3:13, which pictures the future judgment as a harvest. Again, these verses serve as an overview (proleptic summary) of what follows in great detail in chapters 15—19. Christ begins His descent to earth on the white cloud, sickle in hand. He is pictured as the Lord of the harvest, emphasizing that all judgment is under His sovereign dispensation.

Next, three more angels appear, coming "out of the temple" in heaven. We assume that the heavens are still open, revealing the temple of God as in 11:19. Each of these is called "another angel" (vv. 15, 17–18). The first angel signals the beginning of the final judgment. "Put in your sickle and reap," he cries to the son of man (v. 15). Then, a second angel appears, also holding a sharp sickle to assist in reaping the vintage of the grapes of wrath (v. 17). Finally, a third angel comes out of the temple from the altar, having "power [authority] over fire" (v. 18). He cries to the second angel (v. 19) to thrust in his sickle and reap the ripe grapes of earth.

In ancient times, the grapes were harvested, collected, and dumped into the wine press. Then they were stomped until all the juice ran out and was collected in the wine vats. The red stain of the juice and the staining of one's feet and garments make this a powerful picture of divine judgment (cf. Gen. 49:10–11; Is. 63:1–4).

The "wine press of the wrath of God" (v. 19) symbolizes the severity of this judgment. Its location is "with-out [outside] the city," indicating that the last great conflict will be near, but not in, Jerusalem. In 16:16, John will locate the final battle at Armageddon, some fifty miles northwest of Jerusalem.

The Old Testament prophets also predicted the final battle in the Valley of Jehoshaphat, which is adjacent to Jerusalem and the Kidron Valley (cf. Joel 3:12–14; Zech. 14:4). The combined biblical picture of the final conflict portrays a massive invasion of Israel by the forces of the Antichrist. The invading army will overrun the nation from the north and the south all the way to the outskirts of Jerusalem.

The final conflict is so severe that the blood of those killed runs like a river, neck-deep ("up to the horses' bridles"). It covers an area of 200 miles, which is the distance from Bozra (Edom) to Megiddo (cf. Is. 63:1–4). Thomas writes, "The terminology suggests a sea of blood resulting from a direct confrontation on the field of battle. The depth of the blood and the land area covered are both indicative of a massive slaughter and loss of human life."[9]

The destruction described in this chapter is almost beyond human comprehension. Apart from nuclear war or cosmic catastrophe, there is little else to explain such devastation of worldwide proportions. However, whatever the natural means of this destruction may be, the Bible clearly emphasizes that all the judgments are a matter of divine retribution. Whatever means is used is in the hand of God as His instrument of judgment.

Study Questions

1. Read Joel 3:13–14. What key to the prophetic significance of Revelation 14 do you find in these verses?

2. Who appears on Mount Zion with the 144,000 (14:1)?

3. What term is used to describe the moral purity of the 144,000 (14:4)?

4. What does the first angel declare to all the nations (14:6)?

5. What does "Babylon" actually refer to (14:8)?

6. What will happen to those who worship the beast and his image (14:9)?

7. What cup will those who worship the beast be forced to drink (14:10)?

8. What is the eternal punishment of the unsaved (14:10–11)?

9. Who came on a white cloud carrying a sharp sickle (14:14)?

10. In this final harvest, where are the grapes of wrath being thrown as they are gathered (14:19).

11. What proof of the horror of the destruction is as high as the horses' bridles and two hundred miles long (14:20)?

CHAPTER 15

The Seven Last Plagues

Preview:
The final expression of the wrath of God is contained in the bowl judgments.
They are called the "seven last plagues." Before they are poured out upon the
earth, the saved martyrs of the Great Tribulation appear singing the songs of
deliverance and redemption. Then seven angels proceed out of the heavenly
temple with seven golden bowls full of the wrath of God.

The final and dramatic action of the Apocalypse is about to begin. In eight
brief verses, chapter 15 sets the stage for the final drama. The pouring out of
the seven bowls (KJV—"vials") of God's wrath (chap. 16) culminates in the fall
of Babylon (chaps. 17—18) and the return of Christ to earth (chap. 19).

John Walvoord notes that these are the "divine judgments preceding the
second coming of Christ." He points out that the seven seals resulted in the
seven trumpets, which result in the seven bowls. "From this it can be seen that
the order of events is one of dramatic crescendo, the seventh seal being all-
inclusive of the end-time events including the seven trumpets, and the seventh
trumpet including the events described in the seven [bowls]."[1]

The scene shifts to heaven again as it did prior to the seals (Rev. 4—5) and
the trumpets (8:2–6). Some view this chapter as a "celestial interlude" before
all hell breaks loose in the next chapter.[2] What has been anticipated in the cup
of wine (14:10), the harvest (14:14–16) and the vintage (14:17–20) is now
about to happen. But before it does, we are again reminded that God is still
in control. The throne of heaven still overrules the events on earth.

The transition occurs in 15:1 with the words "and I saw." We are again
reminded of the visual nature of this material. John keeps writing as fast as he

can observe the ever-changing events. He refers to this one as "another sign in heaven," following the previous signs of the woman (12:1) and the Dragon (12:3). This third sign (Greek, *sēmion*) is called "great and marvelous" (Greek, *megas* and *thaumastos*). This designation may refer to the ominous and terrible finality of what is about to transpire—both for the earth and for all mankind.

The seven angels may be the same ones who sounded the trumpets in 8:2. But the absence of any definite article may indicate these are seven angels that have not previously appeared. They appear seven times as a group from this point onward (15:1, 6–8; 16:1; 17:1; 21:9). These seven angels are said to have "seven plagues, which are the last." The term *plēgē* ("plague") appears 15 times in the Revelation, always in an eschatological sense. The term "the last" (Greek, pl. of *eschatos*) is the basis of our word eschatology, the study of "last things."

These angels are pictured holding seven "vials" (KJV) or "bowls." The imagery may be drawn from Isaiah 51:17, which says to Jerusalem, "Rouse yourself! Rouse yourself! . . . You who has drunk from the LORD's hand the cup of His anger; The chalice of reeling you have drained to the dregs." Beasley-Murray points out that the Hebrew word used in Isaiah means "cup" or "goblet" and better defines the term used in the Revelation.[3]

The Last Exodus

One cannot miss the obvious symbolism drawn from the Exodus story in this section of the Apocalypse (15:1–8). Mounce calls it "exodus typology," and Beasley-Murray calls it the "last exodus."[4] The final judgments on the Antichrist will be similar to, but much worse than those that fell on Pharaoh in Exodus 7—10. The parallels to the Exodus motif are seen in the "song of Moses" (15:3), the revelation of God's glory in the "smoke" of Sinai (15:8), and the erection of the "tabernacle of testimony" (15:5).

These similarities point to a similar purpose of both *judgment and deliverance.* In the Exodus, the children of Israel are delivered into the Promised Land. In Revelation 15, the redeemed are delivered into heaven where they sing the song of Moses and the song of the Lamb in anticipation of their final victory over the beast.

Suddenly there appears a host of people on the "sea of glass" (cf. Rev. 4:6). These are evidently already in heaven having "come off victorious" over the beast (15:2). These heavenly martyrs are rejoicing in the blessedness and bliss of heaven. No persecution or execution by the beast can touch them now. They are pictured carrying "harps of God." Walter Scott points out that these are the only musical instruments mentioned in the Revelation.[5] The trumpets are used only to sound the call to judgment. All other music in the Apocalypse involves singing.

The song of the harp singers is the victors' song of praise to God. It is called the "song of Moses" (see Ex. 15) and the "song of the Lamb" (see Rev. 5:9–12). While it may represent one great song, it certainly has two separate stanzas. Robert Coleman says, "They are singing of God's wonderful acts in the redemption of His people—'the song of Moses . . . and the song of the Lamb' (15:3). The revelation of the old covenant combines with that of the new, and the law harmonizes with the gospel, in another beautiful exclamation of praise."[6]

Moses sang the song of deliverance in Exodus 15, after God delivered the children of Israel through the miraculous crossing of the Red Sea. The "song of the Lamb" is one of redemption for all people who have put their faith in Him. Thomas observes that the dual specification "the song of" for both Moses and the Lamb indicates two distinct songs. He writes, "John only cites the Song of the Lamb in 15:3–4, however, leaving it to the reader's memory to recall the Song of Moses from Exodus 15."[7] Of course, this assumes his Gentile readers were familiar with Exodus 15.

Throughout the Apocalypse, John clearly distinguishes between saved Jews and saved Gentiles (e.g., the 144,000 Jews in 7:3–8, and the "great multitude" of Gentiles in 7:9–15). Following his typical pattern, it is only appropriate that he make this distinction again by referring to both the "song of Moses" and the "song of the Lamb" as separate, yet similar songs of deliverance and redemption.

In this hymn of praise, God is worshiped for His "great and marvelous" acts. He is praised as the "King of the nations." This praise results in the rhetorical question: "Who will not fear, O Lord, and glorify Thy name?" The question is followed by three "because" (Greek, *hoti*) clauses:

1. Because You alone are holy

2. Because all nations shall worship You

3. Because Your righteous acts are revealed

The Shekinah Glory

The narration moves on again as John says, "After these things I looked" (15:5). Each time John uses this phrase (Greek, *meta tauta*), he indicates a sequential progression to the next event. As John watched, the temple of heaven was opened just as it was in 11:19. There the temple was opened to reveal the Ark of the Covenant. Here it is opened to allow the seven angels to exit from the presence of God. Thomas notes, "Both passages tell of the source of the last plagues, with this one being a further development of the former."[8]

The reference to the "tabernacle of testimony" refers to the place where the tablets of the Law were kept. These angels leave God's presence because that Law has been violated. And they leave with the "seven plagues" (v. 6). They already have the authority to dispense judgment; they need only to be given the means to do it.

One of the four creatures (*seraphim?*) provides the angels with the golden cups filled to the brim with the wrath of God. Mounce observes, "These guardians of the throne appear throughout Revelation (4:6; 5:6; 6:1; 7:11; 14:3; 15:7; 19:4) and are appropriate intermediaries between God and the avenging angels."[9]

As the angels receive their **goblets of divine retribution**, the "smoke" fills the temple with the Shekinah glory of God, as it did in the Tabernacle (Ex. 19:18; 40:34) and the first temple (1 Kin. 8:10–11; 2 Chr. 5:11–14; 7:1–3). Throughout the Revelation, the prophetic seer observes that all is functioning properly in the heavenly temple. Unlike the earthly Tabernacle and temples, this one is indestructible.

Robert Mounce summarizes this chapter beautifully when he writes, "Until the seven plagues are finished, no one is able to enter the temple. Once the time of final judgment has come, none can stay the hand of God. The time for intercession is past. God in His unapproachable majesty and power has declared that the end has come. No longer does He stand knocking: He enters to act in sovereign judgment."[10]

Study Questions

1. Read Psalm 86:9–10. What key to the prophetic significance of Revelation 15 do you find in these verses?

2. In the sign John sees in heaven, what do the seven angels have with them (15:1)?

3. What songs are the redeemed of God singing (15:3)?

4. From what place in heaven did these seven angels come forth (15:6)?

5. What did one of the four creatures give the angels (15:7)?

6. What smoke filled the heavenly temple (15:8)?

CHAPTER 16

Battle of Armageddon

Preview:

The seven angels are sent forth to pour out their goblets ("bowls") of judgment from the cup of God's wrath. The earth is shaken by a series of devastating catastrophes culminating in the Battle of Armageddon. After the seventh goblet, God Himself speaks from the temple of heaven and announces, "It is done."

Armageddon! The mere mention of it causes us to tremble. Armageddon is the ultimate biblical symbol for the great war at the end of the age. Its very name conjures up visions of global destruction, worldwide devastation, and indescribable human suffering. It is the war to end all wars! The people and planet of earth will suffer untold misery, and millions will die.

Revelation 16:14–16 tells us that the ultimate conflict of human history will take place at Armageddon in the Valley of Jezreel. It is the place where the kings of the earth will assemble for battle on the "great day of God, the Almighty." The name "Armageddon" (Har-Magedon) is taken from the plain of Megiddo near Mount Carmel. The ancient ruins of the Old Testament city of Megiddo still stand as gaunt testimony to the strategic significance of this area.

In biblical times, several significant battles were fought there. Deborah and Barak defeated the Canaanites there in the days of the judges (Judg. 5:19). Gideon was victorious there over the Midianites and Amalekites (Judg. 6). King Saul was defeated and slain by the Philistines at Mount Gilboa overlooking the region (1 Sam. 31). Pharaoh Neco of Egypt mortally wounded King Josiah of Judah there in the days of the kings (cf. 2 Kin. 23:29–30; 2 Chr. 35:22–24). The prophet Zechariah (12:11) predicts a great mourning there on the plain of Megiddo.[1] The long history of this location as a strategic battlefield makes it an appropriate place for a modern army of the future to engage in a strategic invasion of Israel in the Last Days. There in the broad valley that separates Galilee from the hills of Samaria, the greatest war of all time will be fought.

The Coming Day of Wrath

The Old Testament prophets called it the "day of the LORD" (Joel 1:15) or the "day of vengeance of our God" (Is. 61:2). They described it as a day of darkness (Amos 5:18) and of fire (Zeph. 1:18), burning as hot as a furnace (Mal. 4:1). "A day of wrath is that day, A day of trouble and distress, a day of destruction and desolation, A day of darkness and gloom . . . Because they have sinned against the LORD" (Zeph. 1:15–17). This day of divine judgment against unbelievers will consume the whole world (Zeph. 1:18).

The Great Tribulation is the period of divine judgment that immediately precedes the coming of Christ in power and great glory. The prophet Ezekiel called it "the day of the LORD . . . a day of clouds, A time of doom for the nations [Gentiles]" (Ezek. 30:3). He even named many of those nations: Egypt, Ethiopia, Put, Lud, Arabia, and Libya (Ezek. 30:5).

In recent years it has been customary for pretribulationists to see two great battles coming in the future: Magog and her Arab allies against Israel, and the Antichrist and his kingdom against Israel.

Older pretribulationists, such as René Pache, believe there is only one great end-time battle, noting that many of the same nations are named as falling on the "day of the LORD" (Armageddon) in Ezekiel 30:1–8.[2] No matter how a person interprets these end-time conflicts, the Bible clearly teaches that Israel, not the Church, is the target of these attacks and that in the final battle Christ will return with His Church saints, His bride, to deliver Israel and complete the unity of God's people.

The final "Battle of Armageddon" is called the . . .

- wrath of the Lord (Is. 26:20)
- fury of the Lord (Ezek. 38:18)
- terror of the Lord (Is. 2:10)
- vengeance of God (Is. 35:4)
- harvest of judgment (Mic. 4:11–12; Rev. 14:14–20)
- grapes of wrath (Is. 63:1–6; Rev. 19:15)
- great supper of God (Ezek. 39:17–20; Rev. 19:17–18)

The devastation of Armageddon will be so extensive that it is probably best viewed as a *war* that destroys most of the earth, as well as a final *battle* focused in the Middle East. This also best explains the development of catastrophic events in Revelation 15—19.

The carnage will be so great that most of the earth's population will be annihilated. The plant life all over the planet will be nearly destroyed. The air and water will be severely polluted. "Babylon" will be burned up. The armies of the Antichrist will be wiped out, and the beast and the False Prophet will be thrown into the lake of fire (Rev. 19:20).

The final devastation will be the self-destructive acts of a world gone mad without God. The Bible says:

- *Darkness will reign (Is. 5:30; Zech. 14:7).*
- *The heavens shall be shaken (Is. 34:4).*
- *The earth will quake (Is. 29:6; Zech. 14:4–5).*
- *Huge hailstones will fall from heaven (Rev. 16:21).*
- *The invading host will destroy itself (Zech. 14:13).*

The prophet Zechariah describes this day in vivid terms:

> . . . the Lord will strike all the nations that fought against Jerusalem: Their flesh will rot while they are still standing on their feet, their eyes will rot in their sockets, and their tongues will rot in their mouths. On that day men will be stricken by the Lord with great panic. Each man will seize the hand of another, and they will attack each other (Zech. 14:12–13 NIV).

As terrible as the Battle of Armageddon will be, it will not mark the end of the earth. Zechariah 14:16 tells us that "any who are left of all the nations that went against Jerusalem will go up from year to year to worship the King, the LORD of Hosts." Revelation 20:1–6 tells us that Satan will be bound one thousand years while we serve as "priests of God and of Christ" (v. 6) and reign with Jesus during those one thousand years.

Seven Bowls of Wrath

The "loud voice" that speaks from within the heavenly temple is the voice of God. He entered into the temple in chapter 15 when it was filled with His glory. During the meantime, no one else enters the temple until the seven plagues, which contain the wrath of God, are disbursed. Isaiah heard the same voice of God speaking from the temple (Is. 66:6).

The word *wrath* is mentioned eleven times in the Revelation. Once it is the wrath of Satan (12:12); once it is called the wrath of the Lamb (6:16); eight times it is the wrath of God (11:18; 14:10, 19; 15:1, 7; 16:1, 19; 19:15); and once it is used of the wrath of the Lamb and of God together (6:17). In some translations, the word "wrath" is also used twice of the "passion" of the harlot's immorality [14:8; 18:3]. As each angel pours out his goblet, the cumulative effect of the wrath of God continually increases.

Bruce Metzger observes, "The writer of the book of Revelation has carefully laid out a series of parallel and yet ever-progressing parallels. These display God's plan from different vantage points, stressing one or another feature. At the same time, the different accounts reinforce one another and bring before the reader, over and over again, the truth that God rules in the affairs of humankind."[3]

Seven Last Plagues: Bowls of Judgment	
1. Into the earth	Malignant sores (16:2)
2. Into the sea	Oceans polluted (16:3)
3. Into the rivers	Fresh waters polluted (16:4)
4. Upon the sun	Scorching heat (16:8–9)
5. Upon the throne of beast	Darkness and pain (16:10–11)
6. Upon river Euphrates	Dried up; kings from the east (16:12–16)
7. Into the air	"It is done"; earthquake and hail (16:17–21)

There are obvious parallels between the trumpet judgments (chaps. 8—11) and the bowl judgments (chap. 16). We have already observed these in chapter 6. The basic similarities have to do with the objects of each of the first six judgments (earth, sea, rivers, sun, darkness, Euphrates River). In both cases, the seventh judgment involves a voice announcing the finality of the judgment, followed by lightening, thunder, hail, and an earthquake.

The differences between the trumpets and the bowls have to do with the more universal extent of the latter. The whole world is affected by the bowl judgments. No one escapes. And they come in rapid succession. As soon as God commands them to go, they move with swift abandonment. Each "pours out" his bowl (cup or goblet) upon its destined target. Thomas notes the irony of the fact that the same verb *ekcheō*, used in Revelation only in this passage, is used in Acts 2:17–33 to refer to the pouring out of God's Spirit on the day of Pentecost.

While there are obvious parallels between the trumpets and the bowls, the bowl judgments are specifically called the "seven last plagues" (15:1). "Seven" is the predominant numeral of the Apocalypse. The seven bowls are poured out in rapid succession. It is too late to repent or to stay the hand of God. The world is nearly wiped out before it knows what hit it!

Thomas states, "This can hardly be recapitulation because the effect is total rather than partial as with the other series. The bowls are universal and far more intense, showing beyond reasonable doubt that this whole series deals with the time of the end."[4] What we do seem to have, though, in 11:15–19 is a panoramic overview of what is now forthcoming. Certainly 11:15–19 foresees the end when the "kingdom of the world has become the kingdom of our Lord, and of His Christ; and He will reign forever and ever" (11:15).

1. **First bowl:** *a loathsome and malignant sore* (Rev. 16:2).

The first bowl or cup is poured out on the earth and affects the followers of the beast who have his mark on them. They are immediately inflicted with "sores" (Greek, *helkos*, "ulcer" or "wound"). These sores recall the sixth Egyptian plague (Ex. 9:9–11) where Pharaoh's magicians were afflicted with sores. Speculation abounds among popular prophecy writers regarding ulcerated sores caused by nuclear radiation poisoning. But this is not farfetched given the nature of the extensive damage done by the trumpet judgments (chap. 8), which may well involve nuclear wars. The greatest tragedy in this account is that the people blasphemed God all the more because of their sores and did not repent (16:11).

2. **Second bowl:** *oceans polluted* (Rev. 16:3).

Again, following the Exodus motif, the plagues are reminiscent of those that came upon Egypt because of Pharaoh's refusal to listen to God. The oceans become "blood" and everything in them dies. Previously, in the trumpet judgments only one-third of the sea became blood. Now it is totally polluted. This would mean all fish and plant life in the oceans would die. The stench alone would be unbearable. The ruination of algae and plankton alone would be life threatening.

3. **Third bowl:** *rivers polluted* (Rev. 16:4–7).

With the pollution of lakes and rivers, all mankind is in jeopardy. The rivers turning to "blood" refers to unprecedented divine judgments. The life-threatening impact would be astounding! Virtually no one could survive. Yet, the angels announce God's justice in allowing this to happen because the recipients have shed "the blood of saints and prophets." Therefore, they "deserve" such judgment. The Greek word for "deserve" is used elsewhere in the Revelation with a positive connotation, where it is translated "worthy" (faithful saints [3:4]; God and the Lamb [4:11; 5:2, 4, 9, 12]).

4. **Fourth bowl:** *sun scorches men* (Rev. 16:8–9).

Whereas the sun was previously blocked out by air pollution (black sun, blood-red moon), now the ultraviolet rays of the sun are scorching men with heat and fire. It is only reasonable to assume that the devastating wars of the Tribulation period have taken a toll on the atmosphere of the earth. The destruction of the ozone layer alone would result in such scorching of people. The sun would burn this planet into a global desert right now were it not for earth's protective atmosphere.

5. **Fifth bowl:** *humiliation of the beast* (Rev. 16:10–11).

Here the parallel with the trumpets totally breaks down. This judgment results in darkness and agonizing pain in the kingdom of the beast. If we are correct in assuming that the Antichrist is from Rome in particular or Europe in general, then we can also presume that Europe will be especially hard hit by this judgment. Whether this is "nuclear winter" one can only guess at this point. Certainly, many of these judgments sound like the devastating effects of nuclear war. If they are, then all the side effects of such war are to be expected.

6. **Sixth bowl:** *Armageddon* (Rev. 16:12–16).

Up until this bowl, the previous bowls have involved a direct outpouring of divine wrath. There is no mention of any specific human instrumentality. These judgments may well be the aftermath of the previous ones (seals and trumpets). But as with the sixth trumpet (9:14–21), so the sixth bowl returns our attention to the armies of men. The "kings of the east" was a common designation in ancient times for the Parthians and other barbarians who lived east of the Euphrates and beyond the borders of the Roman Empire. There is nothing in the text itself to specifically identify these kings. It is pure speculation to suppose that they represent China, Japan, or Korea.

The "kings of the east" may simply refer to the Muslim nations of the east (Iran, Afghanistan, Pakistan, and the former Muslim Soviet republics), all of which are under the sword of Islam. We cannot underestimate the vast Islamic world, which hates Israel and wishes her annihilated. These nations may well be the great enemy who comes in one last *jihad* against Jerusalem from the north, south, and east; whereas, the Antichrist appears to head up the secular powers of the west.

John the seer observes the demonic activity involved in all this when he points out the "three unclean spirits" that motivate the unholy trinity: Dragon [Satan], beast [Antichrist], and False Prophet (16:13). They are the ones orchestrating the march to Armageddon. John tells us that these demonic spirits are gathering the nations to the "great day of God, the Almighty."

It is then and only then that the revelator tells us where all these nations are headed. They are gathering together at "the place which in Hebrew is called Har-Magedon [Armageddon]" (16:16). This is the only place in all the Bible where this name is given in this form. John pronounces the name for his Gentile readers in Asia Minor because they would not otherwise have been familiar with it.

Scholars debate whether Armageddon is literal or figurative. Certainly the general vicinity around Tel Megiddo and the adjacent Valley of Jezreel adequately fits the general description. So does its location between Jerusalem to the south and the Euphrates River to the east. Any army coming into Israel from the east would have to cross through the Jezreel Valley.

Since *Har-Magedon* technically means "Mount Megiddo," John may have in mind the mountains of Israel that surround this valley. In Ezekiel's prophecies (30:1-9; 38:8-21; 39:1-4), the "mountains of Israel" figure prominently in the final conflicts of the End Times. The plain of Megiddo is either the staging area for the invasion of Jerusalem or the location of the final battle. The war itself spreads over two hundred miles from north to south (cf. Rev. 14:20). In addition, the final conflict also has global consequences. The entire planet has been rocked by this great devastation. All that remains for the Antichrist is to control Jerusalem. But alas, he fails miserably.

7. *Seventh bowl: "It is done"* (Rev. 16:17-21).

The seven bowls have been poured out with such rapidity and severity that nothing can stand before them. Our passage indicates that a great earthquake, the worst in the history of the world, rocks the entire planet. Cities collapse, nations fall, islands sink, and mountains disappear. On top of all this, great hailstones fall out of the sky and those who survive blaspheme God all the more.

It is certainly possible that these judgments are cosmic (an asteroid collides with earth) or geological (volcanoes and earthquakes). But the clear references to men fighting, armies marching, and fire falling certainly sound like a great world war involving nuclear weapons. How ironic that John locates this last great conflict between the forces of God and Satan at Armageddon, near Mount Carmel where Elijah stood against the prophets of Baal and called down the fire of God in a demonstration of His mighty power (1 Kin. 18).

When it is all over, God speaks from the heavenly temple and announces, "It is done." In Greek it is one word: *gegonen*. This perfect tense of the verb indicates that what has been in the process of developing is now complete. It summarizes the finality of all that has happened in the bowl judgments, and it anticipates all that will still be explained in detail in chapters 17—19. As we have observed before, the Revelation gives us the big picture in advance, followed by detailed snapshots of the same. Chronologically, at 16:17 we are at the end. But thematically we still see the fall of Babylon and the return of Christ on the horizon.

The statement "It is done" is repeated again in 21:6, after the Millennium and the Great White Throne Judgment when God is making "all things new" in eternity. The statement itself has a ring of permanence and finality about it. Whereas the "It is finished" (Greek, *tetelestai*) of Jesus on the cross in John 19:30 emphasizes the idea that the atonement has been "paid in full." That finished work has ongoing benefits to all who will believe in it. This finished work of judgment is over and done and has no benefit to its recipients. Armageddon has finally come. The world is in ruins!

Study Questions

1. Read Isaiah 34:2–8. What key to the prophetic significance of Revelation 16 do you find in these verses?

2. What was in the seven bowls that the angels pour out (16:1)?

3. What did the first plague bring upon the worshipers of the beast (16:2)?

4. What was the effect of the second plague on the seas (16:3)?

5. What did the third plague cause the rivers to become (16:4)?

6. What plague did the fourth bowl bring upon men (16:8)?

7. Where was the fifth bowl poured out (16:10)?

8. The sixth bowl was poured out upon what river (16:12)?

9. How did this prepare the way for the kings of the east (16:12)?

10. Who gathered the kings of the whole world to battle on the great day of God, the Almighty (16:14)?

11. What is the name of the place where the kings of the east gathered for battle (16:16)?

12. After the seventh bowl was poured out, what caused cities to shake, islands to sink, and mountains to be buried (16:18–20)?

CHAPTER 17

The Great Harlot
and the Scarlet Beast

Preview:
The great harlot who rides a scarlet beast appears. She is called "Babylon the great." But the details of her description clearly indicate she represents the city on "seven mountains"—that great city that "reigns over the kings of the earth." Together, Revelation 17—18 describe the fall of "Babylon" in detail.

The fall of Babylon has already been announced in Revelation 14:8. Its doom has already been certified. Now the seer fills in the details, taking all of chapters 17—18 to do so. Both ecclesiastical and political Babylon come into view in the things that follow. The city itself is pictured as a drunken harlot who is about to fall into judgment. She drains the cup of God's wrath (cf. 16:19), only to be deceived by the very beast that carries her.

Leon Morris emphasizes the sense of finality the reader feels from this point onward. He writes, "Now John fixes his eyes firmly on the end-time. He concerns himself not with the apparent triumph of the evil, but with their final and complete overthrow. He sees God as casting down every stronghold and hurling His judgments against the wicked. No might of theirs avails. God is completely triumphant."[1]

John the revelator is summoned by one of the angels to view the judgment of the great harlot. By contrast, later he will be summoned to view the Bride of the Lamb. The correlation is deliberate. It sets forth the contrast between the kingdom of the Antichrist, the city of the great harlot, and the city of the Bride of Christ, the New Jerusalem. The great harlot is portrayed in direct opposition to the Bride of Christ:

Great Harlot	Bride of Christ
In the wilderness (17:3)	In heaven (19:1–9)
Rides the beast (17:3)	Returns with Christ (19:11–16)
Adorned in luxury (17:4)	Adorned in righteousness (19:8)
Cup of abominations (17:4)	Water of life (22:1)
Great city (17:18)	Holy city (21:2)
War against the Lamb (17:14)	Reigns with the Lamb (22:5)
Ends in destruction (18:21)	Lives forever (21—22)

Whether one views Babylon as the worldly enterprise of John's day, our day, or some future day, Beasley-Murray's observation is valid: "These contrasts will have been readily perceived by John's original readers, and will have served to emphasize the necessity that they should 'depart' from Babylon, so as not to share in its fate, and that they maintain their lot in the city which will endure forever."[2]

The question often debated among evangelicals is whether this "Babylon" is the Babylon of ancient times revived in the Last Days or whether it is symbolic of Rome revived in the Last Days. Either way, those who view the Revelation as a prophecy of the future must look for a future Babylon or future Rome as the fulfillment of this prediction. In this regard, let us consider *several key factors:*

1. The early church unanimously viewed "Babylon" as Rome. None of the early church fathers held that Babylon was to be taken literally. They all viewed it as symbolic of the Roman Empire in general and the city of Rome in particular.

2. The reformers and puritans were also unanimous in taking "Babylon" as a symbol of Rome. The only difference was that they extended it to refer to papal Rome as the apostate church of the Last Days.

3. There is no valid reason today to assume that ancient Babylon will literally be rebuilt and rise to power overnight as the dominant world city and capital of the Antichrist.

Babylon is still in ruins in fulfillment of Old Testament prophecies. Saddam Hussein's attempt to "rebuild" it as a tourist trap hardly qualifies it as the great city of the Last Days. Besides, his attempts have failed. Babylon has no sacred significance to the religion of Islam. Muslims are interested in protecting only their holy sites. They have no interest in rebuilding ancient pagan sites, including Babylon. Therefore, it will likely remain in ruins.

A basic survey of the revelator's description of Babylon quickly reveals that it cannot be ancient Babylon in modern Iraq. Remember, it is portrayed as the city of the Antichrist, who rules the whole world. It is a center of commerce, enterprise, and trade. And it is the city that shed the blood of the "witnesses of Jesus." Babylon does not qualify in any of these regards. Notice also the characteristics of the *apocalyptic "Babylon":*

1. Rich and prosperous (17:4)

2. Immoral and drunken (17:2, 6)

3. Associated with Satan and the beast (17:7–8)

4. City that sits on seven mountains (17:9)

5. Leader of a ten-nation confederacy with Roman (European) roots (17:12–13)

6. City that reigns over many nations (17:15–18)

7. Center of commercial enterprise (18:3, 11–13)

8. Sailors cross the sea to get there (18:17–18)

9. An entertainment capital (18:22–23)

10. Burns up in one hour (18:9–10, 17–19)

Who Is This Great Mystery?

The very fact that John calls her identity a "mystery" ought to be enough to indicate that he does not intend us to take "Babylon" literally. His subsequent description of this great city makes that point all the more clear. David Hocking also emphasizes that she is a "mystery" and says, "This suggests that neither ancient Babylon nor its site is intended. It teaches us to look deeper and to see it figuratively rather than literally."[3]

John's imagery is drawn from Jeremiah 51:7–8, where Babylon is referred to as a "golden cup" that made the nations drunk with the intoxicating desire for power. Thus, John takes the name of Israel's ancient enemy, Babylon, and uses it for Rome. Robert Mounce writes, "Whether Jezebel or Cleopatra sat for the portrait John is now painting makes little difference. The harlot is Rome. Adorned in luxury and intoxicated with the blood of the saints, she stands for a dominant world system based on seduction for personal gain over and against the righteous demands of a persecuted minority."[4]

The real tragedy is that she could well be America! While there is no clear prophecy about the United States in the Bible (nor Canada, Australia, South Africa, etc.), it is possible to infer nations that are European transplants from the "[young lions] of Tarshish" (Ezek. 38:13). It is certainly probable that if a European alliance were to form in fulfillment of these prophecies anytime soon, it would most likely include all the major Western powers. That an American leader could head them is certainly possible, even probable.

The "great harlot" is represented as the "mother of harlots" (17:5). She is pictured as the source of moral evil and spiritual infidelity. She not only seduces men, but she also seductively recruits other "women" to join in her evil enterprise. Hocking again writes,

> This fact alone would control any attempts to limit the meaning of this harlot to one particular religious system. The "mystery" of Babylon the Great is not a reference to ancient Babylon, nor merely the Roman Catholic Church. The false religion symbolized by her has permeated all history from the time of Babylon until the present day. Satan's counterfeits have appeared in many countries and cultures, and they will reach their climax of sinister methods, evil practices and deceptive teachings during the Tribulation period.[5]

I believe John saw the Roman Empire of his day as the greatest satanic threat to the early church. However, we must continually remember that he has been caught up into heaven in a vision since chapter 4. This is a vision of *future events* that reaches all the way down through the End Times to the return of Christ (Rev. 19), the Millennial Kingdom (Rev. 20), and the new heavens and new earth (Rev. 21—22). These final events have not yet occurred! Therefore, it is only reasonable to understand that the final conflict John predicts and the resulting fall of "Babylon" are still future events as well.

Whether apocalyptic Babylon exists today or is still in the process of being formulated, only future generations can judge. What the Revelation does make clear is that it has always existed. It is the epitome of the kingdom of Satan— the "city of Man." It is opposed to and has always been opposed to the "city of God." It is the blatant expression of the finest efforts of finite minds to rule themselves in opposition to the rule of God. Thus, the greatest and most spectacular of our cities without God is an architectural fist in the face of heaven!

A Woman Rides the Beast

Dave Hunt has pointed out that the woman's connection to the beast is critical in this passage. He writes: "Unquestionably, the woman is the central figure in these two important chapters, a major player in the drama of the Last Days. John gives far more attention to *her* than to the beast she rides. And the fact that she *rides* the beast—a beast of such importance that it literally holds the central position in Bible prophecy—demands our special attention."[6]

She is depicted as a great "harlot" (Greek, *pornēs*) involved in fornication *(porneia)*, which is the equivalent to spiritual adultery. The Old Testament prophets brought similar charges against Nineveh (Nah. 3:1–4), Tyre (Is, 23:15–17), Babylon (Ezek. 23:17), and even Jerusalem (Is. 1:21; Jer. 3:8–9). In the symbolism John uses in the Revelation, the great harlot represents apostate religion and its interdependence on and with political power. Hunt makes a very strong case against the Roman Catholic Church for its frequent violations of the relationship of religion and politics. He also points out the terrible persecutions the Roman Church often inflicted on those true believers who dissented with her.

However one interprets the woman's identity, it is clear that she represents the false religion of the Last Days. Thomas writes, "This woman represents all false religion of all time, including those who apostatize from the revealed religion of Christianity."[7] John Walvoord adds, "The picture of the woman as utterly evil signifies spiritual adultery, portraying those who outwardly and religiously seem to be joined to the true God, but who are untrue to this relationship."[8]

Most commentators remind us of the origin of false religion in ancient Babylon, with its occultic practices and deification of the mother goddess symbol. This practice can be traced from Semiramus to Ishtar, Ashtar, Astarte, Aphrodite, Venus, and unfortunately, to the Virgin Mary. Other aspects of Babylonian religion included astrology, black magic, occultic practices, and numerous elements of what today is being popularized in New Age religion. Bob Larsen draws several parallels in his book *In the Name of Satan.*[9]

The great harlot is not only depicted riding the scarlet beast but also riding upon "many waters," which 17:15 describes as "peoples and multitudes and nations and tongues." This depicts the worldwide control and influence the woman has over the earth's population. She is seen as perpetuating and promoting a world religion that engulfs the world political system. After the Rapture of the true Church, all that will be left in Christendom will be *apostate*, be it Catholic, Orthodox, Protestant, evangelical, or charismatic.

False religion will easily and quickly preempt the hollow structures of the religious systems that remain. Pragmatic considerations of economic, social, and political survival will overrule all religious preferences in favor of a global religious system among the Western nations. The religion of the Last Days will be materialism and commercialism of the worst sort. What is frightening is that we are already on the verge of it now!

The Beast and the Bottomless Pit

John takes time to explain his enigmatic figures. He calls our attention again to the beast itself with its seven heads and ten horns. In 17:9 he specifically states that the seven heads are "seven mountains on which the woman sits." Any first-century reader would immediately identify this as Rome, the city on seven hills.

Next, John reminds us of the satanic or demonic origin of the beast from the "bottomless pit" (Greek, *abussos*). Thus, he connects the beast both with the sea (13:1) and the pit (17:8). This dual origin emphasizes that the source of the beast's power is both human and satanic. The beast itself is the symbol of the Antichrist (13:1–10) and of his kingdom, which is opposed to the true kingdom of God.

Then, John tells us there are seven kings (or kingdoms) symbolized here as well (17:10). Five are fallen, one "is" (exists now—the sixth), one will come for a short while (the seventh), and the beast is the eighth, although he originates from the seven. His connection to the seven is similar to his connection to and yet separation from the ten horns (Dan. 7:24–25). Commentators have gone to great detail to trace the Roman emperors of John's day, but no alignment really works out in this pattern.[10] Walvoord argues that the seven kings represent the seven Gentile kingdoms which have followed one another in succession.[11] Egypt, Assyria, Babylon, Persia, and Greece are the five past kingdoms. Rome, of John's day, is the sixth. All six of these kingdoms persecuted the people of God (Israel).

The seventh brief kingdom that gives rise to the eighth kingdom of the Antichrist (17:11) is not as easy to identify. Pagan Rome was eventually succeeded by a Christianized Byzantine Roman Empire with its capital moved to Constantinople. Rome itself was left under the domain of various popes and was later reconstituted as the "Holy Roman Empire," which historians have often noted was neither holy nor Roman, and was not even an empire! It is possible that this is the brief kingdom that John foresaw as the seventh one that would give rise to the eighth kingdom of the Antichrist. It has often been observed that modern Europe is what was left of the various wars involving the Holy Roman Empire, which finally dissolved officially in 1806.

The revival of the old Roman Empire in the future will constitute the reemergence of a united Europe with strong ties to Rome and the Roman Church. The creation of the European Union (EU) in 1993, the establishment of the European Central Bank in 1998, the absorption of the Western European Union in 1999 (making the EU a military power), and the EU's desire for a reunited Europe with its capital in Rome is certainly along the lines of what the books of Daniel and Revelation predict about the End Times. This bears our watching its further developments.

At War with the Lamb

John the revelator points out that ten kings of the future will receive power with the beast for "one hour," or a brief period of time. These ten kings (ten horns) are distinct from the seven heads. They represent ten kings or kingdoms that forge an alliance with the Antichrist in the Last Days. John's symbolism is similar to that of Daniel's in the prophecy about the ten toes of the great statue (Dan. 2:40–44) and the ten horns of the monster (Dan. 7:7, 20–25). Daniel even specifies the same time period as John's Revelation: three and one half "times."

John adds to the prophetic picture that the ten horns will eventually turn against the harlot, destroy her, and give their kingdoms to the beast (Rev. 17:15–18). Thus, raw materialism and intoxication with power will drive the kingdom of the Antichrist to turn against its pseudoreligious perpetrator. The love-hate relationship between the devil incarnate and false Christianity will result in the annihilation of the latter. In the end, the satanic trinity will no longer even pretend to represent anything that can be construed as Christian at all. The ugly head of the beast will demand worship for itself alone.

All-out religious war will follow. Anyone claiming any faith in or allegiance to Jesus Christ will be executed for treason. The beast will declare war against the Lamb and His followers. At the very time of the Great Tribulation when wars and calamities are at their worst, the beast will turn against the offspring of the woman. Converted Israel, represented symbolically by the 144,000, will suffer martyrdom and persecution. But John reminds us, "The Lamb will overcome" because He is "Lord of lords and King of kings" (17:14). Despite all of the efforts of false religion, secular government, and raw military power, Jesus Christ will triumph in the end.

Study Questions

1. Read Daniel 7:24–25. What key to the prophetic significance of Revelation 17 do you find in these verses?

2. Whose judgment was John invited to witness (17:1)?

3. Who is she riding when John sees her (17:3)?

4. What name is she given (17:5)?

5. On what has she become drunk (17:6)?

6. From what place is the beast said to have emerged (17:8)?

7. What do the seven heads of the beast represent (17:9)?

8. What do the ten horns represent (17:12)?

9. Who will make war against the Lamb (17:14)?

10. Who begins to hate the woman and eventually destroys her (17:16)?

11. What identity is given to the woman who "reigns over the kings of the earth" (17:18)?

CHAPTER 18

Fall of Babylon

Preview:

The final aspects of the fall of Babylon are given in detail. The great commercial center of the global economy is destroyed and burned up in "one hour." Sailors and merchants mourn over the "smoke of her burning." But the revelator announces: "Rejoice over her!" Babylon falls that the New Jerusalem may come.

The fall of Babylon announced in 14:8 is now repeated (18:2) as final and decisive. As we have seen so many times in the Apocalypse, we are given the big picture first as a preview. Then the specific details follow in order. That is exactly what we have here. The proleptic announcement was made in 14:8 as a preview of what was coming in chapters 15—18. Now we are given the final details of the destruction of the "city of man."

We have also noted before in chapters 14 and 17 that "Babylon" is used symbolically for Rome (as in 1 Pet. 5:13). It is not a reference to literal ancient Babylon, which was destroyed centuries ago. Nor is it a reference to a rebuilt Babylon of the Last Days. Although such is possible, it is not very probable. The amount of time it would take to rebuild the city and for it to emerge as a world commercial center violates any proper sense of the imminent return of Christ.

The "Babylon" of the Apocalypse is the *New Rome* of the future. It is the revived Roman Empire of a politically and economically resurgent new Europe. Since the days of the Roman Empire, there has never been a truly unified Europe. But today talk of such a reality is commonplace. The European Union (EU) has as its stated goal the establishment of the United States of Europe. Current technological progress and economic development are making this enterprise a reality before our very eyes.

We are fast approaching the final round in the struggle for world dominion. The collapse of communism has removed the last great barrier to a global economy. We are standing on the edge of a new day in world politics. Dramatic changes in Europe, Russia, and the Middle East indicate the world is undergoing a massive transformation. At the same time, there is great concern about where all these changes are taking us. Charles Colson says, "We sense that things are winding down, that somehow freedom, justice, and order are slipping away. Our great civilization may not yet lie in ruins, but the enemy is within the gates. The times smell of sunset."[1]

As John the apostle stood on the precipice of eternity, he foresaw the final collapse of all that we call Western civilization. As apocalyptic "Babylon" burned beyond recognition, its commerce, business, merchandise, and entertainment industries went up in smoke. "Babylon" would again become a desolate and uninhabited place—a "dwelling place of demons" (18:2). And all of this would occur in "one hour" (18:10, 17, 19)!

The massive and instantaneous destruction that John predicts never happened to ancient Rome. To be sure, Rome fell to the barbarians in A.D. 410 and again in A.D. 493. But Rome survived, nevertheless. And it is still standing today. But John foresees a time when the "Babylon" (Rome) of the future will be destroyed and never rebuilt.

The Global Enterprise

John pictures the kingdom of the Antichrist as a place where the "merchants" of earth grow rich and where the people live in prosperity. Yet, they shall all weep one day because her merchandise (gold, silver, precious stones, pearls, linen, silks, ointments, perfumes, and lavish foods) will one day disappear (vv. 12–14). While sailors and merchants weep over Babylon's destruction, heaven rejoices (v. 20). The corporate centers of business and power will collapse. Even the musicians and craftsmen will be silenced (v. 22).

Death stalks the city! Life has been virtually exterminated. Even the merchant sailors are reluctant to land on her shores. They sit in their vessels "at a distance" (v. 17). Something terrible has happened, and it sounds like nuclear war! Notice the various details of *Babylon's final destruction:*

1. Devoid of human life (18:2)

2. Burned up with fire (18:8)

3. Destroyed in one hour (18:10, 17, 19)

4. People afraid to enter her borders (18:10, 17)

5. Wealth laid waste (18:17)

6. Violently overthrown (18:21)

7. Devoid of all activity (18:22–24)

David Jeremiah notes that the sins of Babylon have piled one upon another like the ancient tower of Babel.[2] Each stone stands as an indictment upon the other. Jeremiah points out that Babylon is judged for her influence, infidelity, and inhumanity. Babylon's sins are pictured as having "piled up a high as heaven" (v. 5). Like the unrepentant Babylonians of old, these end-time "Babylonians" will worship the great enterprise they have built and forget the true and living God.

Babylon is pictured as receiving a "double" payment for her sins because she has filled the cup of sin to the double. Here is a great society, not unlike our own, which has forgotten God in all her success. Rather than praising Him for His abundant blessings, they have become obsessed with the pursuit of those blessings. And in the process, they have forgotten the divine One from whom all those blessings come. Worse, they have forgotten there is no permanent satisfaction in that which is temporal. They are caught in an endless and mindless pursuit of that which can never satisfy their souls.

The Two Commands

Two commands are given to the true people of God in the light of Babylon's fall: "Come out of her" and "Rejoice over her." First, a voice speaks from heaven urging the true believers to separate themselves from the false, apostate religion of the End Times. They are told not to partake of her sins lest they also partake of her plagues (v. 4). Second, they are told to rejoice over her demise because "God has pronounced judgment for you against her" (v. 20).

While the merchants of the earth weep over Babylon's destruction, believers are told to rejoice over it. God has no mercy for this evil system that has always persecuted true believers. He shows no mercy and spares no unrepentant soul. So thorough is His punishment that no one can stand before it. It is His final and irrevocable expression of wrath, and it nearly destroys the whole planet.

A "strong angel" appears in 18:21. This is the third such appearance in the Revelation (cf. also 5:2 and 10:1). He picks up a great stone like a "millstone" and casts it into the sea and announces, "Thus will Babylon, the great city, be thrown down with violence, and will not be found any longer."

There can be no question that John predicts the total and violent overthrow of "Babylon." If this is taken only to refer to ancient Rome, the prophecy was never really fulfilled. Rome "fell" to Christianity (A.D. 325) before it fell to the barbarians (A.D. 410). And while it has suffered over the centuries, it still stands intact today. The empire is gone, to be sure, but the city is still there. So is its materialistic heritage: the Western world.

If, on the other hand, we view John's "Babylon" as the Rome (or Europe) of the future, all these ominous warnings remain to be fulfilled. Even as Christians today we dare not underestimate the Satanic lure of materialistic prosperity, human comforts, and the pursuit of pleasure. "Babylon" still tugs at the flesh of every human being. It flirts with our moral sensibilities and calls us to indulge ourselves in that which will destroy us. "Babylon" is not yet dead. Her music can still be heard. Her builders are hard at work. Her commercial enterprises still attract us away from the spiritual and the eternal. But not for long!

The commands to the believers are clear. First, "Come out of her" (v. 4). This is addressed to "my people," and thus to believers. We, too, are vulnerable to the allurements of this Vanity Fair. Therefore, we are told to separate ourselves from it and not to partake of her sins. Second, "Rejoice over her" (v. 20). The true believer is to rejoice, not sorrow, over the judgment and destruction of the materialistic system. Its merchandise is that of fools. It cannot bring lasting joy or peace. It is but a glittering bauble that will ultimately return to the dust of oblivion. It will sink into the ocean like a giant millstone and be forgotten.

Leon Morris observes that the Apocalypse has in view the fall not just of a particular city, but the collapse of civilization itself.[3] All that opposes God shall be overthrown. He quotes Byron who said, "When falls the coliseum, Rome shall fall; and when Rome falls—the World." So be it! Rejoice! The King is coming!

Study Questions

1. Read Isaiah 24:1–10. What key to the prophetic significance of Revelation 18 do you find in these verses?

2. Who will dwell in fallen Babylon (18:2)?

3. Who becomes rich by trading in the city (18:3)?

4. What does God urge His people to do before the judgment comes (18:4)?

5. What portion of vengeance will God call down upon her (18:6)?

6. Who will mourn for her because of the "smoke of her burning" (18:9)?

7. How long does the destruction of the great city take (18:10, 17, 19)?

8. Who remains at a distance and cries out at her destruction (18:17)?

9. What are heaven, the apostles, and the prophets told to do regarding her destruction (18:20)?

10. What symbol did the strong angel use to symbolize the destruction of the city (18:21)?

11. Whose blood is she guilty of shedding (18:24)?

CHAPTER 19

Triumphal Return of Christ

Preview:

This is one of the greatest chapters in the entire Bible! It deals with three of the most important events in our lives: 1) the marriage supper of the Lamb; 2) the return of Christ with His Church; and 3) the final triumph over the Antichrist and the False Prophet. The climax of the entire Revelation is reached in this dramatic and exciting chapter in which Christ returns as the King of kings.

The second coming of Christ is the most anticipated event in human history. It is the ultimate fulfillment of our Lord's promise to return. It is also the culmination of all biblical prophecy. The return of Christ is the final apologetic! Once He returns, there will be no further need to debate His claims or the validity of the Christian message. The King will come in person to set the record straight.

Revelation 19 is probably the most dramatic chapter in the entire Bible. It is the final capstone to the death and resurrection of Christ. In this chapter the living Savior returns to earth to crush all satanic opposition to the truth. He establishes His kingdom on earth in fulfillment of the Old Testament prophecies and of His own promise to return.

Just before the Crucifixion, the disciples asked Jesus, "What will be the sign of Your coming?" (Matt. 24:3). Our Lord replied, "Immediately after the tribulation of those days . . . the powers of the heavens will be shaken, and then the sign of the Son of Man will appear in the sky, and then all the tribes of the earth will mourn, and they will see the Son of Man coming on the clouds of the sky with power and great glory" (Matt. 24:29–30).

As Jesus looked down the corridor of time to the end of the present age, He warned of a time of Great Tribulation that would come upon the whole world (Matt. 24:5–28). Our Lord went on to explain that the devastation of the Great Tribulation will be so extensive that unless those days were cut short, "no one would survive" (Matt. 24:22 NIV). Jesus further described this coming day of trouble as a time when the sun and moon will be darkened and the heavens will be shaken (Matt. 24:29). His description runs parallel to that found in Revelation 16:1–16, where the final hour of the Tribulation is depicted by atmospheric darkness, air pollution, and ecological disaster.

The return of Christ is a twofold event. It marks both the final defeat of the Antichrist and the final triumph of Christ. René Pache writes, "The main event announced by the prophets is not the judgment of the world, nor the restoration of Israel, nor even the triumph of the Church: it is the glorious advent of the Son of God."[1] Without Him, there is no hope of a better future. He is the central figure of the world to come. It is His kingdom and we are His Bride. Oh, what a day that will be!

The Promise of His Return

Jesus promised His disciples in the upper room that He was going to heaven to prepare a place for them. Then He said, "And if I go and prepare a place for you, I will come again, and receive you to Myself; that where I am, there you may be also" (John 14:3). Even though the early disciples eventually died, the Bible promised, "Behold, I tell you a mystery; we shall not all sleep [die], but we shall all be changed [resurrected or raptured], in a moment, in the twinkling of an eye, at the last trumpet; for the trumpet will sound, and the dead will be raised imperishable, and we shall be changed" (1 Cor. 15:51–52).

The apostle Paul reiterates this same hope in 1 Thessalonians 4:14–17, when he comments about those believers who have already died and gone to heaven. He says, "For if we believe that Jesus died and rose again, even so God bring with Him [from heaven] those who have fallen asleep [died] in Jesus. . . . For the Lord Himself will descend from heaven with a shout, with the voice of the archangel, and with the trumpet of God; and the dead in Christ shall rise first. Then we who are alive and remain shall be caught up together with them in the clouds to meet the Lord in the air."

The promise to return for the Church (believers of the Church Age) is the promise of the Rapture. When Revelation 19 opens, the Church is already in heaven with Christ at the marriage supper. The Rapture has already occurred. Jesus is depicted as the groom and the Church as the Bride. The marriage supper celebrates their union after the Rapture and before their return to earth.

One of the greatest interpretive problems for nonrapturists is to explain *how* the Church got to heaven *prior* to the second coming! Surely they were not all martyred, or else Paul's comment about "we who are alive, and remain" (1 Thess. 4:15, 17) would be meaningless! The Rapture must be presumed to have occurred *before* the events in Revelation 19—amillennialists and post-millennialists not withstanding!

The position of the Church (Bride of the Lamb) in Revelation 19:7–10 *in heaven* is crucial to the interpretation of the entire Apocalypse. New Testament scholar Robert Gromacki points out, "The Church is not mentioned during the seal, trumpet, and bowl judgments because the Church is not here during the outpouring of these judgments."[2] He points out that the term for *church* (Greek, *ekklēsia*) appears frequently in chapters 1—3 of the Revelation. In fact, it is used nineteen times in those chapters. But the word *church*, does not appear again until 22:16. In the meantime, the Church is referred to in 19:7–10 as the Bride of the Lamb.

The concept of the Church as the bride or wife of Christ is clearly stated in Ephesians 5:22–33, where husbands are admonished to love their wives as Christ loved the Church and gave Himself for her that He might present her in heaven as a glorious Bride. There can be no doubt, therefore, that John intends us to see the Lamb's "wife" as the Church—the Bride of Christ.

The Nature of Christ's Return

Jesus not only promised to return for His Church, but He also promised to return to judge the world and to establish His kingdom on earth. His brother James refers to believers as "heirs of the kingdom which He promised to those who love Him" (James 2:5). Jesus Himself told His disciples that He would not drink the fruit of the vine after the Last Supper until He drank it with them in His Father's kingdom (Matt. 26:29). After the resurrection, they asked Him, "Is it at this time You are restoring the kingdom to Israel?" (Acts 1:6). He replied that the time was in the Father's hand. All these references imply a future kingdom when Christ returns.

The details of *Christ's return* include the following aspects:

1. *He will return personally.* The Bible promises, "the Lord Himself will descend from heaven with a shout" (1 Thess. 4:16). Jesus promised He Himself would return in person (Matt. 24:30).

2. *He will appear as the Son of Man.* Since Pentecost, Christ has ministered through the Holy Spirit (John 14:16–23; 16:7–20). But when He returns, He will appear as the Son of Man in His glorified human form (Matt. 24:30; 26:64; Dan. 7:13–14).

3. *He will return literally and visibly.* In Acts 1:11, the angels promised, "This Jesus, who has been taken up from you into heaven,
   will come in just the same way as you have watched Him go."
   Revelation 1:7 tells us, "Every eye will see him, even those who
   pierced him; and all the tribes of the earth."

4. *He will come suddenly and dramatically.* Paul warned, "The day of
   the Lord will come just like a thief in the night" (1 Thess. 5:2).
   Jesus said, "For just as the lightning comes from the east, and
   flashes even to the west, so shall the coming of the Son of Man
   be" (Matt. 24:27).

5. *He will come on the clouds of heaven.* Jesus said, "They will see the
   Son of Man coming on the clouds of the sky" (Matt. 24:30 [see
   Dan. 7:13; Luke 21:27]). Revelation 1:7 says, "Behold, He is
   coming with the clouds."

6. *He will come in a display of glory.* Matthew 16:27 promises, "The
   Son of man is going to come in the glory of His Father." Matthew
   24:30 adds, "They will see the Son of Man coming . . . with
   power and great glory."

7. *He will come with all His angels.* Jesus promised, "And He will
   send forth His angels with a great trumpet" (Matt. 24:31). Jesus
   said in one of His parables, "The reapers are angels. . . . so shall
   it be at the end of the age" (Matt. 13:39–40).

8. *He will come with His Bride—the Church.* That, of course, is the
   whole point of Revelation 19. Colossians 3:4 adds, "When
   Christ . . . is revealed, then you also will be revealed with Him in
   glory." Zechariah 14:5 adds, "Then the LORD, my God, will come,
   and all the holy ones with Him."

9. *He will return to the Mount of Olives.* "And in that day His feet will
   stand on the Mount of Olives" (Zech. 14:4). Where the glory
   of God ascended into heaven, it will return (cf. Ezek. 11:23).
   Where Jesus ascended into heaven, He will return (cf. Acts
   1:3–12).

10. *He will return in triumph and victory.* Zechariah 14:9 promises,
    "And the LORD will be king over all the earth." Revelation 19:16
    depicts him as "KING OF KINGS, AND LORD OF LORDS." He
    will triumph over the Antichrist, the False Prophet, and Satan
    himself (Rev. 19:19–21).

Hallelujah, What a Savior!

Chapter 19 opens with a heavenly chorus, a "great multitude" singing the praises of God (v. 1). Beasley-Murray calls it a *"Te Deum* [hymn of praise to God] on the righteous judgments of God."[3] The heavenly choir rejoices with praise because justice has finally been served. "His judgments are true and righteous," they sing, because "He has judged the great harlot" (v. 2). The praise chorus then breaks into a *fourfold hallelujah* (alleluia, KJV) in verses 1–6:

1. "Hallelujah! Salvation and glory and power belong to our God" (v. 1).

2. "Hallelujah! Her smoke rises up forever and ever" (v. 3).

3. They "worshiped God . . . on the throne saying, 'Amen. Hallelujah!'" (v. 4).

4. "Hallelujah! For the Lord our God, the Almighty, reigns" (v. 6).

This is the only place in the New Testament where *hallelujah* occurs. It is a Hebrew word ("Praise Yah [*Jehovah*]"). It was transliterated from the Hebrew into Greek and passed on into English. The same thing occurred with *Amen, hosanna,* and *maranatha.* The use of the four "hallelujahs" emphasizes the magnitude of this praise and worship.

Beasley-Murray observes that these "hallelujahs" are reminiscent of the *Hallel Psalms* (113—118) which were sung at the Jewish Passover meal.[4] The first two (113—114) were sung before the meal and the last four after the meal. Just as Israel sang God's praises for His deliverance in the Passover, so the Church in heaven sings God's praise for His deliverance from the Antichrist. The triumphal praise is very similar to that heard earlier in 11:15–19. But the triumph that is heralded is more than that over the downfall of "Babylon." It is the marriage of the Lamb that takes center stage in this cantata of praise.

Marriage Supper of the Lamb

The sense of movement that is always prevalent in the Apocalypse now reaches a climax. "The marriage of the Lamb has come" (v. 7). It is as though we have finally arrived at what we have been waiting for all along. The wedding is finally here. It is obvious that John the revelator views this as a future (not past) event. The final culmination of their spiritual union has finally arrived.

Beasley-Murray expresses it like this: "The perfection in glory of the Bride belongs to the eschatological future. In this figure, therefore, the *now* and the *not yet* of the New Testament doctrine of salvation in the kingdom of God is perfectly exemplified. The Church is the Bride of Christ now, but her marriage lies in the future."⁵

This is exactly why we cannot say that the consummation of the marriage has already taken place. The apostle Paul says, "For I betrothed you to one husband, that to Christ I might present you as a pure virgin" (2 Cor. 11:2). He also adds that Christ "loved the church and gave Himself up for her . . . that He might present to Himself the church in all her glory, having no spot or wrinkle or any such thing; but that she should be holy and blameless" (Eph. 5:25–27).

Bruce Metzger comments, "The concept of the relationship between God and his people as a marriage goes far back into the Old Testament. Again and again the prophets spoke of Israel as the chosen Bride of God (Is. 54:1–8; Ezek. 16:7, 8; Hos. 2:19). In the New Testament the Church is represented as the Bride of Christ . . . In the words of a familiar hymn: 'With his own blood he bought her, and for her life he died.'"⁶

The New Testament pictures the Church as engaged to Christ by faith at this present time. We are still awaiting the "judgment seat of Christ" (2 Cor. 5:10), presumably after the Rapture and before the marriage supper. The marriage ceremony itself will occur in heaven during the Tribulation period on earth. Dwight Pentecost writes, "At the translation of the Church, Christ is appearing as a bridegroom to take his Bride unto Himself, so that the relationship that was pledged might be consummated and the two might become one."⁷

Christ is still pictured symbolically as the Lamb (19:7), but the picture of the marriage is clearly expressed. The aorist tense of "has come" (Greek, *ēlthen*) indicates a completed act, showing that the wedding is now consummated. Instead of the normal seven-day Jewish wedding ceremony, this one presumably lasts seven years (during the Tribulation period). The marriage is completed in heaven (Rev. 19:7), but the marriage supper probably takes place later on earth where Israel is awaiting the return of Christ and the Church.

This is the only clear way to distinguish the Bridegroom (Christ), the Bride (Church), and the ten virgins (Israel) in the passage in Matthew 25:1–13. There is no way that He is coming to marry all ten (or five) of these girls. They are the attendants (Old Testament saints and Tribulation saints) at the wedding. Only the Church is the Bride. That is how Jesus could say of John the Baptist that there was no one "greater than John [an Old Testament saint], yet he who is least in the kingdom of God [the New Testament Church] is greater than he" (Luke 7:28).

The Triumphal Return

The singular vignette of Christ's return in Revelation 19:11–16 is the most dramatic passage in the entire Bible! In these six verses we are swept up into the triumphal entourage of redeemed saints as they ride in the heavenly procession with the King of kings and Lord of lords. In this one passage alone, all the hopes and dreams of every believer are finally and fully realized. This is not the Palm Sunday procession with the humble Messiah on the donkey colt. This is the ultimate in eschatological drama. The rejected Savior returns in triumph as the rightful King of all the world—and *we* are with Him.

Metzger notes, "From here on the tempo of the action increases. The ultimate outcome cannot be in doubt, but there are some surprises ahead, with the suspense of the drama sustained to the conclusion. From verse 11 to the first verse of chapter 21, we have in rapid succession seven visions preparatory to the end. Each of these begins with the words, 'I saw.'"[8]

The description of the triumphant Savior is that of a king leading an army to victory. The passage itself is the final phase of the seventh bowl of judgment begun in 16:17–21, moving through the details of 17:1—18:24 and on to chapter 19. Robert Thomas observes,

> The final song of 19:1–8 celebrates the marriage of the warrior-Messiah, but this marriage cannot happen until He returns to secure victory on the battlefield (cf. Ps. 45). This agrees closely with traditional Jewish eschatology. The O.T. prophets foresaw the Lord coming in the Last Days as a man of war to dash his enemies in pieces and establish a kingdom over the nations (e.g., Is. 13:4; 31:4; 42:13; Ezek. 38—39; Joel 3; Zech. 14:3).[9]

Triumphal Return of Christ (Rev. 19:11–16)

- • *His character: faithful and true*
- • *His commission: judges and wages war*
- • *His clarity: eyes are a flame of fire*
- • *His coronation: many diadems upon His head*
- • *His code: secret name*
- • *His clothing: robe dipped in blood*
- • *His confirmation: called The Word of God*
- • *His communication: sword of His mouth*
- • *His command: rod of iron*
- • *His celebration: King of kings*

As the scene unfolds, heaven opens to reveal the Christ and to release the army of the redeemed. The description of their being clothed in bright, clean linen (v. 14) emphasizes the garments of the Bride already mentioned earlier (v. 8). In this vignette, the Bride appears as the army of the Messiah. But unlike contemporary apocalyptic dramas of that time (e.g., War Scroll of the Qumran sect), the victory is won without any military help from the faithful. This army has no weapons, no swords, no shields, and no armor. They are merely clad in the righteousness of the saints. They have not come to fight, but to watch. They have not come to assist, but to celebrate. The Messiah-King will do the fighting. He alone will win the battle by the power of His spoken word.

The *twelve-fold description* of the **coming King** combines elements of symbolism from various biblical passages and from the previous pictures of the risen Christ in the Revelation itself. Notice the details of His appearance:

1. He rides the white horse (Rev. 6:2).
2. He is called faithful and true (Rev. 3:14).
3. He judges and wages war in righteousness (2 Thess. 1:7–8).
4. His eyes are a flame of fire (Rev. 1:14).
5. He wears many diadems upon his head (Rev. 6:2).
6. His name is unknown—a wonderful secret (Judg. 13:18; Is. 9:6).
7. He is clothed in a robe dipped in blood (Is. 63:1–6).
8. His name is called The Word of God (John 1:1).
9. A sharp sword is in His mouth (Rev. 1:16; 2:16).
10. He rules with a rod of iron (Ps. 2:9, 27; Rev. 12:5).
11. He treads the wine press of the fierce wrath of God (Is. 63:1–6; Rev. 14:14–20).
12. His written name is King of kings and Lord of lords (Dan. 2:47; Rev. 17:14).

There can be no doubt that the rider on the white horse (19:11–16) is Jesus Christ. He comes as the apostle Paul predicted: ". . . in flaming fire, dealing out retribution to those who do not know God and to those who do not obey the gospel of the Lord Jesus. And these will pay the penalty of eternal destruction . . . when He comes to be glorified in His saints, and to be marveled at among all who have believed" (2 Thess. 1:7–10).

This is the true Christ (Messiah) not the usurper (Antichrist). He rides the white horse of conquest and the outcome of His victory is sure. His greatness is in the spiritual qualities of His Person: faithful, true, and righteous. His eyes of fire penetrate our sinfulness and expose our spiritual inadequacy. His "many diadems" were probably received from those of the redeemed who cast them at his feet in worship (Rev. 4:10). The fact that these diadems (crowns) are "many" totally upstages the seven crowns of the Dragon (Rev. 12:3) and the ten crowns of the beast (Rev. 13:1). His unknown name is a "secret" or "wonder." He is Jehovah God Himself—the *Yahweh* (YHVH) of the Old Testament. He is the "I AM" whose name is "above every name" (Phil. 2:9–11).

John wants us to know for certain who this is, so he calls him by his favorite name: the Word (Greek, *logos*) of God (cf. John 1:1). He is the self-disclosure of the Almighty. He is the personal revelation of God to man. He is the personal Word who is also the author of the written word. The One revealed is the ultimate revelator of the revelation: Jesus the Christ.

The Savior returns from heaven with His Bride at His side. The Church militant is now the Church triumphant. Her days of conflict, rejection, and persecution are over. She returns victorious with her Warrior-King-Husband. The German Pietist A. W. Boehm put it best when he wrote:

> There will be a time when the Church of Christ will come up from the wilderness of her crosses and afflictions, leaning upon her Beloved, and in his power bidding defiance to all her enemies. Then shall the Church . . . appear Terrible as an Army with banners; but terrible to those only that despised her while she was in her minority, and would not have her Beloved to reign over them.[10]

Every true believer who reads the prediction of Christ's triumph in Revelation 19:11–16 is overwhelmed by its significance. We are also overcome by its personal implications, for each of us will be in that heavenly army that returns with Him from glory. In fact, you might want to take a pen and circle the word *armies* in 19:14 and write your name in the margin of your Bible next to it, for *every believer* will be there when He returns!

The destiny of the true believer is now fully clarified. Our future hope includes: 1) Rapture, 2) return, 3) reign. No matter what one's eschatological viewpoint, the Church must be raptured (Greek, *harpazō*, "caught up") to heaven prior to the marriage supper and prior to her return from heaven with Christ. In the Rapture, we go up to heaven. In the return, we come back to earth. In the Millennium, we reign with Christ on the earth for a thousand years (Rev. 20:4).

The Last Battle

The chapter ends with the *final triumph of Christ* over the Antichrist, presumably at or after the Battle of Armageddon. The passage itself merely refers to the carnage as the "great supper of God" (19:17). While Armageddon is only mentioned by name in Revelation 16:16, that one reference introduces the final conflict that is called the "war of the great day of God, the Almighty" (16:14). This includes the sounding of the seventh trumpet (16:17), the great earthquake (16:18-20), and the fall of "Babylon" (17:1—19:6).

The closing verses of chapter 19 (vv. 17-21) summarize the final concluding events of the Battle of Armageddon. Notice the pattern of the Revelation is again the same: panorama followed by snapshots. First the big picture, then the details. The end of the chapter concludes all that has been happening since the first mention of Armageddon in 16:16.

The Antichrist (beast), the kings of the earth, and their combined armies are "assembled" against Christ and the Church to make war. The term *assembled* (Greek, *sunagogē*) in 19:19 is the same word used in 16:16 ("gathered together") in relation to Armageddon. Therefore, it is clear that this is still the same conflict. As we noted earlier, Armageddon may actually be a war of which this is the final battle. The carnage is so extensive that it includes kings, commanders, mighty men, cavalry, small men, and great men (19:18).

Christ returns with His Church, but not to spare His Church. He returns to spare the human race. He Himself predicted, "unless those days had been cut short, no life would have been saved" (Matt. 24:22). Now, He returns in triumph and wins the battle by the power of His spoken word (sword of "His mouth," Rev. 19:21). He but speaks and the battle is over! Just as He spoke, "Hush, be still" and the storm ceased (Mark 4:39), so the greatest conflagration in human history comes to an end—just in time. Jesus the Messiah triumphs by the divine word. He who spoke the worlds into existence, speaks and the enemy is slain. The battle is over, and Christ and His Church are at last victorious.

The chapter ends with the beast (Antichrist) and the False Prophet defeated. Both are cast alive into the lake of fire. This punishment dramatizes the seriousness of their offense and the finality of Christ's victory over them. The rest of the rebel army is slain, but they are not consigned to the lake of fire until the Great White Throne Judgment (Rev. 20:11-15). The fact that the beast and the False Prophet are cast *alive* into the lake of fire, and that they are still there in 20:10, indicates that it is a place of eternal, conscious punishment.

The two prophetic aorists (*seized* and *thrown*) predict the capture and consignment of the two superhuman enemies of Christ. In the meantime, 20:1-2 tells us that Satan will be bound in the bottomless pit for one thousand years before he, too, is cast into the lake of fire. In each case, it is Christ who sends them into the lake of fire, not Satan. Jesus alone will determine the final judgment of unbelievers, as well as that of the unholy trinity.

As dramatic and climactic as this chapter is, it only sets the stage for the Millennium and the eternal state that are to follow. The marriage of the Lamb began with the opening ceremonies in heaven. Now the King and His Bride will rule for one thousand years on earth. During this time, all of God's promised blessings to Israel will be literally fulfilled as the devastated earth again blossoms like a rose.

Study Questions

1. Read Matthew 24:29–30. What key to the prophetic significance of Revelation 19 do you find in these verses?

2. What expression of praise is used four times by the heavenly chorus (19:1, 3, 4, 6)?

3. Why is the choir praising God (19:2)?

4. What special event between Christ and the Church takes place next (19:7)?

5. What does the fine linen worn by the Bride of Christ symbolize (19:8)?

6. On what color of horse does the heavenly rider appear (19:11)?

7. By what attribute will Christ judge and wage war (19:11)?

8. In what has Christ's robe been dipped (19:13)?

9. What is the symbolic name of Christ (19:13)?

10. What weapon will Christ use to smite the nations (19:15, 21)?

11. Into what place will the beast and the False Prophet be thrown (19:20)?

CHAPTER 20

The Millennial Kingdom

Preview:

In a series of incredible events, Satan is bound for one thousand years while Christ, the Bride, and the Tribulation martyrs rule on earth. Then, in one last great surprise, Satan is loosed after the Millennium and makes one final attempt to overthrow the work of God. This time he is cast into the lake of fire. Then the lost of all time stand before Christ at the Great White Throne Judgment.

The idea of the kingdom of God on earth is central to all biblical teaching. The Old Testament prophets predicted it. Jesus announced it. And the New Testament apostles foretold it again. The psalmist said, "God is my king" (Ps. 74:12). Jeremiah said of the Lord, "He is the living God and the everlasting King" (Jer. 10:10). John the revelator refers to Jesus Christ as "King of kings and Lord of lords" (Rev. 19:16).

The concept of the *kingdom* is closely associated with that of the King. Daniel wrote, "The Most High is ruler over the realm of mankind" (Dan. 4:17). The psalmist adds, "His sovereignty [kingdom, KJV] rules over all" (Ps. 103:19). George Ladd observes, "The primary meaning of the New Testament word for *kingdom, basileia,* is 'reign' rather than 'realm' or 'people.' . . . In the general linguistic usage . . . *basileia* . . . designates first of all the existence, the character, the position of the King."[1]

There can be no true kingdom without a king. God has always chosen human representatives to mediate His kingdom on earth. The rule of God through such mediators is called a "theocratic" kingdom. Alva McClain defines such a kingdom as "the rule of God through a divinely chosen representative who speaks and acts for God."[2]

The kingdom of God has always existed and it will always exist. It is the sovereign rule of God from eternity past to eternity future. It has been mediated on earth through the dominion of man over the creation and through the divine institution of human government. In relation to the nation of Israel, the kingdom of God was to be administered by divinely appointed kings in the Davidic line (the line of the Messiah). But only with the coming of the Messiah will the hopes and dreams of a kingdom of God on earth be fully realized.

William S. LaSor states, "The messianic kingdom on earth is a vindication of God's creative activity. . . . The triumph of God over the satanic dominion of this planet is necessary for the glory of God. If there were no messianic age, if God simply picked up the redeemed remnant and took them off to heaven, then we would have to conclude that God was unable to complete what he began."[3]

The term *millennium* comes from the Latin words *mille* ("thousand") and *annus* ("year"). Thus, it refers to the thousand-year reign of Christ. John Walvoord notes, "The Greek word for millennium comes from *chilias,* meaning 'a thousand.' The Greek term is used six times in the original text of the twentieth chapter of Revelation to define the duration of Christ's kingdom on earth."[4] The kingdom of God on earth reaches its apex during the thousand-year reign of Christ.

The Messianic Age

The Old Testament prophets foretold a *golden era* of peace and prosperity when the Messiah would rule on earth. Isaiah said,

> Now it will come about that in the last days, the mountain of the house of the LORD will be established . . . and all the nations will stream to it . . . for the law will go forth from Zion, And the word of the LORD from Jerusalem. And He will judge between the nations . . . and they will hammer their swords into plowshares, and their spears into pruning hooks. Nation will not lift up sword against nation, and never again will they learn war (Is. 2:2–4).

God's promises to Israel include her earthly and spiritual blessings. This explains why the disciples asked Jesus, "Is it at this time You are restoring the kingdom to Israel?" (Acts 1:6). This question was raised after the resurrection and before the Ascension. It reveals that the Jewish disciples were still looking for the promised messianic kingdom. Little did they realize that Jesus was about to return to heaven and postpone that phase of the kingdom until the distant future.

"It is not for you to know times or epochs which the Father has fixed by His own authority," Jesus replied (Acts 1:7). He did not say there would be no future kingdom. He merely indicated that it would come later. In the meantime, He commissioned the disciples to go into all the world and preach the gospel.

During the Church Age, the kingdom of God is "in our midst" (Luke 17:21). Jesus said it does not come with "signs to be observed" (Luke 17:20). We become citizens of that kingdom by faith in Jesus Christ as our King. Thus, our citizenship is in heaven (cf. Phil. 3:20). In the meantime, we are Christ's ambassadors on earth, commissioned to proclaim the gospel to all nations.

As premillennialists, we look forward to the Rapture of the Church. We have no pretensions of thinking that we will be able to bring in the kingdom on earth by our own efforts. This has always been the position of postmillennialists in general, and it is destined to utter failure. If the Church must bring in the kingdom, we will be a long time awaiting its arrival. In fact, by all current measures, we are desperately falling behind.

Beyond the Rapture, we do look forward to the fulfillment of the messianic age. We believe the kingdom of God will come on earth when the King comes back to rule. In the meantime, we continue to declare Him as King and His gospel as the means of salvation. Jesus Himself told us to do this when He said, "And this gospel of the kingdom shall be preached in the whole world for a witness to all the nations; and then the end shall come" (Matt. 24:14).

The Binding of Satan

Revelation 20 opens with an angel descending from heaven with the key to the "abyss" (*bottomless pit*, KJV). This is likely the same angel who unlocked the pit in 9:1. He is also described as carrying a "great chain" by which he bound Satan for "a thousand years" (20:2). Then the angel casts him into the abyss and seals it shut for that duration of time.

Robert Mounce observes, "The purpose of the confinement is not punishment. It is to prevent him from deceiving the nations. The elaborate measures taken to insure his custody are most easily understood as implying the complete cessation of his influence on earth, rather than a curbing of his activities."[5] This point is crucial to one's interpretation of the binding of Satan for one thousand years. Amillennial commentators try to say this is descriptive of the present age. They hold that Satan is currently "bound" and his influence on earth is limited by the power of the gospel. In order to think this, they must view the one thousand years as figurative of the entire Church Age.

John Walvoord points out the problem with this viewpoint when he writes, "Opposed to the amillennial interpretation, however, is the uniform revelation of the New Testament which shows Satan is a very active person. If anything, he is more active than in preceding ages and is continuing an unrelenting opposition to all that God purposes to do in the present age."[6]

Walvoord cites numerous examples of *Satan's current activity*. He is:

1. The god of this world (2 Cor. 4:4)

2. Blinds the minds of the unbelieving (2 Cor. 4:3–4)

3. Prince of the power of the air (Eph. 2:2)

4. Angel of light (2 Cor. 11:14)

5. Prowls about like a roaring lion (1 Pet. 5:8)

These passages make it clear that Satan is anything but bound during the present age. All attempts to picture him otherwise seem rather ludicrous. Therefore, the binding of Satan must be a future event that has not yet occurred. Its relationship to the one thousand years indicates a literal, rather than symbolic period of time. We call this period, therefore, the Millennial Kingdom. Thomas Ice and Timothy Demy write, "Even though the Bible speaks descriptively throughout about the Millennial Kingdom, it was not until the final book—Revelation—that the length of His kingdom is revealed."[7]

While the one thousand years may be symbolic of a long time of peace and prosperity, there is nothing in the text itself to indicate that this period should not be taken literally. Otherwise, all other time indicators in the Revelation would be meaningless. Harold Hoehner says, "The denial of a literal one thousand years is not because of the exegesis of the text but a predisposition brought to the text."[8]

Ruling with Christ on Earth

Beasley-Murray writes, "The essential element of the idea of the Millennium is the appearing of the kingdom of the Messiah in history, prior to the revelation of the kingdom of God in the eternal and transcendent realm of the new creation."[9] In this regard, chapter 19 provides a transition from the fall of "Babylon" (city of man) to the arrival of the New Jerusalem (city of God).

There is no detailed description of the millennial reign here. For that we must rely on the Old Testament prophets. John focuses only on the fact that we will rule with Christ on earth—a promise he introduced earlier in 5:10: "And Thou hast made them to be a kingdom and priests to our God; and they will reign upon the earth." Thus, the idea of a literal earthly kingdom has already been introduced as a future prospect. Now it is portrayed as a present reality.

John foresees the Tribulation martyrs ruling with Christ in the Millennial Kingdom. He also sees "thrones" and those seated on them to whom judgment was given. The scene is similar to the one described by Daniel (7:9–10, 22). While it is possible that these are the thrones of the twenty-four elders, they are not specified as such (cf. Rev. 4:4; 5:8–10; 7:13; 11:15). Since Jesus promised the twelve apostles they would sit on thrones judging the twelve tribes of Israel (cf. Matt. 19:28; Luke 22:30), it seems likely that would be in view here during the earthly kingdom.

The total picture is much greater. The Bride (Church) has returned from heaven with Christ in chapter 19. Now the "Tribulation saints" (believers) are resurrected to rule with them. This is called the "first resurrection" (20:5) to distinguish it from the second resurrection in which the dead are brought to judgment after the thousand years (20:11–15).

The martyrs are described as those who "had been beheaded because of the testimony of Jesus and because of the word of God, and those who had not worshiped the beast or his image, and had not received the mark (20:4). The unsaved dead remain dead for the entire thousand years. But the martyrs are resurrected to rule with Christ during the Millennial Kingdom. This privilege is the reward for their faithfulness to Christ in the face of unprecedented persecution. During this time, the damage of the Tribulation period will be reversed, and the earth will prosper under the personal reign of Christ on the throne of David (cf. Zech. 12:10; Is. 9:6–7). Without such a rule, the return of Christ would be only a "walk among the ruins" after the Battle of Armageddon.[10]

Notice the obvious interplay between the terms *death* and *resurrection* in this chapter. The martyrs die once (physically) and are brought back at the "first resurrection" (20:5). The unsaved die twice (physically and spiritually) when they are thrown into the lake of fire at the "second death" (20:14). The pattern works out like this:

Saved	Unsaved
Born twice (physically and spiritually)	Born once (physically)
Die once (physically)	Die twice (physically and spiritually)
Live forever	Die forever

The Final Revolt

In one of the great surprises of the apocalyptic drama, Satan is loosed from the abyss after the Millennium. John the revelator provides no specific details regarding who, how, or why this occurs. He merely records, "And when the thousand years are completed, Satan will be released from his prison, and will come out to deceive the nations" (20:7–8).

Several things are apparent in this account:

1. Some nations survive the Tribulation period and live into the Millennium.

2. Children continue to be born to the people of earth during the Millennium.

3. Christ will rule during the Millennium with a rod of iron.

4. Mankind will rebel against Christ despite the blessings of the Millennium.

The final revolt is the ultimate proof of human depravity. Unredeemed minds will tolerate Christ's rule, but they will not bow their hearts to Him. As soon as Satan is loosed, they will rebel against the rule of God. Even though Edenic conditions have been restored to earth, mankind will once again fall prey to the deceiver. Beasley-Murray writes, "The full potential of human existence cannot be attained within the limitations of this world, even in the most idyllic conditions, in view of the unceasing possibilities for evil which exist within it."[11]

While some are surprised—even shocked—by this revolt, we must remember two things have not changed: *unrepentant* Satan and *unregenerate* mankind. The devil is still the deceiver, the father of lies (John 8:44). He will not cease from his destructive ways. He has not repented after one thousand years in the abyss. Therefore, God's only possible act of mercy to the rest of the world is to throw him into the lake of fire (v. 10). Notice, it is God, not Satan, who ultimately condemns people to eternal damnation (cf. 19:20; 20:9–10, 12–15).

The *final battle* involves "Gog and Magog" (20:8). It comes after the Millennium and involves many nations attacking the "camp of the saints" and the "beloved city"—presumably Jerusalem. This final act of rebellion is squelched by fire that comes down from God out of heaven. The imagery is typical of non-biblical Jewish apocalyptic writings (cf. 2 Esdras 13:1–12). The reference to Gog and Magog is similar to Ezekiel 38—39, a passage often interpreted to occur before the Millennium. Whether John's usage is identical to Ezekiel or only similar to it is a matter of debate.[12]

The idea expressed in the Revelation is that the unrepentant and unredeemed nations have been deceived into thinking they can attack Christ and the saints successfully. After one thousand years, the memory of His victory at Armageddon has faded sufficiently enough for them to even dare such an enterprise. But the greatest tragedy of all is that they will reject the Savior who has ruled in person for a thousand years. However, this should not surprise us in light of those who personally rejected Him at His first coming. They, too, said, "His blood be on us" (Matt. 27:25). The hearts of men are spiritually cold and dead apart from the regenerating power of God's Spirit. Those in the Millennium will have every chance to believe, but some will remain lost despite their opportunities to be saved.

Satan is finally cast into the lake of fire, from which there is no escape or release (v. 10). The beast and the False Prophet have already been there one thousand years, being tormented day and night. Their condition emphasizes the seriousness of the eternal punishment of the damned. They are condemned forever with no hope of escape or release. That is why consignment there is called the "second death."

Great White Throne Judgment

Next, John sees a "great white throne." This is the judgment throne, not the royal throne. Heaven (atmosphere) and earth (planet) "fled away," and "no place was found for them" (20:11). Many assume it is at this point that the earth and its atmosphere are burned up and destroyed by fire (2 Pet. 3:7–13). This will pave the way for the "new heavens" and "new earth." The earth and its atmosphere are dissolved, and the Great White Throne Judgment takes place in space in eternity.

Robert Thomas reminds us, "A closer examination of most passages that allegedly teach one final judgment shows that *future judgment* will come in several phases."[13] He lists several examples:

1. Judgment of the martyrs (Rev. 20:4–5)
2. Judgment of the nations (Matt. 25:31–46)
3. Judgment Seat of Christ (2 Cor. 5:10)
4. Great White Throne Judgment (Rev. 20:11–15)

This final judgment takes place after the Millennium. It involves all the unsaved dead of all time ("the great and the small"). This is not a judgment of believers, but of unbelievers. This judgment results in the condemnation of all who appear there.

God the Father is the Judge on this occasion. Christ has judged the believers; now the Father judges the unbelievers. Written records of the deeds of all men are kept in books (Greek, *biblia*, "scrolls"). These accounts testify against all men that they have sinned. The Bible is clear in its emphasis on human accountability: "For all have sinned and fall short of the glory of God" (Rom. 3:23). The idea of a written record of men's deeds is found elsewhere in Daniel 7:10, Isaiah 65:6, and Malachi 3:16.

These books of human deeds are only for the purpose of condemnation. They are not a basis for salvation by works. Indeed, good works cannot save anyone (cf. Eph. 2:8–10). These registers of deeds testify against our sins and us. The only hope for salvation is in another register—a list of names. It is the book of life (Greek, *biblion tes zoes*) that settles the eternal destiny of all men. Your name must be written there if you are to have any hope of heaven (cf. Rev. 3:5; 13:8; 17:8; 21:27).

The judgment of one's works also determines the degree of one's punishment. All who are condemned here are consigned to the lake of fire. No one escapes! Both death (*thanatos*) and hell (*hadēs*) are pictured as though they were the city jail, whereas the lake of fire is the penitentiary. Unsaved people go to hell when they die (Luke 16:19–24). But hell is not the end. It is only the holding place while they await final trial at the Great White Throne Judgment. Afterward, the lost are consigned to the lake of fire (Greek, *limnēn tou puros*). In fact, when the judgment is finally over, death and hell themselves are cast into the lake of fire. This is called the "second death" (v. 14).

There is no "hiding place" from God's final judgment. All the dead of all time are resurrected to stand trial before God Almighty. Even hell is turned upside down and emptied out for this great and terrible judgment. There will be no excuses, no blaming of others, no pointing the finger. Each man and woman will stand alone at the great white throne. Each will give an account of his or her own self. Each one's own record—a lifetime of sins for which there is no excuse—will condemn them.

Banishment from the presence of God will be the final result of this judgment. Consignment to the lake of fire will be forever. God has gone out of His way to give mankind every possible chance to repent, but this last act of rebellion after one thousand years of blessing will mark the end of His patience. And all who have rejected Christ as Lord will be condemned to the lake of fire.

All the greatest efforts of mankind are burned up in the end. Armageddon nearly destroyed the planet. Now this battle of Gog and Magog results in earth's final devastation. All the best efforts of the finest minds that have ever lived end in hopeless chaos without God. All is under His judgment. The Bible warns us, "It is a terrifying thing to fall into the hands of the living God" (Heb. 10:31).

Study Questions

1. Read Isaiah 35:1, 6, 10. What key to the prophetic significance of Revelation 20 do you find in these verses?

2. What two items does the angel have in his hands (20:1)?

3. How long will Satan be bound (20:2)?

4. What happens to Satan at the end of the thousand years of the Millennium (20:3)?

5. What group of believers is particularly mentioned as reigning with Christ (20:4)?

6. What is the resurrection of the martyrs called (20:5)?

7. How does Satan's final rebellion end (20:8–9)?

8. After the end of his rebellion, where is Satan condemned to stay (2:10)?

9. What is the final seat of God's judgment (20:11)?

10. Where is the second death (20:14)?

11. Who else is thrown into the lake of fire (10:15)?

SECTION VII: POSTSCRIPT

Seven New Things

Revelation 21—22

CHAPTER 21

New Jerusalem

Preview:

The Revelation now takes us on to its grand conclusion: the eternal state. We are introduced to a "new heaven" and a "new earth." Next, we see the "New Jerusalem"—the Bride of Christ. Finally, all the struggles of earth are over and the glory of God is with redeemed mankind. This is a brand new universe. It is "paradise restored!"

The final chapters of the Revelation take us to the ultimate prophetic vision: eternity. Beyond the Great Tribulation and the Millennial Kingdom lies the final reality: the eternal state. There is a powerful reminder in these chapters that this present world is not the end. There is indeed a new world coming where God dwells among men. Even the blessings of the earthly Millennium cannot compare with the glorious eternity that awaits the children of God.

The Puritan pastor Richard Baxter wrote *The Saints Everlasting Rest* in 1650, in which he expounded the text of Hebrews 4:9, "There remains therefore a Sabbath rest for the people of God." He called the promise of eternity, "the life and sum of all gospel promises and Christian privileges."[1] Yet, the material prosperity of our era has caused some believers to lose sight of our ultimate goal, which is heaven itself. In response to this unfortunate situation, Dave Hunt has written *Whatever Happened to Heaven?* in which he comments, "Unfortunately, too many persons—even dedicated Christians—find such a topic of only minor interest because they consider it to be largely irrelevant to the challenges of this present life."[2]

Joseph Stowell, the president of Moody Bible Institute in Chicago, raises a similar challenge in his book *Eternity*, in which he reminds us: "Life is most despairing when lived as though this world is all we have. . . . Inequities abound in our imperfect world. . . . The world around us tends toward unfairness, danger, and disappointment. . . . It is a world controlled by our adversary. Its intrinsic nature is temporal."[3]

This is why these concluding chapters of the Apocalypse are so important. They take our focus off everything that is temporal and place it on that which is eternal. They remind us that even the blessings of the Millennium are temporary. Those blessings fulfill God's promises to the people of Israel in a wonderful and glorious manner, but they do not compare with the eternal state. There everything will be made new (21:5).

Bruce Metzger writes:

> Whether John would have us think of the new heavens and new earth as a transformation of the existing order, or whether the present cosmos will come to an end and a new creation will replace it, is not quite clear. In any case, the word *new* used by John does not mean simply another, but a new kind of heaven and earth. The new creation will have some kind of continuity with creation as we know it, yet it will be radically different.[4]

John was not the first to see all the way down the canyon of eternity. Isaiah the prophet also foresaw new heavens and a new earth (Is. 65:17–25; 66:22–24). He even went so far as to say, "The former things shall not be remembered or come to mind" (65:17). The apostle Peter, too, spoke of "new heavens and a new earth" (2 Pet. 3:7–13). Peter said the present world is "reserved for fire, kept for the day of judgment and destruction" (3:7). He predicts a time when "the heavens will pass away with a roar and the elements will be destroyed with intense heat. . . . But according to His promise we are looking for new heavens and a new earth, in which righteousness dwells" (3:10, 13).

The New World Order

Revelation 21 introduces us to a whole new series of events. It is not, as some have suggested, the final round of the bowl judgments. Rather, we have entered the final phase of the Apocalypse—the postscript. Just as the Revelation began with a "preface," so it ends with a "postscript." All judgments are now concluded. God shall wipe away all tears from our eyes, and there shall be no more sorrow or death. Even during the blessings of the Millennium, human sufferings were not totally eliminated. But in God's new world order, they are no more.

Walter Scott observes,

The continuity of the passage with the previous chapter is self-evident. There we had the closing up of human history on earth. The unholy dead are raised, the *last* event in time, followed by the *first* recorded act of eternity—the judgment of the wicked dead. What succeeds is a new vision, in which are unfolded some of the main characteristics of the grand eternal state . . . [which] is the grand consummation, the summit of holy desire, the goal of hope in its fullest sense.[5]

Wilbur Smith emphasizes the same point when he writes, "In Revelation 21:1—22:5 we have the most extensive revelation of the eternal home of the redeemed to be found anywhere in the Scriptures, and most suitably it forms the conclusion of all the revelation of the ages recorded in our Bible. The remaining verses (22:6–21) are simply an appendix including an exhortation, warning and promise."[6]

John begins his final vision with the familiar words "and I saw" (21:1), reminding us again that the entire Revelation is a vision of future events. As such, the revelator records what he saw in the vocabulary, language, and descriptive terms of his own time. What he actually means by "streets of gold" or "gates of pearl" may be beyond our wildest imagination or expectation. But that he sees a real place is obvious. He describes it as a city (v. 2). He speaks of its inhabitants (v. 24), its gates (v. 12), its size (v. 16), its foundations (v. 14), and its walls (v. 18). He describes the eternal state as a place of great activity, worship, and service to God. He also speaks of it as our eternal home, where we shall dwell forever.

While the number seven does not appear in these chapters, it is evident that the focus is on *seven "new" things* in the eternal state:

1. New heaven (21:1)
2. New earth (21:1)
3. New Jerusalem (21:2)
4. New world order (21:5)
5. New temple (21:22)
6. New light (21:23)
7. New paradise (22:1–5)

We are immediately swept up into the grandeur of this brand-new world. It is beyond anything of mere human imagination. In these two chapters we have the most detailed account in all the Bible of what heaven will be like. Here we find the redeemed of all time living in perfect peace and harmony in a final fixed moral state in which there is no sin, no rebellion, no pain, no sorrow, no death.

The terms "new heaven" and "new earth" indicate a brand-new world is coming. *Heaven* (Greek, *ouranos*) refers to the atmospheric "heavens" (clouds, etc.), not to the dwelling place of God. It is the old planet and its atmosphere that have vanished and are replaced by a "new heaven and new earth." The heaven where God dwells is often called the "third heaven" (cf. 2 Cor. 12:2) and needs no replacement. It is the place from which the New Jerusalem descends to earth.

The New Jerusalem

The hopes and dreams of the Jewish prophets looked forward to a New Jerusalem (cf. Is. 60; Ezek. 40—48). John has already anticipated it in the promise to the overcomers at Philadelphia (3:12), showing an obvious link between the early and latter chapters of the Revelation. If we are correct in dating the Apocalypse at circa A.D 95, the old Jerusalem would already have been in ashes for about 25 years. Therefore, it should not surprise us that John anticipated the arrival of a brand-new city "coming down" from God out of the third heaven. This event is mentioned three times in the Revelation (3:12; 21:2, 10).

The New Jerusalem is referred to as "a bride adorned for her husband" (21:2). Later, the chapter (vv. 9–10) makes it clear that this is the Bride of the Lamb, who was first introduced in 19:7–10. She returned from heaven with Christ in 19:11–16 and ruled with Him during the Millennial Kingdom (20:4). Now she assumes a new and permanent position as the "holy city."

This time she is called both the "bride" (Greek, *numphēn*) and "wife" (Greek, *gunē*) of the Lamb (21:9). Yet she is also referred to as a city (Greek, *polis*). Robert Thomas comments, "The figure of a bride-city captures two characteristics of the New Jerusalem: God's personal relationship with His people (i.e., the Bride) and the life of the people in communion with Him (i.e., the city)."[7] A.T. Robertson points out that her "adornment" is from the Greek word from which we derive the term "cosmetics." The same term also applies to the adornment of the foundations of the city in 21:19–20.[8]

In anticipation of her arrival, a "loud voice" speaks from heaven announcing that the "tabernacle of God is among men" (21:3). This is a most dramatic announcement. It indicates that God is now accessible to His people. He is no longer on the distant throne of heaven. Nor is He hidden beyond the veil in the holy of holies. Rather:

- *God will dwell with us.*
- *We shall be His people.*

- *He will be our God.*
- *God will wipe away our tears.*
- *There shall be no more death.*
- *There shall be no more sorrow.*
- *There shall be no more pain.*

The summary statement declares, "the first things have passed away" (v. 4). Then God Himself, the One on the throne, said, "Behold, I am making all things new" (v. 5). This one statement summarizes what the entire postscript is all about: "new things." This is not a repair job. Nor is it a major overhaul. It is a brand-new creation. And the New Jerusalem is the apex of that creation.

In addition to telling us what will be in heaven, John also lists *seven things* that will *not* be in the eternal state:

1. Sea (21:1)

2. Death (21:4)

3. Mourning (21:4)

4. Crying (21:4)

5. Pain (21:4)

6. Curse (22:3)

7. Night (21:25)

Some have questioned the absence of the sea, but we must remember it was from the sea that the beast appeared in 13:1. Also, the absence of the sea indicates the eternal city is quite different from the natural world that now exists.

The picture painted in this chapter is that of the New Jerusalem suspended between heaven and earth. It is the final and permanent bond between the two. Notice also that the new earth, not just heaven, is a part of the final state. It would appear that the redeemed saints of God travel from heaven to earth by means of the levels of the eternal city.

The Ultimate Promise

The words "it is done" (Greek, *gegonan*) appear here for the second time in the Revelation. The first time comes after the pouring out of the seventh bowl at Armageddon (cf. 16:17). As the One who is "true and faithful" ushers in the eternal state, the seventh angel pours out his bowl. As we noted earlier, *gegonan* has the sense of finality, whereas the *tetelestai* of Jesus on the cross emphasizes, "Paid in full." The concept of finality is conveyed in all three passages, but the aspect of an atoning payment is only appropriate with Christ's remark on the cross.

There are then three great *"It is finished"* statements in all of Scripture:

1. On the cross: Atonement is paid in full (John 19:30).

2. At Armageddon: Judgment is irrevocable (Rev. 16:17).

3. At the dawn of eternity: A new world order is established (Rev. 21:6).

Alpha and Omega are the first and last letters of the Greek alphabet. The glorified Christ used this phrase in 1:11, when He first appeared to John on Patmos. It appears again in 22:12–13, where Christ promises to return. Here in 21:5–6, it is attributed to "he that sat upon the throne," which appears to be God the Father. The attribution of the title to both the Father and the Son emphasizes the deity of both as to the ascriptions of worship throughout the Revelation (cf. 4:11; 5:10–12).

The promise of God to the believers is that those who overcome (or persevere) will "inherit these things" (21:7). This is the only reference to the believer's spiritual and eternal inheritance in the Revelation. But the concept occurs frequently in other parts of the New Testament, especially in the words of Jesus and Paul (cf. Matt. 5:5; 19:29; 25:34; Rom. 4:13; 1 Cor. 6:9). "These things" refers to all that is really essential and worthwhile for eternity. It is not a promise for earthly wealth and prosperity but for heavenly and eternal blessings. Paul had the same thing in mind when he wrote, "And we know that God causes all things to work together for good to those who love God. . . . He who did not spare His own Son, but delivered Him up for us all, how will He not also with Him freely give us all things?" (Rom. 8:28, 32).

By contrast, the ungodly, unrepentant, and unbelieving multitudes, introduced by the adversative "but," will never see the New Jerusalem. They will be cast into the lake of fire, which burns with fire and brimstone and is the "second death" (21:8). There is no hope of a second chance mentioned. The *rejected* are listed in eight categories:

1. Cowardly

2. Unbelieving

3. Abominable

4. Murderers

5. Immoral persons

6. Sorcerers

7. Idolaters

8. Liars

This is not to say that those who have ever committed these sins cannot be saved, but that those who continue to do so give evidence of an unrepentant and unconverted heart.

The Holy City

One of the seven angels associated with the *bowl judgments* invites John to "come here" and carries him away "in the Spirit" to a great and high mountain (21:9–10). There he shows him the Bride, the Lamb's wife—the holy Jerusalem. This invitation opens a vision of the holy city in 21:11—22:5. What follows now is an extended and detailed explanation of what that city is like. As so many times before, John gives us the big picture first, followed by detailed snapshots.

Beasley-Murray notes that, "the Revelation as a whole may be characterized as *A Tale of Two Cities,* with the subtitle "The Harlot and the Bride.""[9] With the collapse of "Babylon," the "great harlot" (city of man), we were ushered into the Millennium where Christ ruled in the earthly Jerusalem. Now we see the ultimate antithesis: the city of God, the Bride of the Lamb in all her eternal splendor and glory.

The most dominant characteristic of the holy city is the presence of the glory (Greek, *doxa*) of God (21:11). In the Old Testament, the *Shekinah* glory rested on the Ark of the Covenant in the holy of holies, but the prophet Ezekiel tells us that the glory departed before the final destruction of Solomon's Temple (cf. Ezek. 8:4; 9:3; 10:4, 18; 11:23). While the builders of the second temple prayed for the glory to return, there is no record that it ever did (Hag. 2:3). Israel's only hope in those dark days was that the glory would return one day (Hag. 2:7–9).

For over four hundred years the temple was dark and empty. It stood as a gaunt symbol of Israel's empty ritual. No glory. No God. No power. It was not until Christ was born and the angels appeared and the "glory of the Lord shone around them" that the glory returned (cf. Luke 2:9–14). The angels announced the birth of the Savior, Christ the Lord, and sang "Glory to God in the highest." In the person of Jesus Christ, the glory had finally returned. However, Israel officially rejected the Messiah, and the glory was made available to Gentiles who by faith received the Savior and became the temples of the Holy Spirit (cf. 1 Cor. 6:19–20). In the meantime, Jerusalem was destroyed, and the second temple with it, by the Romans in A.D. 70. Even an attempt to rebuild a third temple during the Tribulation period will not bring back the glory in itself.

The glory of God will, however, be in full expression in the New Jerusalem. The "glory" symbolizes God's presence with His people. The fact that He is there is far more significant than the dazzling description of the city itself.

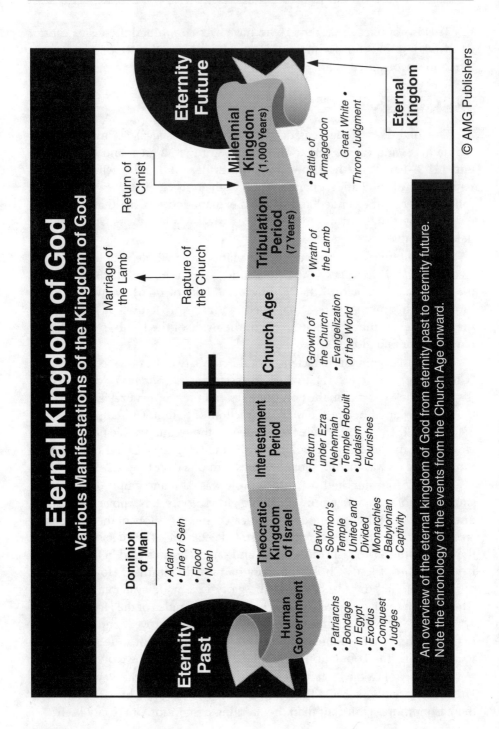

Eternal Kingdom of God
Various Manifestations of the Kingdom of God

Eternity Past

Eternity Future

Dominion of Man
- Adam
- Line of Seth
- Flood
- Noah

Human Government
- Patriarchs
- Bondage in Egypt
- Exodus
- Conquest
- Judges

Theocratic Kingdom of Israel
- David
- Solomon's Temple
- United and Divided Monarchies
- Babylonian Captivity

Intertestament Period
- Return under Ezra
- Nehemiah
- Temple Rebuilt
- Judaism Flourishes

Church Age
- Growth of the Church
- Evangelization of the World

Tribulation Period (7 Years)
- Wrath of the Lamb

Millennial Kingdom (1,000 Years)
- Battle of Armageddon
- Great White Throne Judgment

Eternal Kingdom

Rapture of the Church

Marriage of the Lamb

Return of Christ

An overview of the eternal kingdom of God from eternity past to eternity future. Note the chronology of the events from the Church Age onward.

The *description of the city* by the revelator is as follows:

1. *Splendor:* as a stone of crystal-clear jasper (v. 11)

2. *Wall:* seventy-two yards high (v. 17)

3. *Gates:* giant pearls named for the twelve tribes of Israel (vv. 12, 21)

4. *Measurement:* 1,500-mile cube (v. 16)

5. *City itself:* pure gold, like clear glass (v. 18)

6. *Street:* pure gold, like transparent glass (v. 21)

7. *Temple:* God and the Lamb are its temple (v. 22)

8. *Light:* glory of God and the Lamb (v. 23)

9. *Nations:* those who are saved (v. 24)

10. *Access:* gates shall never be closed (v. 25)

11. *Activity:* no night there (v. 25)

12. *Purity:* no one who practices abomination and lying (v. 27)

A great deal has been written about whether this language is literal or symbolic or phenomenological. In truth, it combines all these elements. The whole book is filled with symbolic language; therefore, we cannot overlook certain obvious symbols here: twelve gates, twelve foundations, foursquare. It is also obvious that John is attempting to describe the indescribable. Human language, though inspired, is not fully adequate to describe the glories of the heavenly city. Thus, we read of "transparent gold" and "gates of pearl."

What is clear is that John is describing a real place where the saved, and only the saved, will dwell with God forever. The unsaved are excluded from this city totally and completely. Satan and those he has deceived are all in the lake of fire, from which there is no escape. The reference to "nations" and "kings" should not surprise us. Jesus promised that the gospel would be preached unto all nations (Matt. 24:14). John has earlier introduced us to those in heaven as "a great multitude . . . from every nation" (Rev. 7:9). He has already referred to believers as "a kingdom and priests" who reign with Christ (Rev. 5:10).

The bottom line is emphasized again in the last verse of the chapter (21:27). Only those whose names are written in the Lamb's book of life can live in the holy city. This includes all the redeemed of all time: Old Testament saints, the New Testament church, Tribulation saints, and millennial saints. Thus, we see the perfect blending of the redeemed in the holy city in that the twelve gates are named for the twelve tribes of Israel and the twelve foundations for the twelve apostles.

Of the final eternal state, Bernard Ramm wrote:

The curtain of Revelation drops with the final vision of glorification. The glorified shall reign forever and ever. It is a *reign!* That is, it is a condition of complete glorification. It is a condition of perfect sharing in the wonder of God. And it is *eternal*. It will last forever and ever. And thus, the vision ends with the redeemed in a state of eternal glory reigning with God and the Lamb.[10]

Study Questions

1. Read Isaiah 65:17–18. What key to the prophetic significance of Revelation 21 do you find in these verses?

2. What happened to first heaven and the first earth (21:1)?

3. What is the name of the holy city (21:2)?

4. How is the city adorned (21:2)?

5. Where is the tabernacle of God (21:3)?

6. How does the Alpha and Omega finalize His promise (21:6)?

7. What other name is given to the Bride (21:9)?

8. What is the real splendor of the holy city (21:11)?

9. Who are the twelve foundations named for (21:14)?

10. Why is there no temple in the holy city (21:22)?

CHAPTER 22

Paradise Restored

Preview:
The book of Revelation ends with a beautiful picture of paradise "restored." The tree of life is once again accessible to mankind. When the entire unveiling of future events was completed, John was told not to seal the prophecy, but to leave it open for all to read. In the meantime, the Revelation closes with an invitation to come to Christ before it is too late.

The aged seer comes now to the final vision of the Apocalypse. The words "and he showed me" indicate one final glimpse of something previously unobserved by any man. There in the center of the New Jerusalem, John the revelator sees the river of life flowing from the throne of God and the Lamb. It is the source of all life that emanates from God. Then he sees something that has been missing from the Bible since Genesis 3: the tree of life!

In the Genesis record, Moses tells us that all was lost in the Garden of Eden when Adam and Eve sinned. They were banished from the tree of life. Death stalked their heels until they succumbed to the grim reaper. From the very moment they sinned, they began to die—physically and spiritually. Walter Scott writes, "Thus Moses and John bridge sixteen centuries, and clasp hands in one united testimony to the truth of Holy Scripture."[1]

Now, in the final chapter of the Revelation, we learn that all that was lost in the beginning will finally be regained. Paradise is restored in the holy city. The biblical story, which began in the garden, ends in the eternal city. In between, there stands the cross of Jesus Christ. It alone has changed the destiny of mankind from death to life.

As in chapters 4—5, God and the Lamb are equal in deity, honor, and power. In 22:1, they share the eternal throne. This is no mere coincidence. Nor is it a casual reference. John's final vision again makes it clear that Jesus Christ is God. To effectively deny the deity of Christ, one would have to rip the book of Revelation from the Bible and throw it away. Even the angel's admonishment to "worship God" (v. 9) is intended to elevate the worship of Christ above that of angels. He is not just a great man. Nor is He the angel of angels. He is Lord of lords. He is God!

Return to Eden

The passage before us clearly indicates that the eternal state will return the new creation to the inherent qualities of the Garden of Eden—only on a grander scale. Then, and only then, will the Creator's true intention for humanity finally be realized. Thomas writes, "Unlimited access to this life-giving water will assure the residents of the new Jerusalem of an everlasting enjoyment of life."[2]

The *river of life* is reminiscent of the river of Eden whose tributaries flowed in four directions (Gen. 2:10, 14). The metaphoric use of a river of spiritual refreshment can be found throughout the Old Testament (Ps. 36:9; Prov. 10:11; 13:14; Is. 12:3; Jer. 2:13; 17:13; Ezek. 47:9; Zech. 14:8). The beautiful picture that is painted by the words of this prophecy remind us that the best of the natural world will be preserved in the eternal world.

The *tree of life* is presented in Genesis 2:9 as a single tree. In Ezekiel's millennial vision, he sees several trees on both sides of the great river (Ezek. 47:12). But the Revelation record reconnects us with the Genesis record. In both accounts, this tree is a singular tree. Here in 22:2 it bears twelve types of fruit—one for each month of the year. Thus, it is perpetually in bloom. There is no winter season in the eternal state.

The reference to using the leaves for "healing" (Greek, *therapeian*) derives from the term *therapeutic*. Walvoord notes that the root meaning of the term conveys the idea of "health-giving."[3] There is no need of healing from sickness or disease since the consequences of sin have been removed and the "first things have passed away" (21:4). Thus, the tree and its leaves are seen as a source of life and health in the eternal state.

The ultimate proof that this indeed is a return to Edenic conditions is the removal of the *divine curse* (22:3). This curse was first pronounced against the participants in the initial act of rebellion in Genesis 3:14–19. The actual objects of the curse were Satan and the earth ("ground") itself. But the implications of the curse affected all involved:

1. *Serpent*—cursed above all animals

2. *Woman*—sorrow and pain in childbirth

3. *Man*—"cursed is the ground because of you"

The Old Testament record of man's rebellion against God begins and ends with a curse. The sin of Adam and Eve is cursed and its consequences are severe (Gen. 3:14–19). Even in the Law of Moses, there is the threat of the curse for those who break the law (Deut. 27:13–26). In the very last book of the prophets, the Old Testament ends with the threat of a curse: "lest I come and smite the land with a curse" (Mal. 4:6).

The Old Testament begins so well ("in the beginning God") and ends so badly ("with a curse"). It starts with all the glorious potential of the divine creation and ends with the threat of divine judgment. It opens in paradise and closes with mankind lost in sin's condemnation. How different the New Testament! It opens with Jesus Christ (Matt. 1:1), and it closes with Jesus Christ (Rev. 22:22). It begins with His first coming and concludes with His second coming.

God Is There!

The removal of the divine curse makes access to God a reality in the new paradise. We are no longer barred from His presence. The throne of God has come to earth and is the central feature of the eternal city. It is the throne of God and the Lamb, who rule jointly over the eternal state. We who believe in Jesus Christ know that He and the Father are One. We believe in Him even though we have never seen Him. But in the eternal city, faith shall become sight—We "shall see His face" (22:4).

The God who has always been there for us shall be there in person. To "see His face" is an ancient idiom meaning we will be granted an audience with the King of kings on a regular basis.[4] His name will be associated with His servants, indicating our close personal relationship to the God of the universe. The biblical view of God's relationship to man is that of a loving Father tenderly caring for His children. It is never the idea of a distant deity of an impersonal nature.

Because of God's presence (v. 5), three things will *not* be found in the new paradise:

1. No night
2. No lamp
3. No sun

The Lord God is all the light the redeemed will ever need. He will outshine all other light sources because He is the Source of light. Remember, in His first account of Creation, He said, "Let there be light" (Gen. 1:3). In eternity, He Himself will be the light. And His servants shall "reign forever and ever" (22:5).

Do not imagine heaven to be a place of inactivity or lazy self-indulgence. We who are even now positionally seated with Christ in "heavenly places" are destined for the throne as joint-heirs with Him (cf. Eph. 1:3, 20; 2:6).

Beasley-Murray writes, "Here is the ultimate reach of the bliss of God's people in the city which descends from heaven: participation in the sovereignty of God and the Lamb, not alone for the duration of the kingdom on earth but in the eternal kingdom of the new creation."[5] The apostle Paul expressed this same idea when he said, "Then comes the end, when He delivers up the kingdom to the God and Father" (1 Cor. 15:24). Thus, the Millennial Kingdom will be merged into the eternal kingdom after the thousand years.

The Final Testimony

The concept of "witness" or "testimony" (Greek, *marturia*) is central to John's writings. The combination "faithful and true" appears four times in the Revelation (3:14; 19:11; 21:5; 22:6). The first speaker here is clearly the angel, whom John inappropriately attempts to worship in verse 8. His testimony is meant to affirm that the whole of the entire revelation of the End Times is true. John adds his testimony in verse 8: "I, John, am the one who heard and saw these things." Then, Jesus speaks in verse 16, affirming, "I, Jesus, have sent My angel to testify to you these things for the churches."

The *threefold "witness"* of the angel, John, and Jesus is intended to assure the reader of the validity and authenticity of the prophecy of the Revelation. It is this assurance that will be necessary to encourage future believers to hold true to their testimonies (Greek, *marturia*) as well, even if it means being martyred for one's faith. Thus, martyrdom is the ultimate testimony, sealed by one's own life.

John is so overwhelmed by his blitz through the future that he falls down at the feet of the angel to worship him (v. 8). But the angel clearly tells him, "Do not do that." Worship of angels is strictly forbidden. True worship is expressed in the two words "Worship God!" He alone is worthy of our worship (cf. chaps. 4—5).

The book closes in an epilogue (vv. 6–21) with a rapid succession of voices, instructions, statements, and promises. Three times the promise is declared: "I am coming quickly" (vv. 7, 12, 20). The term *quickly* means "soon" or "suddenly." It points to the imminent return of Christ. There is no doubt, regardless of one's eschatological view, that the reader of the Revelation is left on the edge of his seat awaiting the coming of Christ at any moment.

Jesus is the speaker of this promise on all three occasions. After the first promise, He adds the sixth beatitude ("blessed") of the seven in the Revelation (cf. 1:3; 14:13; 16:15; 19:9; 20:6; 22:7, 14). Like so many phrases in this final section, it reconnects us to the first beatitude found in 1:3. Thomas observes, "The . . . correspondences of the Epilogue to the book's Prologue demonstrate cohesion and rationality of thought that make this work a superior literary production."[6] This is not the work of some wild-eyed fanatic. Nor is it the babblings of some incoherent idiot. The Revelation is the finest apocalyptic literature ever written. It is purely inspired genius from start to finish.

The *parallels* between the first and last chapters of the Revelation are numerous:

1. A genuine prophecy (1:3; 22:6–10)
2. Addressed to God's bond-servants (1:1; 22:6)
3. To be read in the churches (1:11; 22:16–18)
4. Comes from God (1:1; 22:6)
5. Comes also from Jesus Christ (1:1; 22:16)
6. An angel speaks to John (1:1; 22:6)
7. John is a genuine prophet (1:9–11; 22:8–10)
8. Promises a blessing to all who obey it (1:3; 22:7)
9. Warns of judgment to those who reject it (1:7; 22:11)
10. Focuses on Christ (1:2; 22:16–20)
11. The Alpha and the Omega (1:8, 17; 22:13)
12. Christ is coming soon (1:3, 7; 22:7–12)

The signature of divine inspiration is everywhere in this book. From its symbolic numbers to its symbolic titles, it is a masterpiece of biblical literature. It interconnects Old and New Testament truths with prophetic events and provides a picture of the future with God fully in control. More than anything else, the Revelation uplifts Jesus Christ as the divine Son of God—co-ruler with the Father. Its hymns of praise raise us to the heights of worship. Its vision of the future is frightening. But its promises of the coming King assure us that all will be well in the end.

John is told, "Do not seal up the words of the prophecy of this book" (22:10). This is the opposite of the instruction given to Daniel six hundred years earlier. Daniel was told that his prophecy was "concealed and sealed up until the end time" (Dan. 12:9). By contrast, John is told to leave the Revelation unsealed for the "time is near." Since Christ has already opened the seven seals (chaps. 5—6) to reveal the future to John, it is only appropriate that the entire book remain unsealed for us to read as well.

Jesus again assures, "Behold, I am coming quickly" (v. 12) and emphasizes again that He is the "the Alpha and the Omega" (v. 13). Included is the reminder that at His coming those who do His commandments will be blessed with eternal life (v. 14), but those who reject Him will be excluded from His future blessings.

The Final Appeal

Jesus Himself testifies (Greek, *marturēsai*, "to bear witness") of the validity of this prophecy. The words *I, Jesus* appear nowhere else in the Bible. Therefore, they grab our attention and focus our sight on the divine speaker. He refers to Himself as the "offspring of David," emphasizing His relationship to Israel as their promised Messiah. He also calls Himself the "bright morning star" (cf. Num. 24:17). We call the star referred to by this Greek word, Venus. It is the one that is the brightest and outshines all others. In biblical terminology the star symbolizes the coming Savior. Both of these titles emphasize the fact that Jesus is the Messiah. He is the One who fulfills all the hopes and dreams of the prophets. He is both the "root" of David (5:5) and the "offspring" of David (22:16). In Him the line of Messiah has both its origin and its completion.

Jesus also emphasizes, "these things" (the prophecies of this book) are "for the churches" (v. 16). Thus, the Revelation begins and ends with the Church in mind. John addressed the book "to the seven churches" (1:4). Jesus first appeared among the seven golden candlesticks, which represented the seven churches (1:12–20). He instructed John to record what he saw and send it to the "seven churches" (1:11). Then He took all of chapters 2 and 3 to speak specifically to each of those churches.

The Church is the Bride of Christ. She is designated a special place at His side. The Bible reminds us that Christ "loved the church and gave Himself up for her" (Eph. 5:25). Therefore, we should not be surprised to see this emphasis on the significance of the Church in the closing verses of the Revelation. The fact that she participates in the final invitation (v. 17) reminds us that the church today should be a place where Jesus Christ is worshiped, where the gospel is preached, and where the appeal is made for people to come to Christ as Lord and Savior.

The *final appeal* is threefold: Spirit, Bride, and the one who wishes. The "Spirit" is the Holy Spirit who convicts us of sin, righteousness, and judgment (John 16:8–11). The "Bride" is the Church who publicly issues the invitation of the gospel. The "one who hears" is the same as the "one who wishes," and refers to anyone who is thirsty for a relationship with God. All three say, "Come." The appeal to the reader is to come to Christ before it is too late.

A *final warning* not to add or subtract from the words of this prophecy follows the appeal. Not only does this apply to tampering with the text itself, but it also ought to remind every commentator not to make the book say more or less than it actually says. It has always been a temptation for every generation to read its own current events ("newspaper exegesis") into the text of the Revelation.

New Testament scholar Bruce Metzger observes, "When books were copied by hand, scribes would occasionally add comments of their own or leave out words they thought were unsuitable. John therefore includes at the end of his book a solemn warning declaring that nothing should be added or deleted, for the very good reason that it is a revelation from God (22:18–19)."[7]

The *last words* of Jesus recorded in the Bible are, "Yes, I am coming quickly" (v. 20). Leon Morris observes, "Again we have the thought of testimony, an important concept in this book and in the Johannine writings generally. The witness here is plainly the Lord Jesus."[8] Here at the very end of the Bible, Jesus speaks to us one more time to remind us that He is coming soon. He has repeated this remark three times in this chapter (vv. 7, 12, 20). Each time the reader is left expecting the imminent return of the Savior. Therefore, each generation of Christians must live their lives as though Jesus could come at any moment—and one day He will!

John adds His own "Amen. Come, Lord Jesus" (v. 20). *Amen* is the "truly" (*verily*, KJV) of the Gospels. It means, "so be it." It actually transliterates the Hebrew original in both Greek and English. By saying "Amen," we are confirming or agreeing with what has been said. In this case, John adds his agreement to the promise of Christ's return and adds his own invitation to those already expressed. The words *Come, Lord* (Greek, *erchou kurie*) are the Greek equivalent of the Aramaic *maranatha* ("the Lord comes"), which became the favorite expression of the early church (see 1 Cor. 16:22).

The Revelation ends like an epistle (letter) with a benediction of grace: "The grace of the Lord Jesus be with all" (v. 21). This ending is most appropriate because the prophecy was to be read in the churches. Thus, its practical appeal and personal application are emphasized in the reminder that it is by the grace of God that we can face the uncertain times of the future. We have the confidence that the grace that saved us shall sustain us and take us home to glory.

Throughout the New Testament, the gospel of God's grace is the central teaching of the Christian message. John opens the Revelation (1:4) with *grace* and now he closes it (22:21) with *grace*.

In the Revelation, as in the Gospels, grace has the first and last words. It is the expression of God's love that draws us to the Savior and keeps us at His side. It has been said, "As in the Revelation, so in history—grace shall have the last word!"[9] To which I would add, "And grace shall see us through!"

MARANATHA!

Study Questions

1. Read Matthew 24:42, 44. What key to the prophetic significance of Revelation 22 do you find in these verses?

2. What river did John see coming from the throne (22:1)?

3. What is seen on the side of the river that has not been seen since Genesis 3 (22:2)?

4. What was enacted in Eden, but is removed in the eternal city (22:3)?

5. What does it mean that we "shall see His face" (22:4)?

6. What will we be doing for all eternity (22:5)?

7. What does Jesus say about His coming (22:7, 12, 20)?

8. Who are we to worship (22:9)?

9. List the two "beatitudes" found in this chapter of Revelation (22:7, 14)?

10. Who calls for the unsaved to come to Christ (22:17)?

11. What judgments are promised to those who add or take away words from the book of Revelation (22:18–19)?

Bibliography

Beasley-Murray, G.R. *The Book of Revelation* (New Century Bible). London: Marshall, Morgan & Scott, 1978.

Cohen, Gary. *Understanding Revelation*. Chicago: Moody Press, 1968.

Coleman, Robert. *Songs of Heaven*. Old Tappan, NJ: Fleming H. Revell, 1980.

Hindson, Ed. *Final Signs*. Eugene, OR: Harvest House, 1996.

Hocking, David. *The Coming World Leader*. Portland, OR: Multnomah Press, 1988.

Jeremiah, David. *Escape the Coming Night*. Dallas: Word Publishing, 1990.

LaHaye, Tim. *Revelation Illustrated and Made Plain*. Grand Rapids: Zondervan, 1975.

Metzger, Bruce. *Breaking the Code: Understanding the Book of Revelation*. Nashville: Abingdon Press, 1993.

Michaels, J. Ramsey. *Interpreting the Book of Revelation*. Grand Rapids: Baker Book House, 1992.

Morris, Leon. *The Revelation of St. John* (Tyndale Commentaries). Grand Rapids: Eerdmans, 1969.

Mounce, Robert. *The Book of Revelation* (New International Commentary). Grand Rapids: Eerdmans, 1977.

Pentecost, J. Dwight. *Things to Come*. Grand Rapids: Zondervan, 1958.

Scott, Walter. *Exposition of the Revelation of Jesus Christ*. Grand Rapids: Kregel, 1982 reprint of 1920 edition.

Seiss, Joseph. *The Apocalypse*. Grand Rapids: Zondervan, 1957.

Stott, John. *What Christ Thinks of the Church*. London: Harold Shaw, 1990.

Tenney, Merrill. *Interpreting Revelation*. Grand Rapids: Eerdmans, 1957.

Thomas, Robert. *Revelation 1—7 and 8—22: An Exegetical Commentary*. 2 vols. Chicago: Moody Press, 1992.

Walvoord, John. *The Revelation of Jesus Christ*. Chicago: Moody Press, 1966.

Notes

Introduction: Keys to Unlocking the Future

1. Bruce Metzger, *Breaking the Code: Understanding the Book of Revelation* (Nashville: Abingdon Press, 1993), 12–13.

2. See detailed discussion in Robert L. Thomas, *Revelation 1—7: An Exegetical Commentary* (Chicago: Moody Press, 1992), 40–42. Cf. also W. Graham Scroggie, *The Unfolding Drama of Redemption* (Grand Rapids: Kregel, 1994 reprint), III: 365–70.

3. Scroggie, *The Unfolding Drama*, 357.

4. For details, see Thomas, *Revelation 1—7*, 11–17.

5. For details, see Donald Guthrie, *New Testament Introduction* (Downers Grove, IL: InterVarsity Press, 1990), 939.

6. Metzger, *Breaking the Code*, 16. He notes, for example, that Laodicea was destroyed by an earthquake in A.D. 61, but is described in Revelation as wealthy and prosperous. The Church at Smyrna is described as having suffered persecution for a long time, hardly applicable for the sixties.

7. Scroggie, *The Unfolding Drama*, 363, follows Benjamin Warfield's analysis of the structure of the seven visions.

8. David Jeremiah, *Escape the Coming Night* (Dallas: Word Publishing, 1990), 10.

9. Merrill Tenney, *Interpreting Revelation* (Grand Rapids: Eerdmans, 1957), 28.

10. David Hocking, *The Coming World Leader* (Portland, OR: Multnomah Press, 1988), 21.

11. Thomas, *Revelation 1—7*, 54–56. Attempts to argue for a "soon" return of Christ in the destruction of Jerusalem in A.D. 70 by preterists are woefully inadequate. Cf. Wayne House and Thomas Ice, *Dominion Theology: Blessing or Curse?* (Portland, OR: Multnomah Press, 1988).

12. Cf. Edward E. Hindson, *Isaiah's Immanuel* (Philadelphia: Presbyterian and Reformed, 1978), 33–45. "Shall conceive" (Hebrew, *harah*, should be translated "is pregnant"). Hindson follows Edward Young and Joseph Alexander in suggesting that the term is neither a verb nor a participle, but a feminine adjective connected with an active participle ("bearing") and denotes that the scene is present to the prophet's view. There can be no doubt this is a prediction of the virgin birth of Christ. Thus it is that the virgin is pregnant and is still a virgin!

13. See J.M. Cascione, *In Search of the Biblical Order* (Cleveland: Biblion Publishing, 1987), 1–182. Cf. also, "The Kai Structure," in *God's Word to the Nations* (Cleveland: NET Publishing, 1988), 565–67.

14. Translations are taken from *God's Word to the Nations*. There are scores of these *kaimeter* patterns laid out clearly in this unique translation.

15. For a detailed list of "25 Major Prophecies of the End Times," see Ed Hindson, *Final Signs* (Eugene, OR: Harvest House, 1996), appendix, 197–214.

16. Thomas, *Revelation 1—7*, 32.

17. Scroggie, *The Unfolding Drama*, III, 412.

Chapter 1—What in the World Is Happening?

1. See the excellent study published in Greece by Otto Meinardus, *St. John of Patmos* (Athens: Lycabettus Press, 1974), 1–22. Cf. also Emil Kraeling, *The Disciples* (Chicago: Rand McNally, 1966), 128–55; "John the Apostle," in Walter Elwell, vol. 2 of *Baker Encyclopedia of the Bible* (Grand Rapids: Baker Book House, 1988), 1189–1200.

2. Preterists have often used these terms to argue in favor of the idea that the Revelator believed Christ was coming very soon; therefore, they propose both an early date for the book (circa A.D. 60) and see the fulfillment in the destruction of Jerusalem (A.D. 70). However, the Revelation itself does not predict the fall of Jerusalem (a fact that had already occurred), but the fall of "Babylon" (Rome—city on seven hills) and the arrival of the New Jerusalem as the bride of Christ. See Thomas Ice, "Back to the Future: Keeping the Future in the Future," in Thomas Ice and Timothy Demy, eds., *When the Trumpet Sounds* (Eugene, OR: Harvest House, 1995), 11–24.

3. Some have argued against the authorship of Revelation by John the apostle on the basis that he is named three times in the Apocalypse, since his actual name does not appear in his Gospel or his three epistles. However, most critics who reject his authorship of Revelation also reject his authorship of the other works as well, so the argument is mute. The fact that John had been exiled to a deserted island easily explains why he wanted his readers to know that he had indeed written it. Besides, this was the only prophetic book in the New Testament, and Old Testament prophets always identified themselves in their books. Cf. Robert Thomas, *Revelation 1—7: An Exegetical Commentary* (Chicago: Moody Press, 1992), 1–16.

4. Bruce Metzger, *Breaking the Code: Understanding the Book of Revelation* (Nashville: Abingdon, 1993), 23. Metzger is one of the world's prominent Greek scholars. His simple, but insightful treatment of the Revelation is a delight to read. He views the book as "pastoral encouragement for Christians who were confronted with persecution and cruelty" (106).

5. Thomas, *Revelation 1—7*, 90. Cf. also R.C.H. Lenski, *The Interpretation of St. John's Revelation* (Columbus: Lutheran Books, 1935), 58.

6. David Hocking, *The Coming World Leader* (Portland, OR: Multnomah Press, 1988), 35. He emphasizes the Lord's qualities of majesty, purity, authority, and centrality.

Chapter 2—Judgment Begins at the House of God!

1. Edward Myers, *Letters From the Lord of Heaven* (Joplin, MO: College Press, 1996). I have borrowed Myers' clever arrangement of these letters in his own translation. This arrangement makes each letter more personal and more specific.

2. William Ramsay, *The Letters to the Seven Churches of Asia* (New York: Armstrong,

1904), 191–92. The British archaeologist personally traveled this region in the nineteenth century and was the first to make this observation. He referred to the Roman highway as "the great circular road that bound together the most populous, wealthy and influential part of the Province."

3. C.I. Scofield, *Scofield Reference Bible* (New York: Oxford University Press, 1909). Scofield listed the seven churches as prophetic. His scheme was: Ephesus (Apostolic Age, 30–100), Smyrna (Persecuted Church, 100–300), Pergamum (Roman Church, 300–1200), Thyatira (Medieval Church, 1200–1500), Sardis (Reformation Church, 1500–1700), Philadelphia (Missionary Church, 1700–1900), Laodicea (Apostate Church, 1900–?). There have been many such identifications attempted since medieval times. One of the most popular among the Puritans was Thomas Brightman's *Revelation of the Revelation*, published in 1609. He listed the seven: Ephesus (Apostles to Constantine), Smyrna (Constantine to Gratian), Pergamum (381–1300), Thyatira (1300–1520), Sardis (German Reformation), Philadelphia (Genevan Reformation), Laodicea (Church of England). For other examples, see Ed Hindson, *End Times and the New World Order* (Wheaton, IL: Victor Books, 1991), 65–85.

4. Otto Meinardus, *St. John of Patmos* (Athens: Lycabettus Press, 1974), 1–12. Published in Greece, this is an excellent source on the seven churches.

5. See F.F. Bruce, *Paul: Apostle of the Heart Set Free* (Grand Rapids: Eerdmans, 1977), 475.

6. Meinardus, *St. John of Patmos*, 65–67. Cf. also John Stott, *What Christ Thinks of the Church* (London: Harold Shaw, 1990), 32–33.

7. Ibid., 62.

8. Ibid., 68–69.

9. Myers, *Letters*, 33–34.

10. Cf. Jacques Ellul, *The Subversion of Christianity* (Grand Rapids: Eerdmans, 1986), 113–36; Charles Colson, *Kingdoms in Conflict* (Grand Rapids: Zondervan, 1987), 265–66; Ed Dobson and Ed Hindson, *The Seduction of Power* (Old Tappan, NJ: Revell, 1988).

11. See details in John Stott, *What Christ Thinks*, 42.

12. Ibid., 53. Stott's treatment of Pergamum and photos of its remains are excellent.

13. Myers, *Letters*, 46.

14. Cf. Meinardus, *St. John of Patmos*, 92–94.

15. Robert L. Thomas, *Revelation 1—7: An Exegetical Commentary* (Chicago: Moody Press, 1992), 208.

Chapter 3—Who's That Knocking at My Door?

1. Bruce Metzger, *Breaking the Code: Understanding the Book of Revelation* (Nashville: Abingdon Press, 1993), 29. Metzger also observes: "There is no evidence that these portions of Chapters 2 and 3 originated as separate documents. All Greek manuscripts of the book of Revelation incorporate all of them and none of the seven exists by itself."

2. Ibid., 39.

3. Cf. the discussion in Robert L. Thomas, *Revelation 1—7: An Exegetical Commentary* (Chicago: Moody Press, 1992), 259–67. He quotes Swete, Alford Lenski, and Leon Morris in support of this approach.

4. John Stott, *What Christ Thinks of the Church* (London: Harold Shaw, 1990), 84.

5. Metzger, *Breaking the Code*, 41.

6. Stott, *What Christ Thinks*, 104.

7. For a detailed discussion of the Greek usage of the phrase "kept from the hour of trial," see Robert L. Thomas, *Revelation 1—7*, 283–90.

8. Cf. discussion in Ed Hindson, *End Times and the New World Order* (Wheaton, IL: Victor Books, 1991), 79–85.

9. Edward Myers, *Letters From the Lord of Heaven* (Joplin, MO: College Press, 1996), 76.

10. See details in Otto Meinardus, *St. John of Patmos* (Athens: Lycabethus Press, 1974), 126–29.

11. Stott, *What Christ Thinks*, 114.

12. Metzger, *Breaking the Code*, 46.

13. J. Ramsey Michaels, *Interpreting the Book of Revelation* (Grand Rapids: Baker, 1992), 39–40.

Chapter 4—God Is Still on the Throne

1. G.R. Beasley-Murray, *The Book of Revelation* (London: Marshall, Morgan & Scott, 1978), 108. This excellent commentary combines academic scholarship with spiritual insight in a very effective manner.

2. Ibid., 108.

3. Robert Thomas, *Revelation 1—7: An Exegetical Commentary* (Chicago: Moody Press, 1992), 333.

4. John Walvoord, *The Revelation of Jesus Christ* (Chicago: Moody Press, 1966), 101.

5. Cf. Rudolf Bultmann, vol. 2 of *Theology of the New Testament* (London: SCM Press, 1955), 175; C.H. Dodd, *The Apostolic Preaching and Its Development* (London: SCM Press, 1944), 40.

6. Beasley-Murray, *The Book of Revelation*, 23–25. He notes the inseparability of the Christology from the eschatology of the Revelation.

7. See Bruce Metzger, *Breaking the Code: Understanding the Book of Revelation* (Nashville: Abingdon Press, 1993), 47.

8. Charles Feinberg, "Revelation," in E. Hindson and W. Kroll, eds., *Parallel Bible Commentary* (Nashville: Thomas Nelson, 1982), 2868.

9. Ibid., 2268–69.

10. David Jeremiah, *Escape the Coming Night* (Dallas: Word Publishing, 1990), 87–88.

11. G.B. Caird, *The Revelation of St. John the Divine* (New York: Harper & Row, 1966), 63.

12. Robert Coleman, *Songs of Heaven* (Old Tappan, NJ: Fleming H. Revell, 1980), 29–37. This is the finest work ever done on the songs of the Revelation.

Chapter 5—Worthy Is the Lamb!

1. Walter Scott, *Exposition of the Revelation of Jesus Christ* (Grand Rapids: Kregel, 1962), 135. Scott's commentary on the Revelation is the most worshipful and majestic ever written. No one else does justice to chapter 5 like he does.

2. Robert Thomas, *Revelation 1—7: An Exegetical Commentary* (Chicago: Moody Press, 1992), 374.

3. Bruce Metzger, *Breaking the Code: Understanding the Book of Revelation* (Nashville: Abingdon, 1993), 52.

4. Scott, *Exposition*, 137.

5. David Jeremiah, *Escape the Coming Night* (Dallas: Word Publishing, 1990), 91.

6. Robert Coleman, *Songs of Heaven* (Old Tappan, NJ: Fleming H. Revell, 1980).

7. Ibid., 47. He points out that the word *new* (Greek, *kainen*) here is the same word used for "New Testament," "new creation," "new heaven," "new earth," and "New Jerusalem."

8. See David Jeremiah, *What the Bible Says About Angels* (Sisters, OR: Multnomah Press, 1996).

9. Coleman, *Songs of Heaven* 48.

10. G.R. Beasley-Murray, *The Book of Revelation* (London: Marshall, Morgan & Scott, 1978), 127. He points out the parallels of emphasis on the "passover theology" of John in both his Gospel and the Revelation.

11. Leon Morris, *The Revelation of St. John* (Grand Rapids: Eerdmans, 1969), 99.

12. Some translate this phrase "over the earth," but the implication is still the same. They share in the power and authority of Christ.

13. Beasley-Murray, *The Book of Revelation*, 127–28.

14. See details in Coleman, *Songs of Heaven*, 54–55.

15. Leon Morris, *The Revelation*, 102.

Chapter 6—The Wrath of the Lamb

1. Bruce Metzger, *Breaking the Code: Understanding the Book of Revelation* (Nashville: Abingdon Press, 1993), 55.

2. Robert Thomas, *Revelation 1—7: An Exegetical Commentary* (Chicago: Moody Press, 1992), 414.

3. Merrill Tenney, *Interpreting Revelation* (Grand Rapids: Eerdmans, 1957), 80.

4. Metzger, *Breaking the Code*, 55–56.

5. Norman Geisler, "Revelation" class notes, William Tyndale College, Farmington Hills, MI, 1965.

6. B.R. Beasley-Murray, *The Book of Revelation* (London: Marshall, Morgan & Scott, 1974), 129.

7. R.H. Charles, vol. 1 of *A Critical and Exegetical Commentary on the Revelation of St. John* (Edinburgh: James Clark, 1920), 176.

8. Thomas, *Revelation*, 416.

9. Ibid.

10. Leon Morris, *The Revelation of St. John* (Grand Rapids: Eerdmans, 1969), 102–03.

11. Metzger, *Breaking the Code*, 57.

12. Walter Scott, *Exposition of the Revelation of Jesus Christ* (Grand Rapids: Kregel, 1982), 146.

13. David Jeremiah, *Escape the Coming Night* (Dallas: Word Publishing, 1990), 96.

14. Leon Morris, *The Revelation of St. John*, 105.

15. Jack Van Impe, *2001: On the Edge of Eternity* (Dallas: Word, 1996), 35.

16. Metzger, *Breaking the Code*, 58.

17. Scott, *Exposition*, 154.

Chapter 7—From Tribulation to Jubilation

1. John F. Walvoord, *The Revelation of Jesus Christ* (Chicago: Moody Press, 1966), 139.

2. Bruce Metzger, *Breaking the Code: Understanding the Book of Revelation* (Nashville: Abingdon Press, 1993), 60–62.

3. See Ed Dobson and Ed Hindson, "Apocalypse Now? What Fundamentalists Believe about the End of the World," *Policy Review* (Fall 1986), 16–22. Cf. also Lorraine Boettner, *The Millennium* (Philadelphia: Presbyterian and Reformed, 1957); David Chilton, *Paradise Restored* (Tyler, TX: Dominion, 1984); G.C. Berkouwer, *The Return of Christ* (Grand Rapids: Eerdmans, 1962); P.E. Hughes, *Interpreting Prophecy* (Grand Rapids: Eerdmans, 1976); J.D. Pentecost, *Things to Come* (Grand Rapids: Zondervan, 1958); Paul Benware, *Understanding End Times Prophecy* (Chicago: Moody Press, 1995).

4. Walvoord, *The Revelation of Jesus Christ*, 142.

5. Benware, *Understanding End Times Prophecy*, 259.

6. Walvoord, *The Revelation of Jesus Christ*, 149.

Chapter 8—The World at War

1. Quoted by John Phillips, *Only God Can Prophesy!* (Wheaton: Harold Shaw, 1975), 27.

2. Ibid., 105–07.

3. Arthur Levine, *When Dreams and Heroes Died: A Portrait of Today's College Student* (San Francisco: Jossey-Bass, 1980).

4. Phillips, *Only God Can Prophesy!* 111–12.

5. Alfred Edersheim, *The Temple* (Grand Rapids: Eerdmans, 1963), 162–68.

6. Bruce Metzger, *Breaking the Code: Understanding the Book of Revelation* (Nashville: Abingdon Press, 1993), 63.

7. W. Graham Scroggie, *The Book of Revelation* (Edinburgh: The Book Stall, 1920), 167.

8. Phillips, *Only God Can Prophesy!* 113.

9. Leon Morris, *The Revelation of St. John* (Grand Rapids: Eerdmans, 1969), 124.

10. Ibid., 122.

Chapter 9—Demons Unleashed

1. See this discussed at length in Richard Lee and Ed Hindson, *Angels of Deceit* (Eugene, OR: Harvest House, 1993), 11–24.

2. A.T. Pierson, *The Bible and Spiritual Life* (Fincastle, VA: Scripture Truth, n.d., reprint of 1887 Exeter Hall Lectures), 169.

3. C.S. Lewis, *Mere Christianity* (New York: MacMillan, 1960), 53–54.

4. Billy Graham, *Angels: God's Secret Agents* (Garden City, NY: Doubleday, 1975), 60.

5. Hal Lindsay, *Satan Is Alive and Well on Planet Earth* (Grand Rapids: Zondervan, 1972), 77–82.

6. Graham, *Angels*, 65.

7. David Jeremiah, *What the Bible Says About Angels* (Sisters, OR: Multnomah Press, 1996), 211.

8. Robert Mounce, *The Book of Revelation* (Grand Rapids: Eerdmans, 1977), 192.

9. Bruce Metzger, *Breaking the Code: Understanding the Book of Revelation* (Nashville: Abingdon Press, 1993), 65.

10. Robert Thomas, *Revelation 8–22: An Exegetical Commentary* (Chicago: Moody Press, 1995), 38.

11. Ibid., 44.

12. Dave Hunt, *Global Peace and the Rise of Antichrist* (Eugene, OR: Harvest House, 1990), 220. Cf. also Ed Hindson, *Final Signs* (Eugene, OR: Harvest House, 1996), 123–43.

13. Tim LaHaye, *Revelation: Illustrated and Made Plain* (Grand Rapids: Zondervan, 1975), 141.

Chapter 10—Can It Get Any Worse?

1. Bruce Metzger, *Breaking the Code: Understanding the Book of Revelation* (Nashville: Abingdon Press, 1993), 67.

2. Robert Mounce, *The Book of Revelation* (Grand Rapids: Eerdmans, 1977), 205.

3. Robert Thomas, *Revelation 8—22: An Exegetical Commentary* (Chicago: Moody Press, 1995), 57–58.

4. Tim LaHaye, *Revelation: Illustrated and Made Plain* (Grand Rapids: Zondervan, 1975), 144.

5. Mounce, *The Book of Revelation*, 211.

6. Thomas, *Revelation 8–22*, 71.

7. Metzger, *Breaking the Code*, 68.

8. Mounce, *The Book of Revelation*, 217.

9. Ibid., 213.

Chapter 11—Hell on Earth!

1. John Walvoord, *The Revelation of Jesus Christ* (Chicago: Moody Press, 1966), 175.

2. Charles Feinberg, "Revelation," in E. Hindson and W. Kroll, *Parallel Bible Commentary* (Nashville: Thomas Nelson, 1982), 2782.

3. Bruce Metzger, *Breaking the Code: Understanding the Book of Revelation* (Nashville: Abingdon Press, 1993), 68.

4. G.R. Beasley-Murray, *The Book of Revelation* (London: Marshall, Morgan & Scott, 1978), 176–82.

5. Cf. "Temple," in A.C. Meyers, ed., *Eerdmans Bible Dictionary* (Grand Rapids: Eerdmans, 1987), 989–92.

6. Thomas Ice and Randall Price, *Ready to Rebuild* (Eugene, OR: Harvest House, 1992), 12–16.

7. Robert Mounce, *The Book of Revelation* (Grand Rapids: Eerdmans, 1977), 226.

8. Leon Morris, *The Revelation of St. John* (Grand Rapids: Eerdmans, 1969), 150.

9. Robert Thomas, *Revelation 8—22: An Exegetical Commentary* (Chicago: Moody Press, 1995), 98–99.

10. William Barclay, vol. II of *The Revelation of John* (Philadelphia: Westminster Press, 1960), 89.

11. Mounce, *The Book of Revelation*, 230.

Chapter 12—War in Heaven?

1. Robert Mounce, *The Book of Revelation* (Grand Rapids: Eerdmans, 1977), 236.

2. Robert Thomas, *Revelation 8—22: An Exegetical Commentary* (Chicago: Moody Press, 1995), 115.

3. Ibid., 117.

4. Cf. John Walvoord, *The Revelation of Jesus Christ* (Chicago: Moody Press, 1966), 187.

5. Bruce Metzger, *Breaking the Code: Understanding the Book of Revelation* (Nashville: Abingdon Press, 1993), 72.

6. Douglas Moo, "The Case for the Posttribulation Rapture Position," in *The Rapture: Pre, Mid, or Post-Tribulation?* (Grand Rapids: Zondervan, 1984), 171.

7. John Walvoord, *The Rapture Question* (Grand Rapids: Zondervan, 1979), 22.

8. Paul Benware, *Understanding End Times Prophecy* (Chicago: Moody Press, 1995), 203.

9. Cf. Leon Morris, *The Revelation of St. John* (Grand Rapids: Eerdmans, 1969), 156.

10. Mounce, *The Book of Revelation*, 236.

11. Thomas, *Revelation 8—22*, 122.

12. Metzger, *Breaking the Code*, 73.

Chapter 13—Rise of the Antichrist

1. Robert Mounce, *The Book of Revelation* (Grand Rapids: Eerdmans, 1977), 248.

2. G.R. Beasley-Murray, *The Book of Revelation* (London: Marshall, Morgan & Scott, 1978), 207.

3. Dave Hunt, "Discerning the Times" 1990 Prophecy Conference, Niagara Falls, Canada. Quoted in Peter Lalonde, *One World Under Antichrist* (Eugene, OR: Harvest House, 1991), 32.

4. For a detailed discussion, see J. Dwight Pentecost, *Things to Come* (Grand Rapids: Zondervan, 1964), 332–39.

5. Richard Trench, *Synonyms of the New Testament* (London: Kegan Paul & Co., 1906), 107.

6. Mounce, *The Book of Revelation*, 255.

7. John Hagee, *Beginning of the End* (Nashville: Thomas Nelson, 1996), 135.

8. Robert Thomas, *Revelation 8—22: An Exegetical Commentary* (Chicago: Moody Press, 1995), 172.

9. Jack Van Impe, *2001: On the Edge of Eternity* (Dallas: Word Publishing, 1996), 123.

10. Lalonde, *One World Under Antichrist*, 23.

Chapter 14—Wine Press of the Wrath of God

1. Robert Thomas, *Revelation 8—22: An Exegetical Commentary* (Chicago: Moody Press, 1995), 192.

2. Ibid.

3. H.B. Swete, *The Apocalypse of St. John* (Grand Rapids: Eerdmans, 1951), 182.

4. Cf. Charles Dyer, *The Rise of Babylon* (Wheaton: Tyndale House, 1991). Contra, Dave Hunt, *A Woman Rides the Beast* (Eugene, OR: Harvest House, 1994).

5. For details, see Ed Hindson, *Final Signs* (Eugene, OR: Harvest House, 1996), 137–43. Cf. also E. Yamauchi, "Babylon," in R.K. Harrison, ed., *Major Cities of the Biblical World* (Nashville: Thomas Nelson, 1985), 32–48.

6. Thomas, *Revelation 8—22*, 207.

7. David Reagan, "Two Important Questions Concerning End Time Bible Prophecy," 5.

8. Thomas, *Revelation 8—22*, 210.

9. Thomas, *Revelation 8—22*, 224.

Chapter 15—The Seven Last Plagues

1. John Walvoord, *The Revelation of Jesus Christ* (Chicago: Moody Press, 1966), 225.

2. Robert Thomas, *Revelation 8—22: An Exegetical Commentary* (Chicago: Moody Press, 1995), 228.

3. B.R. Beasley-Murray, *The Book of Revelation* (London: Marshall, Morgan & Scott, 1978), 231.

4. Robert Mounce, *The Book of Revelation* (Grand Rapids: Eerdmans, 1977), 285, and Beasley-Murray, *The Book of Revelation*, 233.

5. Walter Scott, *Exposition of the Revelation of Jesus Christ* (Grand Rapids: Kregel, 1982), 314.

6. Robert Coleman, *Songs of Heaven* (Old Tappan, NJ: Fleming H. Revell, 1980), 125.

7. Thomas, *Revelation 8—22*, 235.

8. Ibid., 241.

9. Mounce, *The Book of Revelation*, 289.

10. Ibid., 290.

Chapter 16—Battle of Armageddon

1. "Armageddon," in A.C. Myers, ed., *Eerdmans Bible Dictionary* (Grand Rapids: Eerdmans, 1987), 85.

2. René Pache, *The Return of Jesus Christ* (Chicago: Moody Press, 1955), 248–89.

3. Bruce Metzger, *Breaking the Code: Understanding the Book of Revelation* (Nashville: Abingdon Press, 1993), 80.

4. Robert Thomas, *Revelation 8—22: An Exegetical Commentary* (Chicago: Moody Press, 1995), 247.

Chapter 17—The Great Harlot and the Scarlet Beast

1. Leon Morris, *The Revelation of St. John* (Grand Rapids: Eerdmans, 1969), 202.

2. G.R. Beasley-Murray, *The Book of Revelation* (London: Marshall, Morgan & Scott, 1978), 251.

3. David Hocking, *The Coming World Leader* (Portland: Multnomah, 1988), 247.

4. Robert Mounce, *The Book of Revelation* (Grand Rapids: Eerdmans, 1977), 307.

5. Hocking, *The Coming World Leader*, 247–48.

6. Dave Hunt, *A Woman Rides the Beast* (Eugene, OR: Harvest House, 1994), 14.

7. Robert Thomas, *Revelation 8—22: An Exegetical Commentary* (Chicago: Moody Press, 1995), 283.

8. John Walvoord, *The Revelation of Jesus Christ* (Chicago: Moody Press, 1966), 244.

9. Bob Larsen, *In the Name of Satan* (Nashville: Thomas Nelson, 1996). Cf. also his *Straight Answers on the New Age* (Nashville: Thomas Nelson, 1989).

10. Beasley-Murray, *The Book of Revelation*, 256–58, discusses this at length, finally assuming John's symbolism was not intended to approximate the Roman historical situation.

11. Walvoord, *The Revelation of Jesus Christ*, 245ff.

Chapter 18—Fall of Babylon

1. Charles Colson, *Against the Night* (Ann Arbor, MI: Servant Publications, 1989), 19.

2. David Jeremiah, *Escape the Coming Night* (Dallas: Word Publishing, 1990), 178–79.

3. Leon Morris, *The Revelation of St. John* (Grand Rapids: Eerdmans, 1969), 214.

Chapter 19—Triumphal Return of Christ

1. René Pache, *The Return of Jesus Christ* (Chicago: Moody Press, 1955), 353.

2. Robert Gromacki, "Where is 'the Church' in Revelation 4–19?" in Thomas Ice and Timothy Demy, eds., *When the Trumpet Sounds* (Eugene, OR: Harvest House, 1995), 355.

3. G.R. Beasley-Murray, *The Book of Revelation* (London: Marshall, Morgan & Scott, 1978), 270.

4. Ibid., 271.

5. Ibid., 273–74.

6. Bruce Metzger, *Breaking the Code: Understanding the Book of Revelation* (Nashville: Abingdon Press, 1993), 90.

7. J. Dwight Pentecost, *Things to Come* (Grand Rapids: Zondervan, 1958), 226.

8. Metzger, *Breaking the Code*, 90.

9. Robert Thomas, *Revelation 8—22: An Exegetical Commentary* (Chicago: Moody Press, 1995), 381.

10. A.W. Boehm, "Preface" to Johann Arndt's *True Christianity* (London: Brown & Downing, 1720), xxii.

Chapter 20—The Millennial Kingdom

1. George Ladd, *Crucial Questions About the Kingdom of God* (Grand Rapids: Eerdmans, 1952), 78.

2. Alva McClain, *The Greatness of the Kingdom* (Chicago: Moody Press, 1959), 17, 41.

3. William S. LaSor, *The Truth About Armageddon* (Grand Rapids: Baker, 1982), 160–61.

4. John Walvoord, *Prophecy* (Nashville: Thomas Nelson, 1993), 139.

5. Robert Mounce, *The Book of Revelation* (Grand Rapids: Eerdmans, 1977), 353.

6. John Walvoord, *The Revelation of Jesus Christ* (Chicago: Moody Press, 1966), 292.

7. Thomas Ice and Timothy Demy, *The Millennium* (Eugene, OR: Harvest House, 1996), 8. Cf. also Mal Couch and Gordon Johnston, "Millennium," in Mal Couch, ed., *Dictionary of Premillennial Theology* (Grand Rapids: Kregel, 1996), 267–72.

8. Harold Hoehner, "Evidence from Revelation," in D. Campbell and J. Townsend, eds., *A Case for Premillennialism* (Chicago: Moody Press, 1992), 249–50.

9. G.R. Beasley-Murray, *The Book of Revelation* (London: Marshall, Morgan & Scott, 1978), 287.

10. René Pache, *The Return of Christ* (Chicago: Moody Press, 1955), 381.

11. Beasley-Murray, *The Book of Revelation*, 292–93.

12. Robert Thomas, *Revelation 8—22: An Exegetical Commentary* (Chicago: Moody Press, 1995), 429.

13. Ibid.

Chapter 21—New Jerusalem

1. Richard Baxter, *The Saints Everlasting Rest* (London: Epworth Press, 1962 edition), 27.

2. Dave Hunt, *Whatever Happened to Heaven?* (Eugene, OR: Harvest House, 1988), 7.

3. Joseph Stowell, *Eternity* (Chicago: Moody Press, 1995), 13–24.

4. Bruce Metzger, *Breaking the Code: Understanding the Book of Revelation* (Nashville: Abingdon Press, 1993), 98.

5. Walter Scott, *Exposition of the Revelation of Jesus Christ* (Grand Rapids: Kregel Publications, 1982), 416.

6. Wilbur Smith, *The Biblical Doctrine of Heaven* (Chicago: Moody Press, 1968), 239.

7. Robert Thomas, *Revelation 8—22: An Exegetical Commentary* (Chicago: Moody Press, 1995), 442.

8. A.T. Robertson, vol. VI of *Word Pictures in the New Testament* (Grand Rapids: Eerdmans, 1933), 467.

9. G.R. Beasley-Murray, *The Book of Revelation* (London: Marshall, Morgan & Scott, 1978), 315.

10. Bernard Ramm, *Them He Glorified* (Grand Rapids: Eerdmans, 1963), 136.

Chapter 22—Paradise Restored

1. Walter Scott, *Exposition of the Revelation of Jesus Christ* (Grand Rapids: Kregel, 1982), 439.

2. Robert Thomas, *Revelation 8—22: An Exegetical Commentary* (Chicago: Moody Press, 1995), 482.

3. John Walvoord, *The Revelation of Jesus Christ* (Chicago: Moody Press, 1966), 330.

4. See Bruce Metzger, *Breaking the Code: Understanding the Book of Revelation* (Nashville: Abingdon Press, 1993), 103.

5. G.R. Beasley-Murray, *The Book of Revelation* (London: Marshall, Morgan & Scott, 1978), 333.

6. Thomas, *Revelation 8—22*, 494.

7. Metzger, *Breaking the Code*, 106.

8. Leon Morris, *The Revelation of St. John* (Grand Rapids: Eerdmans, 1969), 262.

9. Beasley-Murray, *The Book of Revelation*, 350.

About the Author

Dr. Ed Hindson is the Assistant Chancellor, Professor of Religion, and Dean of the Institute of Biblical Studies at Liberty University in Lynchburg, Virginia.

He has authored over twenty books, including *Isaiah's Immanuel, Final Signs,* and *Is the Antichrist Alive and Well?* He also served as general editor of the Gold Medallion award-winning *Knowing Jesus Study Bible,* the *King James Study Bible* and the *King James Bible Commentary,* and was one of the translators for the New King James Version of the Bible. He is also an associate editor of the *Tim LaHaye Prophecy Study Bible.*

An executive board member of the Pre-Trib Research Center in Arlington, Texas, he is also a Life Fellow of the International Biographical Association of Cambridge, England. Dr. Hindson holds degrees from several institutions: B.A., William Tyndale College; M.A., Trinity Evangelical Divinity School; Th.M., Grace Theological Seminary; Th.D., Trinity Graduate School; D.Min., Westminster Theological Seminary; D.Phil., University of South Africa. He has also done graduate study at Acadia University in Nova Scotia, Canada.

Dr. Hindson has served as a visiting lecturer at Oxford University and the Harvard Divinity School, as well as numerous evangelical seminaries including Dallas, Denver, Trinity, Grace, and Westminster. He has taught over fifty thousand students in the past twenty-five years. His solid academic scholarship, combined with a dynamic and practical teaching style, communicate biblical truth in a powerful and positive manner.

Dr. Mal Couch, one of the general editors of the Twenty-first Century Biblical Commentary Series, is founder and president of Tyndale Theological Seminary and Biblical Institute in Fort Worth, Texas. He has taught at Philadelphia College of the Bible, Moody Bible Institute, and Dallas Theological Seminary.